James & Emma,

Some choice recipes to make your marriage & life together "Sweet as"!..

Best wishes & Kiwi love,

Louise, Tim & Patrick

X

THE GREAT NEW ZEALAND Cookbook

thom & PQ Blackwell

CONTENTS

"Well, *of course* we need another bloody cookbook!" was Tui Flower's response when I outlined our plans over the phone. Despite being highly skeptical, she still allowed us to pop around, share what we had in mind and even make a date to capture her contribution.

We had bought a very large map of New Zealand, hung it on the office wall and showered it with Post-it notes, identifying the many, many talented cooks, chefs and bakers from one end of the country to the other. After much discussion and having settled on our list of contributors, we thought we could set off on a leisurely trip around the country, region by region.

That plan was quickly shattered when we discovered that Peter Gordon was over from London with a very small window of availability. So we raced out the door, immediately after visiting Tui, to photograph Peter whipping up spaghetti toasts and his dad's soufflé omelette. It doesn't get more Kiwi than that!

Shoot No. 3 was at Mrs Clark's Cafe in Riverton. Pat is the cook and Caz front of house. Caz greeted us as though we were old friends reuniting, and we loved her from that moment. It turned out it was her birthday, and did we want to come to her party after the shoot, and would we all like to stay at their house for the night? Surely this much fun and this much warmth couldn't last!

We were actually in the deep south to catch the final week of the oyster season, so shoot No. 4 saw the alarm go off in our Invercargill motel at 1.30 a.m. Oystering in the Foveaux Strait with Willie Calder and the *Argosy* crew will remain one of my life's highlights. Even though we didn't know it then, it would be one of many truly special moments we were to have throughout the project.

No lingering down south, though, as Anthony Hoy Fong was back in the country from New York for a short visit. So shoot No. 5 saw us at his family home in Epsom for a full Chinese banquet, and the joy of sharing it with four generations of his family.

These first five shoots gave us an early indication that what lay ahead could well be a once-in-a-lifetime experience. Everywhere we went, and I do mean everywhere, we were met with so much generosity and warmth as we were welcomed onto boats and into restaurants, cafés and family homes.

Travelling the length and breadth of New Zealand made us realise afresh just how privileged we are to live in such a beautiful country. We've battled storms and road closures but any inconvenience has truly been compensated for by serendipitous moments such as the tranquility of whitebaiting at dawn or the solitude of hunting in the bush at sunset. We all feel so fortunate to have had these incredible experiences.

To my travelling team – Tim Harper, Lottie Hedley and Hayley Thom – you have done such an amazing job capturing the spirit of the people, the uniqueness of the moment and the splendour of the food. It was the ultimate road trip made so much smoother because of the fabulous support back home from Wendy Nixon and Mary Wells. Great job, team!

Finally, huge thanks to all eighty of our amazing contributors. Every single shoot was a delight, and each one of you so accommodating. It has been an honour to meet such hard-working, dedicated people whose greatest joy is to share their food, prepared with passion and commitment and served with such love and care. I remain so very grateful to you all.

With great respect,

Murray Thom

MURRAY THOM, LOTTIE HEDLEY
TIM HARPER & HAYLEY THOM
THE TRAVELLING COOKBOOK TEAM

Kohimarama,
Auckland

THE COOK'S COMPANION
CLOSE-ENOUGH CONVERSIONS

LIQUID/VOLUME

1 TBSP	½ FL OZ	3 TSP	15 ML
2 TBSP	1 FL OZ	6 TSP	30 ML
¼ CUP	2 FL OZ	4 TBSP	60 ML
⅓ CUP	2½ FL OZ	5 TBSP	75 ML
½ CUP	4 FL OZ	8 TBSP	125 ML
⅔ CUP	5 FL OZ	10 TBSP	150 ML
¾ CUP	6 FL OZ	12 TBSP	175 ML
1 CUP	8 FL OZ	16 TBSP	250 ML
1¼ CUPS	10 FL OZ		310 ML
1½ CUPS	12 FL OZ		350 ML
1 PINT (2 CUPS)	16 FL OZ		500 ML
2½ CUPS	20 FL OZ		25 ML
1 QUART	32 FL OZ		1 LITRE
1 GALLON	128 FL OZ		4 LITRES

DRY/WEIGHT

¼ OZ	7 G
½ OZ	15 G
1 OZ	30 G
2 OZ	55 G
3 OZ	85 G
4 OZ	115 G
5 OZ	140 G
6 OZ	170 G
7 OZ	200 G
8 OZ (½ LB)	225 G
9 OZ	255 G
10 OZ	285 G
11 OZ	310 G
12 OZ	340 G
13 OZ	370 G
14 OZ	400 G
15 OZ	425 G
16 OZ (1 LB)	450 G

TEMPERATURE

VERY COOL	275°F	140 °C
COOL	300°F	150 °C
WARM	325°F	160 °C
MEDIUM	350°F	180 °C
MEDIUM HOT	400°F	200 °C
HOT	425°F	220 °C
VERY HOT	450°F	240 °C

FRIZZELL/14

TUI FLOWER

RAISIN LOAF
BRAN BISCUITS

One of my earliest memories of learning to cook is helping to make this Raisin Loaf. I wondered if I would ever know how to judge when the oven was the right temperature to bake it. I watched as my mother held the handle of the oven door on the coal range or opened the door and held her hand in the oven briefly. This easy, modest, good-keeping loaf has been a staple throughout my life.

Another regular baking-day recipe of my youth was for Bran Biscuits. I think it was the rolling and cutting them out that I liked best. It is a process I still enjoy when baking.

Tui

Mt Eden,
Auckland

RAISIN LOAF

Servings: 8 | Prep Time: 15 mins | Cook Time: 1 hour | Skill Level: 1 (Easy)

INGREDIENTS

1 cup milk
2 tbsp golden syrup
2 cups plain flour
3 tsp baking powder
pinch of salt
¾ cup sugar
1 cup raisins

METHOD

Pre-heat the oven to 180°C. Line the bottom of a 22 cm loaf tin with baking paper and grease the tin.

Put milk and golden syrup together in a pan and heat gently to combine. Leave to cool. Sift flour, baking powder and salt into a bowl, add sugar and raisins and stir to combine. Add the milk mixture, stirring to make a soft batter. Turn into the prepared tin.

Bake for about 1 hour. Allow to cool in the tin for 15–20 minutes, before removing to cool completely. Serve sliced, with or without buttering.

TIP

This is a forgiving recipe, so if you find measuring golden syrup tricky, a little inaccuracy will be allowed. It will also tolerate milk starting to sour.

BRAN BISCUITS

Makes: 20–30 | Prep Time: 15 mins | Cook Time: 20 mins | Skill Level: 1 (Easy)

INGREDIENTS

100 g butter
⅓ cup sugar
¼ cup milk
1¼ cups plain flour
3 tsp baking powder
1 cup bran

METHOD

Pre-heat the oven to 180°C. Lightly grease two oven trays.

Soften butter, add sugar and beat well together until light and creamy. Stir in milk. The mixture will not be smooth. Mix flour, baking powder and bran in a bowl. Add to the butter mixture and stir to form a stiff dough.

Lightly flour a flat surface. Place about half the dough on it, cover with plastic wrap and roll out to about 3 mm thick. Remove plastic wrap and cut dough into rectangular pieces. Put the trimmings with the remaining dough and repeat rolling and cutting. Place biscuits on prepared trays.

Bake for about 20 minutes. Remove from tray to cooling rack. When cold, store in an airtight container. Serve plain or buttered.

SIMON WRIGHT
THE FRENCH CAFE

ROASTED LAMB RACK, KŪMARA, PEAS, MINT & PANCETTA
A TWIST ON LEMON MERINGUE PIE

Kiwi lamb is world famous and the lamb rack is such a delicious, decadent cut – perfect for those special occasions. You can't go wrong with this dish which is very easy to prepare and has a classic combination of summery flavours to go alongside a velvety smooth kumara mash. My twist on a classic lemon meringue pie is simpler than making a tart and gives you an explosion of flavours and textures in one scoop. Bon Appetit!

Simon

Eden Terrace,
Auckland

ROASTED LAMB RACK, KŪMARA, PEAS, MINT & PANCETTA

Servings: 4 | Prep Time: 20 mins | Cook Time: 2 hours | Skill Level: 1 (Easy)

INGREDIENTS

24 small Roma
  tomatoes
olive oil
a little icing sugar
4 bulbs garlic
2 sprigs thyme
500 g peeled golden
  kūmara
120 g unsalted butter
50 ml milk

Lamb racks

2 French-trimmed
  lamb racks
  (approx. 400 g each)
50 ml olive oil
4 sprigs thyme
4 cloves garlic, peeled
50 g butter

Garnish

8 slices pancetta
50 ml olive oil
100 g cooked fresh peas
80 g feta, diced
fresh mint leaves
2 tbsp chopped chives
aged balsamic vinegar

METHOD

Pre-heat the oven to 100°C. Make a small criss-cross in the top of each tomato with a small knife; plunge tomatoes into boiling water for 10 seconds and refresh in iced water to stop them cooking. Drain, and remove the skins. Lightly toss tomatoes in a little olive oil, place on a baking sheet lined with baking paper and sprinkle a little icing sugar over each one. Place tomatoes in the oven for about an hour to slightly dehydrate them and intensify their flavour. Remove from the oven and keep to one side.

Turn the oven up to 200°C. Cut garlic bulbs in two, slightly above halfway, with a sharp knife to give you a large cross-section. Place bulbs on a large square of tinfoil, drizzle with a little oil, add thyme and some sea salt, and wrap the garlic up in the foil – not too tightly. Place on a baking tray and cook in the oven for about 40 minutes or until the garlic has nicely caramelised. Remove from the oven and keep warm.

Dice kūmara and cook in boiling salted water until soft. Drain and allow to steam dry for a few minutes. Place kūmara and butter into a food processor and purée to a fine consistency, stopping the machine every so often to scrape down the sides. Add milk, adjust seasoning with a little more salt and continue to process until smooth. Place mash in a clean saucepan and keep warm.

Turn the oven up to 230°C. Season lamb racks well with sea salt and freshly ground black pepper. Heat olive oil in a large ovenproof frying pan, and when hot add the lamb racks, fat side down, and fry until nicely browned. Turn racks over, add thyme and garlic cloves and place in the oven for 8 minutes for medium rare or 11 minutes for medium. Once lamb is cooked, place the pan back onto the heat on the stovetop, add butter and baste the lamb continuously for 1 minute. Remove lamb from frying pan and keep in a warm place to rest for 6 minutes.

For the garnish, cut pancetta slices in half, place in a hot frying pan and fry until crispy, then remove and keep warm. Gently warm olive oil in a medium-sized saucepan, add peas and warm for 1 minute. Add dried tomatoes, feta, mint and chives, toss together gently to warm and season to taste.

To serve, carve the lamb rack between the bones and place two cutlets onto each plate. Place a spoonful of kūmara mash and caramelised garlic next to the lamb, and spoon the tomato, pea, feta and mint mixture over the lamb. Top with a few slices of crispy pancetta and drizzle with a little aged balsamic vinegar and some olive oil and roasting juices.

A TWIST ON LEMON MERINGUE PIE

Servings: 6 | Prep Time: 2¼ hours | Skill Level: 3 (More challenging)

INGREDIENTS

Meringue
200 g caster sugar
200 ml water
4 egg whites
1 small lemon

Passionfruit gel
200 ml passionfruit
  juice (no seeds)
125 g sugar
125 ml water
2 tsp powdered agar

Pastry crumbs
120 g cold butter, diced
60 g sugar
130 g plain flour
15 g rice flour

Lemon curd
1 gelatine leaf
100 ml freshly squeezed
  lemon juice
120 g sugar
3 egg yolks
150 g cold unsalted
  butter, diced
150 ml semi-whipped
  cream

White chocolate powder
35 g white chocolate
75 g maltodextrin

Garnish
fresh blueberries
freeze-dried blueberries
lavender tips
1 tub good-quality white
  chocolate ice cream

METHOD

Pre-heat the oven to 80°C. Combine sugar and water in a small saucepan and bring to the boil, stirring continuously with a wooden spoon until sugar has dissolved. Reduce heat slightly and continue to cook the syrup until it reaches 115°C. Place egg whites in the bowl of an electric mixer with a whisk attachment, grate zest of lemon over egg whites using a micro grater and start whisking whites until they reach soft peaks. Once the sugar syrup reaches 120°C, remove from the heat and slowly pour onto the egg whites while whisking. Continue to whisk at medium speed until meringue has cooled and is thick and glossy. Spread a quarter of the meringue thinly on a baking sheet lined with baking paper and place in the oven to dry for about 2 hours. Place remaining meringue into a piping bag and refrigerate until required. Once meringue sheet has dried completely, break it into large shards and store in an airtight container.

Place all passionfruit gel ingredients into a medium-sized saucepan and gently heat to dissolve the sugar. Bring to the boil and whisk continuously for about 1 minute or until thickened slightly. Remove from the heat, pour into a clean container and refrigerate. Once the mixture has cooled completely and has set slightly, pour it into a liquidiser and blend at high speed for 20 seconds to emulsify. Pour passionfruit gel into a squeeze bottle and refrigerate until required.

Turn the oven up to 170°C. Place all pastry crumb ingredients in a bowl and use your fingers to rub the mixture together until you have a rough crumb. Spread mixture onto a lined baking sheet and place in the oven for about 20–30 minutes, or until slightly browned. Allow to cool, then place in a food processor and quickly process into a fine crumb. Store in an airtight container until required.

Soak gelatine in cold water to soften. Place lemon juice, sugar and egg yolks in a bowl set over a pot of simmering water and whisk continuously until the mixture thickens. Add butter, piece by piece, until fully emulsified. Squeeze excess water from gelatine and add to lemon curd, whisking until completely dissolved. Pour curd into a clean bowl and refrigerate. Once completely cooled, gently fold cream in. Place curd in a piping bag and refrigerate until required.

Melt white chocolate. Place maltodextrin into a food processor and, with the motor running, slowly add chocolate until you have a fine powder resembling icing sugar. Store chocolate powder in an airtight container until required.

To serve, pipe three mounds of meringue onto each plate and lightly brown with a blowtorch, being careful not to burn them. Pipe three mounds of lemon curd in between the meringue and top with a spoonful of pastry crumbs. Squeeze a few drops of passionfruit gel around the plate and lightly sprinkle meringue with a little white chocolate powder. Scatter plate with fresh and freeze-dried blueberries and lavender tips, place a scoop of ice cream in the centre and lean two meringue shards up against the ice cream.

AL BROWN

TUATUA FRITTER BUTTIES
MUM'S GINGER CRUNCH

I'm a proud New Zealander and I'm proud to tell stories about this country through its food. To be able to go and collect tuatuas and make tuatua fritter butties, as simple as it sounds, is absolutely priceless.

Food doesn't have to be perfect; it's people and place that create the memory and those are the special ingredients that make it taste so good.

A recipe is like a culinary love letter — you keep passing it on. Someone will take my recipe and add something to it and then it will become their recipe and then they will hopefully pass it on. My Mum's ginger crunch will be passed on and, who knows, in a couple of years' time, it might be being made in Canada or wherever; there's something inherently wonderful about that.

— Al

TUATUA FRITTER BUTTIES

Servings: 6 | Prep Time: 10 mins | Cook Time: 5 mins | Skill Level: 1 (Easy)

INGREDIENTS

1.2 kg tuatua, washed
splash of white wine
⅓ cup finely diced
   red onion
zest and juice of 1 lemon
¼ cup finely chopped
   fresh coriander leaves
¼ cup fresh finely
   chopped basil leaves
2 tbsp sweet chilli sauce
4 eggs (size 7)
⅓ cup self-raising flour
2 tbsp milk (optional)
cooking oil

To serve
fresh white bread, sliced
good-quality mayonnaise
lemons

METHOD

Heat a large saucepan to high heat. Add tuatua and wine, then cover tightly with a lid. Cook for 3 minutes, then check to see if the shellfish are opening. As they pop open, remove from the saucepan, discarding any that don't open. Pull the meat from the shells and refrigerate until cool.

Chop tuatua meat into a coarse mince with a knife or food processor. Transfer to a large mixing bowl, then add onion, lemon zest plus 1½ tablespoons of lemon juice, coriander, basil and sweet chilli sauce. Season with sea salt and freshly ground pepper, and combine.

Whisk eggs and flour together in a large mixing bowl until smooth. If the batter is too thick, loosen with a dash of milk. The consistency should be similar to that of golden syrup. Fold 1 cup of the batter mix through the tuatua mix. Cook off a little mix, and check consistency and seasoning. You can add a little more batter if the fritters are not holding together. Refrigerate remaining mix until required (it will keep for 1–2 days).

Heat up a skillet or griddle top on your barbecue to a medium heat. Add a little cooking oil to the surface, then spoon out small amounts of fritter mix. Cook for a couple of minutes either side until golden and cooked through.

Slather bread (two slices per serving) with mayo and stack half the slices with hot fritters. Give them a squeeze of lemon juice and a dash of seasoning before putting the bread lids on.

MUM'S GINGER CRUNCH

Makes: 20 | Prep Time: 8 mins | Cook Time: 25 mins plus setting | Skill Level: 1 (Easy)

INGREDIENTS

Base
175 g butter
¾ cup sugar
1¼ cup plain flour
1½ tsp ground ginger
1½ tsp baking powder

Icing
100 g butter
1 cup icing sugar
2 tbsp golden syrup
4 tsp ground ginger

METHOD

Pre-heat the oven to 180°C. Grease and line a 25 cm x 20 cm baking tin. Cream butter and sugar together until pale. Sift in flour, ginger and baking powder and mix until combined. Press evenly into lined tin.

Bake for 20–25 minutes until base is firm to the touch. Remove from the oven and gently level out the base with the back of a spoon. Ice while the base is still warm.

Heat icing ingredients in a small saucepan. Stir until melted and combined. Pour the icing over the warm base and spread out evenly. Leave to cool in the tin before cutting into squares.

TIP

It is best to cut this slice in the tin, just before the icing is fully set, using a warm, wet knife.

KIM EVANS
LITTLE AND FRIDAY

BRIOCHE DOUGH
CINNAMON & WALNUT BRIOCHE
CREAM DOUGHNUTS
CRÈME DIPLOMAT

Food is something to be enjoyed.
to be grateful for.

These days we are in such a rush—
- we buy food without knowing where it came from
- we heat it in the microwave & gobble it down ....

The ceremony has gone out of eating

That's why I'm big on sharing recipes ...
The more people who are inspired to cook
the better !!!

Both of these recipes, the doughnut
& the brioche, are made from the same dough.
I recommend you use fresh, organic
ingredients & I hope that you
enjoy making the dough
from scratch.

Kim.

Belmont,
Auckland

BRIOCHE DOUGH

Makes: 1 large quantity dough | Prep Time: 40–50 mins | Skill Level: 2 (Moderate)

INGREDIENTS

550 ml milk
60 g fresh yeast
 (crumbled) or
 3 tsp dry yeast
½ cup sugar
6½ cups plain flour
3 tsp salt
3 eggs
140 g unsalted butter

METHOD

Heat milk over a medium heat until lukewarm. Remove from heat and pour over yeast, stirring until yeast has dissolved.

Place dry ingredients in a mixing bowl. Using an electric mixer with a dough hook, mix at low speed (or mix by hand to fully combine). Add milk/yeast mixture and eggs to the bowl, continuing to mix at low speed until a sticky dough forms. Stop the mixer.

Scrape down the dough and then turn the mixer speed on to medium for 10 minutes until an elastic, shiny dough forms and pulls away from the bowl. If doing this by hand, knead the dough on a lightly floured surface.

Cut butter into small pieces and gradually knead into the mixture until well combined. Cover the bowl with a tea towel and allow dough to rise until almost doubled in size. Tip dough onto a floured surface. It is now ready to use.

TIPS

Traditional brioche recipes require the dough to be chilled prior to it being used – overnight or for at least 2 hours. I tend to avoid this as the dough comes out slightly firmer and less fluffy. My method means you have to work faster once the dough is ready, to stop it from over-rising, especially during summer. If it does rise too quickly, place it in the refrigerator for short periods to slow down the process.

CINNAMON & WALNUT BRIOCHE

Makes: 9 | Prep Time: 30 mins plus dough | Cook Time: 20–30 mins | Skill Level: 2 (Moderate)

INGREDIENTS

1 cup walnut halves
1 cup brown sugar
1 cup chopped dates
1 tbsp ground cinnamon
1 recipe brioche dough
1 egg
2 tbsp milk
50 g unsalted butter

METHOD

Make brioche dough (see above). Pre-heat the oven to 180°C. Blitz walnut halves, sugar, dates and cinnamon in a food processor, until the mixture starts resembling coarse breadcrumbs. Set aside.

On a floured surface, roll dough into a rectangle 1 cm thick. Beat egg and milk together to make egg wash and use to brush the entire dough. Spread a layer of cinnamon and walnut mix, 1 cm thick, right up to the corners of your dough. Roll up dough, rolling from the widest part. Using a sharp knife or a serrated-edge knife, slice pieces 5 cm thick.

Grease large muffin tins with baking spray or butter. Place the scrolls into the tins, cut side up. Brush with egg wash. Bake for 20 minutes or until golden brown. Cool before removing from tins.

CREAM DOUGHNUTS

Makes: about 15 | Prep Time: 20–30 mins plus dough and filling | Cook Time: 30 mins
Skill Level: 2 (Moderate)

INGREDIENTS

1 recipe brioche dough
oil, for frying
raspberry coulis or jam
1 recipe crème diplomat
a large bowlful of
  icing sugar

METHOD

Make brioche dough (see previous page) and crème diplomat (see below). Roll dough out on a floured surface to 4 cm thick. Using a cookie cutter, cut into circles. Allow to prove for 10–15 minutes – it is ready when a dry skin forms on the dough.

In a large saucepan, add oil to 2 cm deep and heat to 180°C. It is best to use a thermometer to get the temperature just right. If you are not using one, heat the oil over a medium heat – once it starts smoking, it is too hot.

Drop a few doughnuts into the hot oil at a time. You do not want them to touch or they will stick together. Cook for 3 minutes on each side, until they are quite dark and crisp. Remove and allow to cool on a wire rack covered with baking paper.

Once cool, poke a hole into each doughnut, creating a cavity. Fill a piping bag with raspberry coulis or jam and squeeze about 1 teaspoon's worth into each cavity. Next, use a clean piping bag full of crème diplomat to fill each doughnut until it starts to expand. Dust each doughnut generously with icing sugar.

CRÈME DIPLOMAT

Makes: 2½ cups | Prep Time: 20 mins plus chilling | Skill Level: 2 (Moderate)

INGREDIENTS

250 ml milk
½ tsp vanilla essence
  or paste
¼ cup caster sugar
2 egg yolks
2 tbsp cornflour
150 ml cream

METHOD

Combine milk, vanilla and half the caster sugar in a saucepan, and bring to the boil. In a separate bowl, beat together remaining caster sugar and egg yolks until pale and thick. Slowly pour half the milk mixture into the egg mixture, whisking constantly.

Return remaining milk to the heat. When it has reached boiling point, leave on the heat and quickly add the egg mixture, whisking constantly. Keep whisking vigorously until it returns to the boil, then remove from the heat. Pour into a bowl and place a circle of baking paper on top, to stop a film forming on the surface. Cool, then chill. (This is called crème pâtissière.)

Whip cream until firm. Beat chilled crème pâtissière until smooth and fold gently through whipped cream with a metal spoon. Refrigerate in an airtight container for up to three days.

ANTONIO CRISCI
PODERI CRISCI/NON SOLO PIZZA

POACHED CHICKEN SALAD WITH CHARGRILLED VEGETABLES
PIZZA WITH PROSCIUTTO, ROCKET & MUSHROOM
BEEF & SPINACH RAVIOLI WITH SAGE BURNT BUTTER

I grew up in Naples where my Grandmother had a restaurant. Both my Mother and Grandmother were excellent cooks and from my Grandmother I learnt that, apart from skill and technique, food requires the additional ingredient of passion that you put into the food as you prepare it.

In Italy, like a lot of warm countries, most people have a break from 1:30-4:30pm; it's too hot to work. Also, school finishes at 1pm and the children can reunite with their parents around the focal part of the house; the dining table. A proper sit-down lunch is an important part of the day and when it's Sunday, the day of rest, this becomes a more leisurely and long event where extended family and friends are invited. That is what we call the "Long Lunch". This is how I was brought up. So, for me, I want people to embrace the whole experience of food ambience and wine as a way of life.

— Antonio

Waiheke Island

INSALATA DI POLLO A VAPORE E VEGETALI ALLA GRIGLIA
POACHED CHICKEN SALAD WITH CHARGRILLED VEGETABLES

Servings: 4 | Prep Time: 50 mins plus marinating | Cook Time: 1 hour
Skill Level: 3 (More challenging)

INGREDIENTS

2 free-range chicken breasts
1 tsp curry powder
1 tsp ground coriander
1 tsp chopped fresh
   fennel leaves
50 g carrots, assorted colours
50 g celery, white part
50 g partially peeled and
   de-seeded cucumber
2 medium-sized zucchinis
1 clove garlic
2 sheets of filo pastry
50 g butter, melted, or a
   little oil
200 g Stracchino cheese
10 g chopped fresh chives
80 ml extra virgin
   olive oil
50 ml balsamic reduction
20 g salt and pepper
a few herbs, for garnish

METHOD

Trim any fat off the chicken and place in a bowl. Mix with curry powder, coriander, fennel and some salt and pepper, cover with plastic wrap and leave to marinate overnight, or for a minimum of 4 hours, in the fridge. Cut carrots, celery and cucumber into julienne strips and place in cold water. Also leave in the fridge to crisp up.

Remove the marinated chicken and roll each breast in plastic wrap. Tie off the ends of the plastic and then wrap in tinfoil – you want to form a roll shape. Place rolls in cold water on a low heat, and warm until small bubbles form in the water. Leave not quite simmering for almost 1 hour. The inside temperature of the chicken should be 75°C. If you own a sous vide cooker, you can cook the chicken for 1 hour at 75°C.

Slice zucchinis lengthwise, grill until slightly softened and dress with a little oil, chopped garlic, salt and pepper.

Pre-heat the oven to 160°C. Brush 1 sheet of filo with a little melted butter or oil. Cover with the second sheet and then cut both together into four squares. Place one quarter in each of four ramekins. Place ramekins on a tray and bake until coloured, to obtain four baskets – this should take a couple of minutes. Remove and allow to cool down.

Whisk cheese with chives (or any other herb you prefer). Remove foil and plastic from chicken and slice as thin as you can with a sharp knife. Drain the julienned vegetables, pat dry and dress with olive oil, salt and pepper and a little balsamic.

To serve, place a small dot of cheese on each serving plate and put a filo basket on top. This will stop the filo basket sliding. Divide the julienned vegetables between the baskets, and add the remaining cheese, chargrilled zucchini and sliced chicken. Dress with olive oil and a little balsamic, and garnish with fresh herbs.

TIPS

You can use 1 tsp chopped fresh coriander leaves in the marinade instead of the ground coriander.

Stracchino cheese can be found in specialist food stores, or you can use any other soft cheese you may have or prefer. If you use different cheese, add a little cream (up to 50 ml) if needed to obtain a smooth consistency.

PIZZA CON PROSCIUTTO CRUDO & RUCOLA
PIZZA WITH PROSCIUTTO, ROCKET & MUSHROOM

Servings: 4 | Prep Time: 5¾ hours including proving | Cook Time: 5—6 mins
Skill Level: 2 (Moderate)

INGREDIENTS

Dough
400 ml water
100 g ice cubes
4 g dried yeast granules
900 g '00' pizza flour
30 g salt

Topping
360 g button mushrooms
65 g parmesan cheese
60 ml cream
300 g fresh rocket leaves
250 g prosciutto
10 ml extra virgin olive oil

METHOD

Mix water with ice and yeast in your mixer, and start to add flour until you reach a soft, homogenous consistency. Add salt and let it mix slowly for 20 minutes more. Remove dough from mixer, place on a lightly floured surface, cover with a damp tea towel and leave to rest for 30 minutes.

Divide into 230 g balls and place on a floured tray to prove for 3–4 hours. If not needing to use straight away, store it in the fridge, then bring up to room temperature before rolling.

Rolling the pizza is an art that requires practice and experience. Try to do it with your hands without the use of a rolling pin, otherwise that will compress all the balls of air and create a biscuit base instead of a traditional light base.

Place a ball of dough on a lightly floured surface. With one hand, try to open up the ball of dough. Rotate it so as to obtain a circular base, approx. 30 cm in diameter. If you want to be a little more adventurous, when you have opened the base let it roll between your hands as if you are shaking flour from your hands. Repeat with remaining dough.

As I said, it will take time and practice so start by being happy with the consistency of your pizza more than its shape.

Turn your oven on to a high heat, 300°C, and if cooking on a pizza pan or stone put that in to heat up.

For the topping, slice mushrooms and grate 25 g of parmesan, shaving the rest and setting it aside. Cover pizza with cream, grated parmesan and mushrooms, and season with salt and pepper. Bake high in the oven – depending on the heat of your oven, it will take 5 or 6 minutes to cook.

Remove from the oven, plate and cut if required. Garnish with rocket leaves, prosciutto and shaved parmesan. Drizzle with extra virgin olive oil.

TIPS

There are many different ways to make pizza dough – at Non Solo Pizza we use an old traditional way that requires a slow proving. Don't hesitate to give us a call and check whether we can provide you with some pizza dough for your dinner!

RAVIOLI ALLA PIEMONTESE
BEEF & SPINACH RAVIOLI WITH SAGE BURNT BUTTER

Servings: 6 | Prep Time: 1¼ hours | Cook Time: 8 minutes | Skill Level: 2 (Moderate)

INGREDIENTS

Ravioli
6 tbsp butter
3 tbsp olive oil
1 small onion
1 clove garlic
1 sprig of fresh rosemary
500 g lean beef
  (or ½ beef and ½ pork)
2 tbsp flour
1 cup beef stock
3 cans tomatoes, puréed
300 g fresh spinach leaves
60 g grated parmesan cheese
3 eggs
2 pinches of salt
pinch of pepper
pinch of ground nutmeg
500 g fresh pasta sheets

Sauce
6 fresh sage leaves
2 tbsp butter
30 ml cream
90 ml reduced beef stock
50 g rock salt

To serve
10 g shaved parmesan cheese
30 g grated parmesan cheese
5 ml truffle oil

METHOD

Heat butter and oil together in a pan. Finely chop onion, garlic and rosemary and add to pan to sauté. Cut meat into a large dice, season to taste with salt and pepper and add to pan, browning well on all sides. Sprinkle with flour and add stock and tomato. Cover and simmer for just under 1 hour, until the meat is tender.

Cool slightly, then shred the meat, reserving the cooking juices. Finely chop spinach and sauté gently in a little butter. Add parmesan and blend together with meat, spinach, 2 lightly beaten eggs, salt and pepper and nutmeg.

Decide what shape you want for your ravioli according to the size and shape of your pasta sheets and the cutter you have. Lay a pasta sheet on a lightly floured surface; depending on its size, you will either be folding half the sheet over or placing a second sheet on top. Lightly whisk remaining egg and brush onto the sheet where the filling is going to go. Use the cutter to lightly mark out your ravioli shapes. A nice size is between 6 and 7 cm in diameter or inside length. Place a dollop of filling in the centre of each shape. Fold over the pasta sheet or place a second sheet on top. Press around the edge of each ravioli shape, then cut.

For the sauce, pan-fry sage in most of the butter for a few minutes. Add the juices from the meat along with cream and reduced beef stock, and let cook for a few more minutes until all is well combined.

Bring a large pot of water to the boil. Add rock salt and ravioli and cook until ravioli floats (at least 7–8 minutes). Drain. Toss ravioli in a bowl with the remaining butter and then in the pan with the sauce.

Serve with shaved parmesan over the top, a grind of pepper and a drizzle of truffle oil, with the grated parmesan on the side.

WILLIE CALDER
OYSTERMAN

OYSTERS KILPATRICK

I've been an oysterman for thirty-eight years, ever since the day I turned sixteen. My great-great-grandfather was the first man ever to catch commercial oysters in 1861 and the family's been catching them ever since. You really can't beat Bluff oysters 'cause, when they come out of the shell, they are totally clean and ready to eat. Some people like them with a squeeze of lemon, but I actually like them Kilpatrick style: a bit of bacon, a bit of cheese, a bit of Worcestershire sauce... it doesn't get any better than that.

-Willie

Bluff

OYSTERS KILPATRICK

Servings: 3 | Prep Time: 10 mins | Cook Time: 3 mins | Skill Level: 1 (Easy)

INGREDIENTS

12 Bluff oysters (raw)
12 oyster shells, cleaned
3 rashers bacon
¾ cup grated
  tasty cheese
Worcestershire sauce

METHOD

Pre-heat the oven grill. Place an oyster in each oyster shell.

Grill or fry bacon until just crispy. Chop bacon and split evenly between oysters. Add a dash of Worcestershire sauce to each oyster and sprinkle cheese evenly over all 12.

Put under a hot grill and cook until cheese has just started to bubble – oysters should only be warmed through (approx. 3 minutes).

PETER GORDON

SPAGHETTI & CHEESE TOASTS
BRUCE GORDON'S SOUFFLÉ OMELETTE

When I think back to my childhood in Whanganui, the dish that most stands out is Dad's soufflé omelette. Bruce is your typical Kiwi bloke - so where he conceived of the idea to beat egg whites into an omelette escapes me. And him actually! My favourite birthday treat was spaghetti toasts. It's probably my simplest recipe to date and I just love them. At my last book launch in London, a major newspaper editor was so impressed he asked for the secret to making the spaghetti. My reply - "Open the can!"

Peter

Whanganui

SPAGHETTI & CHEESE TOASTS

Servings: 6 | Prep Time: 10 mins | Cook Time: 20 mins | Skill Level: 1 (Easy)

INGREDIENTS

60 g butter, melted

6 slices soft white
  sandwich bread

1 x 400 g tin spaghetti
  in tomato sauce

3 tbsp grated cheddar

METHOD

Pre-heat the oven to 180°C. Butter the bases of a 6-hole patty pan or muffin tin.

Butter bread on one side, flip it over and press into the tin butter-side down. Brush with remaining butter, making sure you use it all up. Spoon in spaghetti and top with cheese.

Bake until bread is crisp and golden, around 20 minutes. Leave in the tin for a few minutes to firm up, before gently removing. These are lovely eaten straight from the oven, or at room temperature.

TIP

You could make these in smaller tins and get even more!

BRUCE GORDON'S SOUFFLÉ OMELETTE

Servings: 4 | Prep Time: 5 mins | Cook Time: 20 mins | Skill Level: 1 (Easy)

INGREDIENTS

½ large onion
  (I use a red one)

2 tomatoes

6 rashers smoked
  streaky bacon

6 eggs

a few knobs of butter

2 tbsp grated cheddar

METHOD

Dice onion and tomatoes, and cut bacon into lardons. Separate eggs into two largish bowls. Turn the oven grill on.

Heat some butter in a frying pan over medium heat until sizzling. Add onion and cook until beginning to caramelise, stirring often. Add bacon and cook until it begins to crisp up a little. Add tomatoes and cook for a few minutes until any extra moisture is evaporated, stirring.

Meanwhile, beat egg whites with a pinch of salt until thick and foamy.

Tip bacon mixture onto yolks and mix together well. Fold beaten whites into egg yolk mixture.

Put the pan back on the heat and add a knob of butter. Once butter is sizzling, tip omelette mixture back into the pan and put a lid on. Cook over medium-low heat for 3 minutes, until the whites firm up a little.

Take the lid off, sprinkle with cheese and place under the grill. Once golden and bubbling, remove the pan from the heat and cut into four. Serve on buttered toast.

Epsom,
Auckland

ANTHONY HOY FONG

CRISPY PORK & CABBAGE SPRING ROLLS
CHINESE ROASTED PORK BELLY WITH QUICK-PICKLED CUCUMBER

Any member of a big Chinese family will tell you that food is a huge part of their identity. Crispy roasted pork belly was a "special occasion" food growing up; it reminds me of my Ma-ma, birthday parties, extended family gatherings and, of course, cold roast-pork sandwiches for lunch the next day! Each generation makes it their own with subtle, signature nuances ... But always the common denominator is: tender, juicy, melt in your mouth meat and crispy crackling that you could light a match on! Home-made pork & cabbage spring rolls were the definition of "fast food" in our house growing up. Making them was always a family event where we'd sit around the table rolling them together, seeing who could make the best rolls. Being Kiwis, we'd always have ours with Worcestershire sauce, the perfect complement – yum!

– Anthony

CRISPY PORK & CABBAGE SPRING ROLLS

Servings: 4–6 | Prep Time: 40 mins | Cook Time: 20 mins | Skill Level: 2 (Moderate)

INGREDIENTS

Filling
2 tbsp canola oil
2 tbsp minced ginger
2 tbsp minced garlic
250 g lean pork mince
1 tbsp light soy sauce
1½ cups finely sliced carrots
½ cup finely sliced onions
½ cup finely sliced bamboo shoots
1½ cups finely sliced rehydrated
  shiitake mushrooms
¼ tsp sea salt
1 tsp toasted sesame oil
2 cups finely sliced green cabbage
3 tbsp oyster sauce
¼ cup finely chopped fresh coriander

To finish
12 large Chinese spring roll wrappers
  (24 cm x 24 cm), thawed
2 eggs, beaten
canola oil, for shallow-frying
fresh coriander leaves and sliced spring onions,
  to garnish
Worcestershire sauce, for dipping

METHOD

Heat a large non-stick sauté pan over high heat. Add 1 tablespoon of canola oil, then sauté ginger and garlic for 30 seconds until fragrant. Add pork and cook for 5 minutes until browned, breaking up with a wooden spoon as it cooks. Season pork with soy sauce, then transfer to a large bowl.

Return pan to heat and add remaining tablespoon of canola oil. Sauté carrots, onions, bamboo shoots and shiitake mushrooms for 3–4 minutes until just cooked through. Season with salt and add sesame oil. Turn off heat, fold in cabbage (the residual heat will wilt the cabbage), then transfer vegetable mix to the bowl with the pork. Add oyster sauce and mix well. Cool, uncovered, in fridge for 15–20 minutes. Pour off any excess liquid in bowl, then fold in fresh coriander.

Working with one wrapper at a time, brush with egg. With one corner facing you, place approx. 2½ tablespoons of filling in a log shape across the corner. Roll over opposite corner and tuck in neatly, then firmly roll the log over itself to secure. Fold in both sides, then roll until sealed by final top corner of wrapper. Repeat with remaining wrappers and filling.

Heat canola oil, 3–4 cm deep, in a heavy pan to 180°C. Working in batches, fry the spring rolls in hot oil for 3–4 minutes per side until golden and crispy. Drain well, then cut on the bias and serve with garnish and Worcestershire sauce.

TIPS

For a vegetarian version, simply omit the pork and increase the amount of shiitake mushrooms to 3 cups total; also substitute oyster sauce with a vegetarian sauce.

Spring roll wrappers can be found in the freezer section at your local Asian grocery store.

CHINESE ROASTED PORK BELLY WITH QUICK-PICKLED CUCUMBER

Servings: 6 | Prep Time: 15 mins plus marinating | Cook Time: 2 hours | Skill Level: 2 (Moderate)

INGREDIENTS

Pork belly
1½ kg boneless slab of pork belly, skin on
1 tsp mānuka honey
1 tsp sugar
3 cloves garlic, crushed
3 tbsp hoisin sauce
1 tbsp soy sauce
1 tbsp sea salt, plus extra for rubbing
½ tsp five-spice powder
1 tbsp canola oil
fresh coriander leaves, to garnish
spring onions, to garnish

Pickled cucumber
1 large cucumber
2½ tbsp seasoned rice vinegar
2 tbsp water
1 tbsp sugar
1 tbsp toasted sesame oil
1 tsp sea salt
1 medium-sized fresh red chilli, finely sliced

METHOD

Place pork skin-side down on board and slice three-quarters deep into the flesh at 4 cm intervals (this will allow the marinade to get deep into the meat). Place pork on roasting rack in a clean sink and pour boiling-hot water over both sides 2–3 times to tighten skin (this helps the crackling process). Pat dry with paper towels and place in foil-lined roasting pan.

Make marinade by combining honey, sugar, garlic, hoisin, soy, 1 tablespoon salt and five-spice powder. Rub marinade all over flesh of pork, getting it deep into the slices but avoiding the skin – if you get any on the skin, wipe it off with a paper towel as it will prevent the skin from crackling.

With pork skin-side up in pan, use the tip of a sharp knife to dock the skin all over with small slashes. Rub skin with canola oil and a little salt. Place in fridge to marinate for 2–3 hours.

Pre-heat the oven to 240°C. Place pork in centre of oven and cook for 20 minutes. Add 2 cups of water to pan, then reduce heat to 160°C and cook for 1½ hours. Finish under grill for 3–4 minutes to crackle skin further if required (use foil to cover any edges that get too brown). Remove from oven and rest for 15 minutes before slicing.

Peel cucumber, then slice lengthwise in half. Using a small spoon, scrape out seeds and discard. Slice halves lengthwise into thirds, then cut into small wedges (approx. 2 cm). In a medium-sized bowl, place vinegar, water, sugar, sesame oil, salt and chilli. Whisk together, then add cucumber. Cover with plastic wrap and place in fridge for 30 minutes before serving.

Cut pork into strips using the original deep cuts as a guide. Slice each strip into bite-sized pieces and arrange on platters. Serve with pickled cucumber. Garnish with coriander and sliced spring onions.

JEREMY RAMEKA
PACIFICA

PAN-FRIED JOHN DORY
BUTTER LIME SCALLOPS

My earliest memory of cooking was with my grandfather while eeling. He'd cut the top of his fingers, drawing out blood so that the eels would latch onto his fingers, then he'd pull them out. After the initial preparation we'd cook them over an open fire. When we were kids, that was a strong foundation towards respect for food and the cooking of it.

I remember travelling to the Hawke's Bay as a kid and being in awe of the different types of fruit and veg. We were from the King Country where such things never really existed.

These days, we have our own garden at home and grow everything and anything. The menu at the restaurant is formed around what I can pick on the day, so that changes every day.

Jeremy

Napier

PAN-FRIED JOHN DORY

Servings: 4 | Cook Time: 8 mins | Skill Level: 2 (Moderate)

INGREDIENTS

50 g butter
40 ml soya oil
1 brown onion, diced
1 Oxo beef stock cube
 or 200 ml beef stock
200 ml water (if using
 stock cube)
8 spears white
 asparagus
4 John Dory fillets,
 skin on (120 g each)

METHOD

In a saucepan over a moderate heat, add 20 g of butter and 20 ml of oil, then the diced onions. Turn the heat up gradually. Once onions are browned or caramelised, add beef stock and water (if needed), and leave on a moderate heat until reduced to required thickness.

Pre-heat the oven to 180°C. Slice asparagus into 3 cm lengths. Add remaining oil to medium-to-hot oven-safe frying pan. Pan-fry fillets, skin-side down, for approx. 30 seconds to a minute, or until crispy. Don't be tempted to move the fillets until they are completely crispy underneath.

Add remaining butter together with the asparagus, then immediately put into the oven for 2 minutes. Return to the heat on the stovetop, and turn fillets over for 10–15 seconds only. Remove and rest for 2–3 minutes before serving.

BUTTER LIME SCALLOPS

Servings: 4 | Cook Time: 5 mins | Skill Level: 2 (Moderate)

INGREDIENTS

170 g butter
20 scallops (roe on)
30 ml Pernod
juice of 2 limes
raw oyster mushrooms,
 for garnish

METHOD

Heat a pan over medium to high heat, then add 100 g of butter and the scallops. Pan-fry, only turning once they are toasted brown. Place on clean paper towels to absorb excess butter.

Return pan to a moderate heat, and add Pernod and lime juice with the remaining butter. Drizzle butter-lime sauce over the scallops and serve with fresh raw oyster mushrooms.

TIP

If wanting an aerated sauce, use a stick blender while the sauce is at a simmering temperature. Do not boil the sauce as the fat will separate, making the sauce difficult to foam.

BEN BAYLY

LAMB MEATBALLS
HERB PASTA
CHOCOLATE SOUFFLÉ

As a chef, you often get so tied up in what you are doing you can forget you have a family at home.

Saturday was my day off but I had to pop into the restaurant... I told my daughter Ella, who is 4, I'd be home at 1pm but I got home at 4.30pm and she told me off. We had to play beads straight away. I now wear a bracelet she made me as a reminder that when I say I'm going to be home at a certain time, I'll be home at that time!

I LOVE COOKING with my girls – they are interested in food and just love to get in there and help. It's important for kids to get their hands dirty and lick spoons; it's all part of developing their palates and having fun...

— Ben.

Te Awamutu

LAMB MEATBALLS

Servings: 6 | Prep Time: 30 mins | Cook Time: 30 mins | Skill Level: 1 (Easy)

INGREDIENTS

Meatballs
2 brown onions
good splash of olive oil
200 g wholemeal bread
75 ml milk
1 whole lamb
  shoulder, boned
100 g spinach,
  chard or kale
50 g fresh rosemary leaves
50 g fresh thyme leaves
30 g salt

Sauce
3 shallots, sliced
2 cloves garlic
pinch of chilli flakes
10 g salt
75 ml good-quality olive oil
500 g good-quality canned
  tomatoes
1 tbsp honey

METHOD

Slice onions and caramelise in olive oil until sweet and soft; cool them down in the fridge. Soak bread in milk and cut lamb into strips. Pre-heat the oven to 220°C.

Set up your mincer with a medium-sized grinder plate (with holes of about 4 mm). Mix onion and bread with remaining meatball ingredients in a bowl until evenly dispersed. Turn mincer on and feed mixture through into the bowl of your electric food mixer.

Using a paddle on your food mixer, beat meatball mixture for about 1 minute on medium speed until everything is well incorporated and the mixture is sticky.

Wet your hands slightly and divide the meatball mixture into 40 g portions. Roll into a nice round shape and place on a baking tray. Place meatballs in the oven for 4 minutes to set the outside and make them easy to barbecue or pan-sear.

For the sauce, sweat the shallots, garlic, chilli flakes and salt in the olive oil until they soften – do not colour. Add tomatoes and honey and simmer for 5 minutes, or until the tomatoes have broken up to make a sauce. In another pan, sear the meatballs until they are nicely caramelised. (Alternatively, barbecue the meatballs on a nice high heat.)

Pour tomato sauce over meatballs in the pan and simmer for 5 minutes until meatballs are cooked inside.

TIP

If you don't have a mincer, ask your local butcher to mince the lamb shoulder for you.

HERB PASTA

Servings: 4 | Prep Time: 1¼ hours | Cook Time: 1 min | Skill Level: 2 (Moderate)

INGREDIENTS

300 g '00' flour
5 egg yolks
1 egg
pinch of salt
20 g fresh chervil leaves
20 g fresh parsley leaves
a little olive oil

METHOD

Blend flour, egg and salt together in a food processor. Place on a lightly floured work surface and knead until it forms a tight dough. Cover with plastic wrap and allow to rest for 30 minutes.

Roll the pasta out through a pasta machine until 2–3 mm thick. Fold the pasta over in a book fold and re-roll through the pasta machine until 2–3 mm thick (this will help develop the dough).

With your sheet of pasta laid out on the work surface, cover half the sheet with herb leaves. Fold the other half of the pasta over the top, sandwiching the herbs between the pasta. Roll through the pasta machine again until you have a thin pasta sheet 1–2 mm thick. All the herbs will be pressed into the pasta and become a part of it.

Slice pasta into pappardelle (strips 2½ cm wide) with a sharp knife. Cook in boiling water for 1 minute, then drain and toss with olive oil and serve.

CHOCOLATE SOUFFLÉ

Servings: 4 (plus extra base) | *Prep Time: 40–50 mins* | *Cook Time: 10 mins*
Skill Level: 2 (Moderate)

INGREDIENTS

Soufflé base
95 g butter
450 g good-quality
  dark chocolate
105 g egg yolk,
  at room temperature

Mould preparation
50 g butter
50 g sugar

Soufflé
150 g egg white
60 g sugar
150 g soufflé base
40 g white chocolate,
  chopped
20 g icing sugar

To serve
icing sugar, for dusting
fresh berries

METHOD

Melt butter and chocolate together carefully. Fold egg yolks through. This will make about three batches of four soufflés.

To prepare the moulds, soften butter and use to grease four soufflé moulds, using a pastry brush. Place in the fridge and leave to set, then 're-paint' with the butter to create a nice thick layer. Be generous with the butter – you don't want the soufflés to stick! Pour sugar into the buttered moulds and roll the sugar around to coat all of the butter. As the soufflé cooks, the sugar will melt and combine with the butter to create a protective layer between the soufflé mould and the soufflé mix and stop it sticking to the sides of the mould.

Pre-heat the oven to 180°C. Have two bowls ready. Place egg whites in one bowl with 5 g of sugar. While whisking continuously, slowly add the rest of the sugar, then whisk until you have soft peaks.

In the other bowl put the soufflé base. Give it a good mix to soften it a little, add white chocolate, then add one-third of the whites and mix. Carefully add the other two-thirds of the whites and fold in carefully. Spoon into your prepared soufflé moulds and bake for 10 minutes.

The soufflés will rise nice and high! Serve immediately with a dusting of icing sugar and some fresh berries.

Whakatane

ANNE THORP
KAI ORA

TĪTĪ (MUTTONBIRD) & WATERCRESS
PORK & PŪHĀ

I was reared on pork & pūhā but for a treat we would often have tītī (muttonbird) + watercress.

Tītī has incredible flavour + is considered a delicacy to Māori & many would kill for a feed of it!

When I was a kid, pork & pūhā was very much in vogue. It still is. It was called 'the pot'.

The aroma of the cooking of the pot evokes nostalgia for most Māori. Everything went into the one pot although today I like to cook the root vegetables separately. The pork bones are simmered and, when the meat is practically falling off the bones, the pūhā is chucked into the pot and cooked gently until wilted.

I remember my mother would send me out with my siblings to gather pūhā. We had a kete each and weren't allowed back until our kete were full!

These days, I head to the Ōtara Market most Saturday mornings for all my fresh produce before heading up to my home at Pakiri Beach to cook for my family & friends. – Anne.

B-Burn Apples
$1-79¢
Kilo

TĪTĪ (MUTTONBIRD) & WATERCRESS

Servings: 4 | Prep Time: 20 mins | Cook Time: 3 hours | Skill Level: 1 (Easy)

INGREDIENTS

2 or 3 tītī/muttonbirds
2 bay leaves (optional)
big bunch of watercress
  (about 750 g)
4 small kūmara, peeled
  and cut into chunks

METHOD

Bring a large pot of water containing the tītī and bay leaves (if using) to the boil, then simmer very gently (*blip blip*) for 1–1½ hours. Turn off the heat and leave tītī in the pot with the lid on for another hour. Meanwhile, prepare watercress by removing long stalks and rinsing thoroughly. Cut watercress in half.

After an hour, take tītī out of the pot and discard most but not all of the liquid, to get rid of the fatty oil. Add water to make a weaker stock, just enough to flavour the watercress and kūmara. Bring pot back to the boil, reduce heat to a gentle simmer and add kūmara. After 5 minutes, add watercress – once kūmara is cooked, the watercress will be too. Remove from the heat.

Pre-heat the oven grill to 200°C. Place tītī onto baking paper on an oven tray, skin-side up, and roast under the grill for 10–15 minutes, longer if you wish. This crisps up the skin and removes even more oil! Break tītī into segments, removing any fatty deposits and the skin if you find it too rich. Many Māori love the crispy skin and eat all of the tītī except the bones – and these too are sucked dry! Serve with the kūmara and watercress.

TIP

Leave kitchen windows wide open when cooking tītī. It has a strong aroma during cooking. Don't be put off, though – it's delicious!

PORK & PŪHĀ

Servings: 4 | Prep Time: 20 mins | Cook Time: 2–3 hours | Skill Level: 1 (Easy)

INGREDIENTS

1–2 kg pork bones
2 bay leaves (optional)
2 tsp salt, for the pot
big bunch of pūhā
  (about 1 kg)

*Any root vegetables,
  such as:*
2 carrots, cut into chunks
¼ pumpkin,
  cut into chunks
2 kūmara, cut into chunks
4 small or gourmet
  potatoes
1 tsp salt, for the
  vegetables

METHOD

Put pork bones and bay leaves (if using) into a large pot and drown them in cold water. Add salt and bring to the boil with the pot lid off. Still with the pot lid off, simmer very gently (*blip blip*) for an hour or so, until the meat is falling off the bone.

Meanwhile, prepare pūhā. Remove flowers, tarnished leaves and long stalks and rinse thoroughly. (You will end up with approx. half the weight after removing all the unusable bits.) Cut pūhā in half.

Add pūhā to pot once pork is ready, i.e. falling off the bone. With pot lid on, simmer very gently for about 5–8 minutes. Turn heat off, and allow pūhā to steam in the pot with lid on for 5–10 minutes. Meanwhile, steam or gently boil your vegetables of choice in another pot with salt until soft.

Before serving, gently turn pūhā over in the stock of the pot. Plate up and finish off by pouring a little of the stock water over the dish. Season to taste. 'The pot' heated up the next day is divine.

MICHAEL COUGHLIN
PIER 24

SLOW-COOKED BEEF SHORT RIBS WITH CANDIED BABY ONIONS
APRICOT CRÈME BRÛLÉE
PISTACHIO BISCOTTI

I come from a big family with seven children, where everything was centred around the dinner table. Even after thirty-five years in the business, I'm still excited about getting into the kitchen, discovering new flavours and textures and using them to tell a story. I chose to share my slow-cooked beef short-rib because we all love that slow-cooked intense stickiness, while the inspiration for my crème brûlée comes from the intensely flavoured sun-dried apricots from the orchard across the river from where I used to live in Clyde. Just make sure that you don't have the heat too high or it will curdle on you!
— Michael

St Clair,
Dunedin

SLOW-COOKED BEEF SHORT RIBS WITH CANDIED BABY ONIONS

Servings: 4 | Prep Time: 30 mins | Cook Time: 4–5 hours | Skill Level: 1 (Easy)

INGREDIENTS

100 g onion
100 g carrot, peeled
1 stick celery
4 portions beef short
  rib on the bone
  (200 g each)
100 g rice bran oil
1 clove garlic
2 star anise
200 ml beef stock
50 ml Madeira wine
80 ml light soy sauce
50 ml sweet chilli sauce
20 g hoisin sauce

Sauce
30 g butter
400 g baby onions
  or shallots
40 ml sherry vinegar
100 g brown sugar

METHOD

Pre-heat the oven to 140°C.

Lightly chop onion, carrot and celery. Season beef ribs with plenty of salt and pepper, and brown in a heavy frying pan with the oil until caramelised. Remove from the pan and set aside on a plate.

Brown off onion, carrot and celery in the same pan, add garlic and star anise, then pour on beef stock, Madeira, soy, chilli sauce and hoisin and deglaze all the sediment and flavour from the pan.

Place ribs in an oven bag that has been placed in a roasting dish or casserole dish and pour vegetable and pan juices onto ribs. Seal up the bag, leaving a small vent to avoid pressure building up, and cook in the oven for 4–5 hours or until the meat comes easily away from the bone. Carefully remove ribs from the bag and place on a plate to keep warm until required. Strain the juices from the bag, remove all the fat and set aside for completing the sauce.

For the sauce, melt butter in a clean, large frying pan, and on a moderate heat caramelise onions on all sides. Pour on sherry vinegar and sugar (be wary of a sudden rush of steam). Pour on the reserved braising stock, carefully place the ribs in and simmer the stock, occasionally coating ribs, until stock reduces and becomes thick and syrupy. Carefully place onto serving plates.

TIPS

Don't rush this dish – allow the juices to cook down until shiny and thick so that the ribs become well coated for that lip-sticking feeling and flavour.

I use Silver Fern Farms' short ribs; these are readily available wholesale – try your local butcher and ask if they can cut the ribs into three strips about 7–8 cm long, which will require a bandsaw or hacksaw to achieve, and will create a shorter rib that is much more presentable and elegant on the plate.

To remove unwanted fat from stocks and sauces, cut strips of good-quality baking paper and float from one end of the paper to the other across the surface of the liquid. The fat will be attracted to the paper; you can then discard that strip with the fat attached. You can only use the paper for one run each, so cut half a dozen strips or more depending on how much fat has formed on top of the stock.

Serve with creamy kūmara purée – the earthy, sweet flavour is just a wonderful partner with the sticky, rich flavours of the rib – and how about a crisp, green vegetable salad such as fresh asparagus, thinly sliced red onion and zucchini tossed with a light citrus dressing and sprinkled with toasted sesame seeds.

APRICOT CRÈME BRÛLÉE

Servings: 4 | Prep Time: 20 mins plus cooling | Cook Time: 50 mins plus chilling | Skill Level: 2 (Moderate)

INGREDIENTS

Apricot filling
100 g dried apricots
100 ml hot water
100 g caster sugar
150 ml orange juice
  plus zest of 1 orange

Brûlée
500 ml cream
5 g vanilla paste
5 egg yolks
160 g caster sugar

METHOD

Slice apricots thinly and place in a pot with remaining filling ingredients. Bring to the boil, stirring constantly. Remove from the heat, cover and stand for approx. 2 hours, until apricots have softened and plumped up.

To make brûlée, place cream and vanilla in a medium-sized saucepan over a medium-high heat and bring to just below boiling point. Remove from heat, cover and sit for 15 minutes.

In a medium-sized bowl, whisk together egg yolks and 60 grams of sugar until well blended and just starting to lighten in colour. Add vanilla cream a little at a time, stirring constantly.

Pre-heat the oven to 150°C. Place a spoonful of soaked apricots into four 220 ml ramekins, then carefully ladle in the custard. Place ramekins in a large cake tin or roasting pan. Pour enough hot water into the pan to come halfway up the sides of the ramekins. Cover the tin/pan with tinfoil and bake until the custard is just set but still trembling in the centre – approx. 45–50 minutes. Remove ramekins from the tin/pan and refrigerate for at least 2 hours (up to three days).

To serve, place a dessertspoonful of the remaining caster sugar evenly on top of each custard. Using a blowtorch, melt sugar to form a crispy top. Allow crème brûlées to sit for at least 5 minutes before serving with 3–4 crisp pistachio biscotti (see below) on the side.

TIPS

The difficulty – and success – in this recipe lies in constant checking of the baking custard. Lower the temperature to 140°C on your first batch if you are unsure what will work for you; and never allow the heat to exceed 150°C.

PISTACHIO BISCOTTI

Makes: 24 | Prep Time: 20 mins | Cook Time: 55 mins | Skill Level: 1 (Easy)

INGREDIENTS

125 g egg whites
125 g caster sugar
125 g plain flour
125 g pistachio nuts
5 g vanilla paste

METHOD

Pre-heat the oven to 175°C. Line a loaf tin with non-stick baking paper.

In a large bowl and using an electric mixer, beat egg whites with a pinch of salt until they just form stiff peaks. Gradually beat in sugar, beating until meringue mixture forms stiff, glossy peaks. Sift flour over mixture and fold in with nuts and vanilla, gently but thoroughly.

Spoon meringue mixture into loaf pan, smoothing the top, and bake in middle of oven until golden, 25–30 minutes. Cool loaf in tin on a rack for 15 minutes, then turn out onto rack to cool completely.

Reduce oven temperature to 150°C. Peel baking paper off and use a serrated knife to cut loaf crosswise into slices 3 mm thick. Arrange slices about 1 cm apart on two baking sheets and bake for about 20 minutes or until pale golden and crisp, switching position of the sheets halfway through. Cool biscuits on sheets placed on racks. Biscuits keep in an airtight container at a cool room temperature for up to 10 days.

JAY SHERWOOD
AMISFIELD WINERY

DUCK LIVER &
PORK CHEEK PÂTÉ
PICKLED RADISH
MUSHROOM & HERB
PAPPARDELLE

We have a great team here at
Amisfield where the main focus of
our kitchen is on being creative and proud
of what we do every day. I feel really
fortunate to have such amazing chefs
working for me and so lucky to live here
in the Queenstown region. We have access
to the most stunning ingredients and talented
local suppliers who I can call up at a
moment's notice. They come to our doorstep
with shopping bags full of rocket, fresh herbs
and other produce, all picked earlier that
morning. Where else in the world could
you do that?!

Jay

Lake Hayes

DUCK LIVER & PORK CHEEK PÂTÉ

Servings: 8 | Prep Time: 13 hours | Cook Time: 40 mins | Skill Level: 3 (More challenging)

INGREDIENTS

Pâté spice

1 tbsp ground cloves
1 tbsp ground nutmeg
1 tbsp dried ginger
2 tbsp ground cinnamon
1 tbsp ground white pepper

Pâté

40 g salt
600 g pork cheek
1 kg duck fat
1 leek
400 g duck liver
600 g diced pork shoulder
½ onion, diced
1 bunch fresh Italian parsley, chopped
2½ tbsp sea salt
½ tbsp ground black pepper
½ tbsp pâté spice
5 cloves garlic, minced
2 eggs
3 tbsp brandy
½ cup cream

METHOD

Place all pâté spice ingredients in a spice grinder or mortar and pestle and grind to a powder. Store in an airtight container.

Rub salt into pork cheek and stand for 3 hours. Place in a deep baking tray and cover with duck fat. Cover the tray with tinfoil and place in a 90°C oven for 12 hours. Remove from oven and allow to cool to room temperature. Remove the meat from the fat and break it apart with your fingers. Pre-heat the oven to 150°C.

Cut leeks in half lengthways so that each layer is a long rectangular piece. Blanch for 30 seconds in a large pot of boiling water then place in ice water immediately. Remove from ice water and pat dry. Use leeks to make a rectangle shape the same length as your pâté mould. Spoon pork cheek onto leek to the width of a large coin. Carefully roll the leek up around the pork and set aside.

Combine all other ingredients in a large bowl and mince through a large die. Keep both bowls on ice to keep the liver from spoiling. Cover the insides of the pâté mould (standard 1.5 litre) with plastic wrap, using a tea towel to push the plastic into the corners. Add pâté mixture to halfway up the mould, place the leek/pork roll in and cover with the rest of the pâté mixture. Cover the top with plastic wrap.

Cover the pâté mould with its lid and place in a large, deep oven tray. Pour hot water into the tray to three-quarters of the way up the mould. Place in the oven for 1 hour or until the internal temperature of the pâté reaches 65°C. The cooking time depends on the oven, water temperature and tray size, so start checking the internal temperature of the pâté with a meat thermometer after 45 minutes.

Once the correct temperature has been reached, remove the mould from the water bath and rest at room temperature for 30 minutes. Remove the lid and replace with a rectangular piece of wood or plastic the same size as the inside of the mould. Use something slightly heavy on top to press down the pâté and place it in the chiller overnight.

Serve with pickled radish (see below) as a garnish.

PICKLED RADISH

Servings: 4 | Prep Time: 10 mins plus maturing time | Skill Level: 1 (Easy)

INGREDIENTS

500 g radishes
¾ cup red wine vinegar
½ cup water
¼ cup sugar
1 tsp mustard seeds
1 tsp salt

METHOD

Top and tail the radishes and place in sterilised jars with metal lids. Bring vinegar, water, sugar, mustard seeds and salt to a simmer and stir to dissolve the sugar. Pour the liquid over the radishes and put the lids on firmly.

Place the closed jars into the dishwasher (without soap) to heat, sanitise and seal the jars. Store in a cool, dry place. The pickled radishes will be ready in 10 days.

DF GF V

MUSHROOM & HERB PAPPARDELLE

Servings: 8–10 | Prep Time: 15 mins | Cook Time: 3¼ hours | Skill Level: 2 (Moderate)

INGREDIENTS

1 kg pasta flour
pinch of salt
2 tbsp oil
10 eggs

200 g dried
  porcini mushrooms
8 portobello mushrooms
oil, for cooking
knob of butter
150 g parmesan cheese,
  grated
small bunch of chopped
  fresh parsley, chervil
  and chives

METHOD

Mix flour and salt together in a food processor. With the motor running, add oil and slowly add eggs until the mixture turns into small pebbles of dough, then empty onto a clean, flat work surface. Alternatively, place flour and salt in a large bowl, in a volcano shape with the middle big enough to hold the oil and eggs. Add oil and eggs and whisk, slowly incorporating the flour from the edges until a thick paste is formed. Then use your hands to mix in the rest of the flour. Knead dough until smooth and well mixed. Wrap in plastic wrap and rest in the fridge for at least 1 hour.

Put porcini in a small pot and cover with 500 ml of hot water. Leave for at least 1 hour.

Bring pasta dough out of the fridge 15 minutes before using, to allow it to come to room temperature. Pass through a pasta roller four times, folding it end to end between rollings, then roll into thin sheets and cut into ribbons about 2 cm wide. Keep dough covered to stop it drying out.

Heat a sauté pan on high until hot. Chop portobellos, add to pan and drizzle with oil. Cook until golden brown. Add some porcini stock and bring to a simmer. Meanwhile, cook pappardelle in a large pot of boiling water. Add pasta to the mushrooms along with some pasta water. Cook for 3 minutes until the sauce comes together and thickens slightly. Remove from the heat, and add butter, 100 g parmesan and salt, pepper and herbs. Toss to incorporate all ingredients. Top with the remaining parmesan.

because my mum was a good cook and my dad comes from a big family, we were always at the marae in and around food. I remember I wanted to be a cop or a cook but, after my first year cooking I was hooked. I go back to the marae every now and then and Im allowed to do a bit of cooking now Im a chef. I remember a few years back I was asked to make a gravy. It was a packet gravy; it turned out lumpy so everyone had a good laugh at that: "flash chef eh, cant even follow instructions!"

Rex

REX MORGAN
BOULCOTT STREET BISTRO

LAMB SHANKS
HERB POLENTA
RHUBARB &
APPLE CRUMBLE

Wellington
Central

LAMB SHANKS

Servings: 4 | Prep Time: 20 mins | Cook Time: 3 hours | Skill Level: 1 (Easy)

INGREDIENTS

1 medium-sized onion

4 cloves garlic

4 hind lamb shanks, trimmed

8 tbsp canola or olive oil

2 tbsp tomato paste

1 tbsp chopped fresh rosemary or thyme

1 cup red wine (optional)

410 g canned crushed tomatoes

400 ml chicken stock or water

2 tbsp chopped fresh parsley

METHOD

Pre-heat the oven to 180°C. Coarsely chop onion and peel and crush garlic. Pat lamb dry with a paper towel and season with salt and pepper. Heat oil in an ovenproof pot over a medium-high heat and brown lamb well on all sides for approx. 8 minutes. Remove from the pan.

Add onion and garlic to pan and cook for a few minutes until soft. Stir in tomato paste and rosemary/thyme for 1 minute. Add wine and simmer until liquid is almost reduced. Stir in tomatoes and stock, then bring to the boil. Return shanks to pan, place a circle of greaseproof paper directly on surface of lamb and cover with a lid. Cook in the oven for 2–2½ hours, or until meat is very tender.

Remove paper and shanks from pan and keep shanks warm. Skim any fat from the surface of the sauce and discard. Purée sauce in a food processor or with a stick blender and return to the pan. Correct seasoning if needed. Place shanks back into the sauce, and add parsley. Serve with herb polenta (see below) and buttered green beans.

HERB POLENTA

Servings: 4 | Prep Time: 10 mins | Cook Time: 10–15 mins | Skill Level: 1 (Easy)

INGREDIENTS

400 ml water

1 tbsp salt

100 g instant polenta

1 tbsp olive oil

2 tbsp grated parmesan (optional)

2 tbsp finely chopped fresh parsley

olive oil or butter, for cooking

METHOD

Bring water to a vigorous boil, add salt, and let polenta fall into the pot in a steady stream while whisking. Cook, stirring continuously with a wooden spoon to avoid lumps forming or the polenta sticking and burning, for 3–5 minutes or until the mixture comes together (check the time required on the packet). Stir in oil, parmesan and parsley until combined. Pour onto an oiled baking sheet or chopping board and shape into a smooth, flat rectangle. Allow to cool until firm, about 10 minutes.

Cut into four pieces. Place a non-stick frying pan with a little olive oil or butter on a medium-high heat. Fry polenta for approx. 2 minutes each side, or until slightly golden. Add a little salt and pepper to the polenta while frying. Keep warm until ready to serve.

RHUBARB & APPLE CRUMBLE

Servings: 4 | Prep Time: 10 mins | Cook Time: 10–20 mins | Skill Level: 1 (Easy)

INGREDIENTS

Fruit mixture
3 cooking apples
½ cup water
400 g fresh rhubarb
½ cup sugar
1 tsp finely grated
  orange zest

Crumble
100 g butter, chopped
½ cup self-raising flour
½ cup soft brown sugar
½ cup rolled oats
icing sugar, for dusting

METHOD

Pre-heat the oven to 180°C.

Peel, quarter and core apples, then cut into slices 2 cm thick and place in a saucepan with water. Simmer for 5–8 minutes.

Meanwhile, wash rhubarb and chop into 1 cm lengths. Add rhubarb, sugar and orange zest to apple; return to the boil and simmer for 3 minutes.

Pour mixture into a greased shallow ovenproof dish or four small individual ones.

Make the crumble by rubbing butter into flour with your fingers, then mix in brown sugar and oats. Sprinkle crumble evenly over the fruit mixture.

Bake for approx. 20 minutes for a large dish and 10 minutes for small dishes. Dust with icing sugar and serve warm with vanilla ice cream.

TIPS

If you are using individual dishes, you may not need to bake for so long. Look for them to be turning golden brown and bubbling a little.

Rhubarb can be substituted with ripe stone fruit.

We've been making these citrus berry & white chocolate muffins since the day we opened. A couple of hundred thousand of them so far! Funnily enough we asked our local plumber to cut up some stainless steel tubes to use as moulds — just something to give them that something extra — but you can use normal muffin tins at home.

The caramelised onion scones come out of the oven around 8.20 every morning, & there's a bit of a rush in the café when the scone lovers come in. I hope our favourites become your favourites.

Bruce Murrell.

BOSCO CAFE

BLUEBERRY, ORANGE & WHITE CHOCOLATE MUFFINS

CARAMELISED ONION & CHEDDAR SCONES

Te Kuiti

BLUEBERRY, ORANGE & WHITE CHOCOLATE MUFFINS

Makes: 18 | Prep Time: 10 mins | Cook Time: 30–35 mins | Skill Level: 1 (Easy)

INGREDIENTS

4 oranges
1¼ cups sugar
1¼ cups soya oil
1 tsp vanilla essence
4 eggs
1¼ cups yoghurt
1¾ cups milk

8 cups self-raising flour
2 tsp baking soda
pinch of salt
3 cups frozen berries
  – blueberries, blackberries or raspberries
3 cups white chocolate buttons
extra berries and chocolate for topping

METHOD

Pre-heat the oven to 150°C. Put oranges, including skin but not pips, into blender and blend until mushy. Add sugar, oil, vanilla, eggs, yoghurt and milk and blend together.

In a large bowl, sift flour, baking soda and salt together. Mix in wet ingredients and add berries and chocolate.

Spoon into lightly greased muffin tins using a wide-mouthed funnel and a spoon. Fill each tin three-quarters full. Bake for 30–35 minutes. Cool until warm. Top each muffin with melted white chocolate and some berries.

CARAMELISED ONION & CHEDDAR SCONES

Makes: 16 | Prep Time: 30 mins | Cook Time: 20 mins | Skill Level: 1 (Easy)

INGREDIENTS

6 onions
4 tbsp oil, for cooking
6 cups flour
2 tbsp baking powder
2 tsp salt

4 tsp caster sugar
6 cups grated tasty cheese
600 ml milk (approx.)
extra milk and grated tasty cheese, for topping

METHOD

Pre-heat the oven to 180°C on fan-bake. Finely slice onions and sauté in oil until soft and caramelised, stirring as needed to prevent them sticking to the pan.

Sift flour, baking powder and salt together and add sugar. Stir in cheese and add milk. Mix well to combine, adding a little more milk if necessary. Turn out onto floured surface and shape into a rectangle. Cut in half, and roll each half to form two even squares approx. 1 cm thick.

Spread one square with caramelised onion. Carefully lift the other square and place on top. Cut into 16 even-sized pieces. Place on baking trays and brush with milk. Sprinkle with a little grated cheese. Bake for approx. 15 minutes until golden brown, and not too soft to the touch.

JIM BYARS
THE FRIDAY SHOP
_____

LEMON TART
CROISSANTS

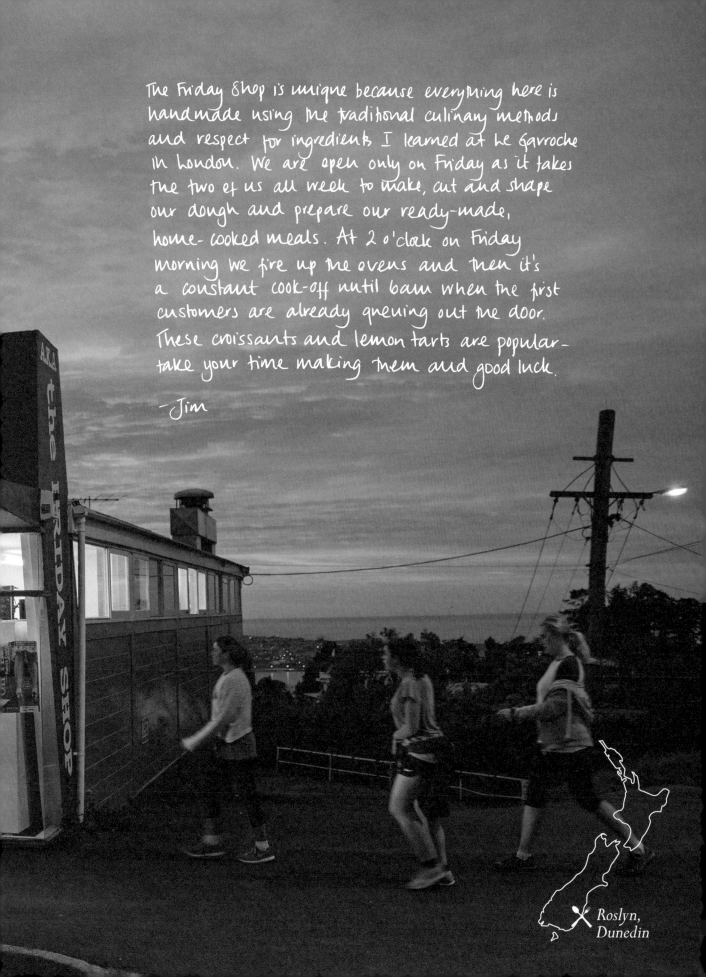

The Friday Shop is unique because everything here is handmade using the traditional culinary methods and respect for ingredients I learned at Le Gavroche in London. We are open only on Friday as it takes the two of us all week to make, cut and shape our dough and prepare our ready-made, home-cooked meals. At 2 o'clock on Friday morning we fire up the ovens and then it's a constant cook-off until 6am when the first customers are already queuing out the door. These croissants and lemon tarts are popular – take your time making them and good luck.

—Jim

Roslyn, Dunedin

LEMON TART

Servings: 6–8 | Prep Time: 25 mins plus pastry | Cook Time: 1½ hours | Skill Level: 2 (Moderate)

INGREDIENTS

400 g sweet pastry
125 g icing sugar
125 g lemon juice
250 g eggs
175 g cream
icing sugar, for dusting

METHOD

Line a 20 cm flan ring with pastry, leaving a good overlapping edge. Rest for 15 minutes in the fridge. Pre-heat the oven to 200°C (or 165–180°C fan-bake). Line the pastry with greaseproof paper and weigh it down with baking beans. Bake for 20 minutes, then remove paper and beans and bake for another 5–10 minutes, until golden brown. Turn oven down to 100°C.

Mix icing sugar, lemon juice, eggs and cream together until smooth. Fill the flan base and bake until set (approx. 60 minutes). Allow to cool, then remove from the ring and dust with icing sugar.

CROISSANTS

Makes: about 20 | Prep Time: 2 hours plus proving | Cook Time: 15–20 mins
Skill Level: 3 (More challenging)

INGREDIENTS

1 kg high-grade flour
500 ml milk, lukewarm
100 g sugar
100 g egg
13 g instant dried yeast
500 g butter, chilled

METHOD

Make a dough using flour, milk, sugar, egg and yeast. Mix until smooth – usually I leave the dough covered in the refrigerator overnight to prove.

Lightly pat butter out to a flat rectangle. Take dough and knead it a little, then roll into a rectangle. Place butter on one half of this and fold the other half of the dough over the butter to enclose it completely. Press the edges closed and gently roll the dough into a rectangle again.

Fold one-third of the dough over, then fold one-third at the opposite end over the top (single turn), roll lightly to press the layers together and rest in the refrigerator for at least 15 minutes. With the long side facing you, roll the dough out to a rectangle again. Fold one side of the dough into the centre, then fold the other side in to meet it, then fold dough in half, like closing a book (double turn). Roll lightly to press layers together and rest again in the refrigerator for at least 15 minutes.

Give the dough another single turn; allow to rest in the refrigerator for 30 minutes. Pre-heat the oven to 180°C.

Roll the dough out to a rectangle 2½ mm thick, at least 20 cm wide. Using a large knife, cut triangles 10 cm across the base and 20 cm high. Roll up to form your croissants and place on a baking tray. Prove until doubled in size (about 2 hours) and bake for 15–20 minutes, until golden. (Note that this recipe can easily be halved.)

MARY BENNETT
BENNETTS OF MANGAWHAI

MINT TRUFFLES
FRUIT & NUT SLAB
CANDIED CITRUS PEEL

When we were growing up in Ireland, grapefruit was a luxury. As children, we would have it on Christmas morning as a treat. I think that's why I love to use citrus fruit in chocolate so much. When my husband Clayton and I moved to New Zealand — his home and now mine — I noticed that many Kiwis had fruit trees in their back gardens: grapefruit, oranges and lemons and mint was always to be found.
I took those memories as inspiration for my recipes so hopefully you have half the ingredients already!
As a chocolate lover I dont obsess about the percentage of cocoa solids, as long as it's good that's what matters to me. You can't think of chocolate as a superfood, it's simply something to enjoy!
— Mary

Mangawhai

MINT TRUFFLES

Servings: 40 | Prep Time: 2¾ hours plus drying | Skill Level: 2 (Moderate)

INGREDIENTS

Decoration
1 egg white
a few fresh mint leaves
1 tbsp caster sugar

Ganache
small handful of fresh
  mint leaves
200 g cream
80 g caster sugar
200 g Bennetts' dark
  chocolate

Coating
600 g Bennetts' dark
  chocolate

METHOD

Start by making the decoration the day before. Whisk the egg white lightly with a fork. Dip mint leaves to coat both sides. Dust with caster sugar. Lay on a tray lined with baking paper and leave to dry overnight.

To make the ganache, place mint, cream and sugar in a saucepan. Bring to the boil, then turn off the heat. Allow to rest for 1 minute, then discard the mint. Meanwhile, break the chocolate in pieces and put in a bowl. Pour the hot cream over and whisk until smooth and glossy. Allow to cool, then cover and place in the fridge until set. Scoop out teaspoons of the ganache, roll into round shapes and place the truffles on baking paper. Set aside.

To make the coating, break up chocolate and place 400 g in a stainless-steel bowl. Place the bowl over a pot of water. Simmer on a low heat, allowing chocolate to melt slowly for up to an hour. Do not allow water to boil.

Once chocolate is melted, remove bowl from the heat. Add the remaining chocolate pieces and stir in until dissolved. The chocolate will cool fairly quickly. When it is at body temperature, place the bowl back over the warm water. After a few minutes, dip the tip of a knife into the chocolate – if it sets smooth and glossy, the chocolate is tempered and ready to use.

With the help of a fork, dip the truffles one by one into the chocolate, shake off excess chocolate, and place on baking paper in the fridge for 15–20 minutes until set. To finish, decorate with pieces of candied mint leaf. A drop of liquid chocolate helps the decoration stick to the truffle.

TIPS

Rolling truffles is a messy business, so dip your hands in cocoa powder every so often.

When melting the chocolate, the bowl must not touch the water below as it simmers.

FRUIT & NUT SLAB

Servings: 12 | Prep Time: 10 mins | Skill Level: 2 (Moderate)

INGREDIENTS

1 kg Bennetts' dark chocolate

250 g candied citrus peel (see below)

100 g toasted macadamia nuts

METHOD

Temper your chocolate in a bowl over water, as for truffles (see previous page). Add peel and nuts. Combine.

Pour into a shallow lined tray, no more than 2 cm thick. Place in the fridge for 15–20 minutes or until set. Turn out onto the work surface and break the slab up.

TIPS

A plastic tray makes for an easier time when turning out your slab.

Warm the macadamia nuts in a warm oven before adding to the tempered chocolate.

CANDIED CITRUS PEEL

Makes: about 250 g | Prep Time: 2–3 days | Skill Level: 1 (Easy)

INGREDIENTS

1 grapefruit

1 orange

1 lemon

500 ml water

500 sugar

METHOD

Wash fruit. Using a knife, score the fruit top to bottom into six wedges. Remove peel wedges from fruit and place in a pot. Cover with boiling water and simmer for 2 minutes, then strain and repeat twice more.

Bring water and sugar to the boil. When sugar is dissolved, add peel. Lower heat and keep on a gentle simmer for 3 hours. Leave to rest in the syrup overnight.

Next day, remove peel from syrup and place on a wire rack to drain and dry. This might take a couple of days (up here in Mangawhai it gets pretty humid – mine can sit on the bench for up to three days).

TIPS

The sugary poaching syrup has great flavour and makes an excellent ham glaze.

Thick-skinned citrus is best, but I always just use what's in the garden.

FLEUR SULLIVAN
FLEURS PLACE

SEAFOOD CHOWDER
SMOKED FISH PIE

When I first opened Fleurs Place, I would have people sitting at tables, cutlery in hands and I would have to say See the boat coming around the corner, it's got your fish on it!
Every day from the moment I open my eyes I look down into the Bay – what's the weather like, where are the fishermen are the boats out, will I get any fish today?
Each day when the restaurant fills with people from all over the world, I am reminded – how fortunate I am.
Every day is a highlight for me. I am now on peoples Bucket Lists and I think that's pretty amazing!

Fleur.

Moeraki

SEAFOOD CHOWDER

Servings: 8–10 | Prep Time: 10 mins | Cook Time: 15 mins
Skill Level: 1–2 (Easy–Moderate)

INGREDIENTS

200 g butter
1 onion, diced
2 carrots, diced
2 sticks celery, diced
200 g plain flour
100 ml white wine
150 g tomato paste
2 litres fish stock, warmed
1 tsp fennel seeds, ground
1 tsp smoked ground
  paprika
2 bay leaves
1 tsp chopped fresh thyme
500 g fish, diced
20 mussels, picked
  and washed
30 littleneck clams,
  washed
20 queen scallops, washed

METHOD

In a large heavy-bottomed pot, melt butter and add diced vegetables. Sweat for a couple of minutes but do not allow to colour. Add flour and cook for a further 2 minutes or until mixture has a sandy texture.

Slowly pour in the wine and tomato paste, and bring together as it thickens to remove all the lumps.

Add the warmed fish stock slowly, stirring continuously, and drop in the herbs and spices. Allow all this to come to the boil, taking care not to let it catch the bottom of the pan.

Add all the fish and shellfish, and simmer until the shells begin to open (only 2–3 minutes) and the fish is cooked through. Discard any shellfish that doesn't open.

TIP

Making your own stock is the key to an adventurous and infectious journey into naturally good food. 'Prep time' depends on whether you gather your ingredients from the wild and your garden or the supermarket!

SMOKED FISH PIE

Servings: 4 | Prep Time: 30 mins | Cook Time: 20—22 mins | Skill Level: 1—2 (Easy—Moderate)

INGREDIENTS

4 large potatoes

100 g butter

splash of cream

1 kg smoked fish fillets

12 smoked mussels,
  shells removed

200 g spinach leaves

400 ml fish stock

50 ml lemon juice

50 ml white wine

50 g plain flour

1 tbsp seeded mustard

40 g chopped fresh parsley
  or other fresh herbs

METHOD

Pre-heat the oven to 180—190°C.

Peel, boil and mash potatoes with 50 grams of butter, some salt and pepper and the cream. Break up fish and roughly chop mussels, and set aside. Wash and chop spinach leaves.

Bring fish stock to the boil together with lemon juice and wine. In a separate pan, melt remaining butter, then slowly add flour, stirring well and being careful not to burn it. Then gradually add your stock – add the hot liquid a ladleful at a time, mixing well each time, until you have a smooth, glossy velouté sauce. Add the mustard and herbs.

Mix the sauce with the fish and mussels, place in large ramekins or pie dish and top with spinach and then mashed potato. Bake until hot (20—22 minutes), and serve hot with salad.

I have blissful memories of
life growing up on the farm,
running around doing whatever
we wanted and having animals
everywhere. In time, I grew
to have a bit of respect for
the rabbits and wanted to do
more than just shoot them.
This is a lovely, easy dish with
classic flavours: essentially a
rabbit stew - it's a one-pot
wonder! Likewise, the rhubarb
is as simple as it can be
but simple things are always
the best!

Josh

JOSH EMETT

AGRIA POTATO &
CELERIAC GRATIN

RABBIT CASSEROLE WITH
BRANDY & PRUNES

POACHED RHUBARB
WITH MASCARPONE

Hamilton

AGRIA POTATO & CELERIAC GRATIN

Servings: 4 | Prep Time: 15 mins | Cook Time: 30–40 mins | Skill Level: 1 (Easy)

INGREDIENTS

3 cloves garlic
2 large Agria potatoes
1 large celeriac
50 g Gruyère cheese
200 ml cream
200 ml milk

METHOD

Pre-heat the oven to 180°C. Finely slice garlic, potatoes and celeriac (2 mm slices for the potato and celeriac). Grate cheese.

Place garlic, cream and milk in a pan and bring to the boil. Remove from heat and add potato and celeriac. Bring back to the boil, then remove from heat again.

Take an ovenproof dish and layer some potato and celeriac on the base, then top with cheese. Repeat to fill the dish, finishing with cheese. Pour the milk and cream mixture over to cover the potato and celeriac. Bake uncovered for 35–40 minutes until golden and potato is cooked through.

RABBIT CASSEROLE WITH BRANDY & PRUNES

Servings: 6 | Prep Time: 40 mins | Cook Time: 30–40 mins | Skill Level: 1 (Easy)

INGREDIENTS

225 g shallots, peeled
3 cloves garlic, peeled
150 g carrots, sliced
100 g button mushrooms, halved
2 tbsp rice bran oil
1 large rabbit, cut into pieces
50 ml brandy
100 ml riesling

1 cinnamon quill
2 star anise
2 bay leaves
12 g fresh ginger, peeled and sliced
400 ml veal stock
250 g chicken stock
12 prunes

METHOD

In a large casserole pot, sweat down shallots, garlic, carrots and mushrooms in oil until they pick up a little colour. Add rabbit pieces and lightly colour. Add brandy and reduce by half, then add riesling and also reduce by half. Add cinnamon, star anise, bay leaves, ginger and both stocks.

Bring to a simmer and skim. Lastly, add prunes then cover with a cartouche (greaseproof paper folded and torn to the same size as the pot) and continue to simmer slowly for 30–40 minutes until the rabbit is tender.

POACHED RHUBARB WITH MASCARPONE

Servings: 4| Prep Time: 8 mins | Cook Time: 10 mins | Skill Level: 1 (Easy)

INGREDIENTS

3 sticks rhubarb
1 orange
80 g sugar
120 g water
1 sprig fresh rosemary
150 ml cream
50 g mascarpone
1 tsp grated pistachio
  nuts

METHOD

Cut rhubarb into 3½ cm batons. Pare zest from orange in strips, using a sharp knife.

Heat sugar and water together with rosemary and orange zest until sugar is dissolved. Poach the rhubarb in this syrup on a very gentle heat for 2–3 minutes. Remove rosemary and orange zest.

Whip cream, then fold mascarpone through.

Serve rhubarb with a spoonful of mascarpone cream on top and a scattering of grated pistachio nuts.

LEYTON ASHLEY
CRAGGY RANGE

SCAMPI TAIL WITH
ESSENCE OF BORA BORA
CITRUS FROMAGE BLANC

MY FIANCÉE & I SPENT A PERIOD OF TIME IN
TAHITI WHERE WE ATE A FAIRLY CLASSIC DIET OF
LOCAL POISSON CRU. THIS SUPER-FRESH SALAD
OF YELLOW FIN TUNA MARINATED IN VIBRANT GREEN
LIME JUICE, SALT & FRESHLY SQUEEZED COCONUT
MILK ALWAYS HIT THE SPOT. WITH COCONUTS &
LIMES DROPPING EVERYWHERE YOU GO (IT'S NOT
EVEN FORAGING WHEN IT'S THAT EASY!), IT'S JUST
MEANT TO BE.
MY FAVOURITE FOOD IS UNQUESTIONABLY NEW ZEALAND
SCAMPI &, BEING RESPECTFUL OF THE OVER-FISHING
OF TUNA AROUND THE WORLD, I HAVE REPLACED
TUNA WITH SCAMPI IN THIS RECIPE.

I CREATED THIS DESSERT FOR MY GIRLS,
FLEUR, RUBY & WILLOW XXXX
Leyton

Havelock
North

SCAMPI TAIL WITH ESSENCE OF BORA BORA

Servings: 4 | Prep Time: ½ day in advance | Cook Time: 20 mins | Skill Level: 2 (Moderate)

INGREDIENTS

250 g mānuka wood
  chips, for smoking
3 large ripe tomatoes
1 tbsp soft brown sugar
pinch of ground
  Espelette pepper
1 cucumber
1 small shallot
5 threads of saffron
150 ml water
2 gelatine leaves
1 coconut
12 scampi tails, shelled
  and de-veined
juice of 2 limes
¼ tsp soy lecithin
4 large fresh sorrel
  leaves

METHOD

Set up a smoking tray with the wood chips in the bottom and heat over a flame. Peel tomatoes and rub sugar and pepper into them, then sprinkle with sea salt and place on a tray inside the smoker. Cover and leave for 3–5 minutes, then remove and cool. Peel and chop cucumber and shallot.

In a blender combine tomatoes, cucumber, shallot, saffron and water, then strain through a fat-filter or muslin cloth. Leave to hang for half a day, then discard the solids. Gently heat the clear tomato liquid in a saucepan. Soak gelatine in cold water, squeeze it out and add it to the tomato water. Stir until dissolved, then cool. Pour liquid into a mould and place in the fridge.

Line a bowl with a clean, damp cloth or tea towel. Pierce the coconut and reserve the water. Remove coconut flesh and grate it into the cloth, then fold up the sides and twist hard to squeeze out the coconut milk.

In a clean bowl, place scampi tails, lime juice and a couple of good pinches of sea salt and grinds of black pepper. Gently fold the tails through the juice a couple of times. After 1–2 minutes, the scampi should be cured and white – tip off the excess juice, add the coconut milk to the tails and fold together.

To finish, combine the coconut water and soy lecithin in a jug, and use a stick blender with the blade held on the surface to create bubbles. Arrange the scampi between four bowls, wrapped in the sorrel leaves. Remove the tomato jelly and break it up with a fork, then drop this over the scampi and drizzle with coconut bubbles.

CITRUS FROMAGE BLANC

Servings: 4 | Prep Time: 4–5 hours plus overnight | Cook Time: 12 hours
Skill Level: 3 (More challenging)

INGREDIENTS

Fromage blanc sorbet
500 ml sheep's milk
  (non-homogenised)
0.25 g fromage blanc culture
500 ml water
300 g caster sugar
juice of 1 lime
pinch of sea salt

Lime meringue
220 g caster sugar
½ kaffir lime leaf
1 egg white
1 tsp lime juice
¼ tsp citric acid
pinch of sea salt

Milk wafers
500 ml sheep's milk
1 tbsp liquid glucose

Verjus granita
250 ml verjus

Lemon tapioca
300 ml loose tapioca
  maltodextrin
2–3 tbsp lemon-flavoured
  extra virgin olive oil

Lemon jelly
275 ml limoncello
1 tsp liquid glucose
2½ gelatine leaves

To finish
4 tbsp lemon curd
a few freshly picked
  chrysanthemum petals
a few freshly picked
  lemon thyme leaves
¼ tsp freeze-dried Fresh As!
  yuzu flakes

METHOD

Make fromage blanc one day ahead. In a clean plastic bowl, stir together sheep's milk and fromage blanc culture. Leave overnight at around 24°C (warm room temperature). The next day, strain the mixture through a muslin cloth over a clean bowl, hanging it up until it stops dripping. Remove the curd from the cloth. If you're keen, keep the whey for your Weetbix in the morning.

In a saucepan, heat together the water, sugar and lime juice utill the sugar dissolves, then cool. Slowly mix together the cooled sugar liquid and your fromage blanc, adding the salt. Churn in an ice cream machine until creamy or freeze in a Pacojet canister if you have one. Keep in the freezer until required.

Start lime meringue ahead of time. Pre-heat the oven to 55°C. Place sugar and kaffir lime leaf in a spice grinder and blend until the leaf is very fine; the sugar will turn light green. Place this sugar in a bowl and add egg white, lime juice, citric acid and salt. Whisk until the mixture turns pale and creamy, then spread it onto the second oven tray and place in the oven. Leave for up to 12 hours or until a crisp meringue texture results. Reserve in an airtight container.

To make the milk wafers, line two flat oven trays with baking paper. In a saucepan, heat sheep's milk and glucose together to around 65°C (do not boil), then froth with a stick blender to create a good foam on the surface. Spoon the foam off the top and place onto one of the baking trays in an even layer, then place in the oven at 55°C for around 5 hours or until it forms a crisp wafer. Reserve in an airtight container.

For the verjus granita, put verjus in a suitable container and place in the freezer. Once it starts to freeze, remove once an hour and agitate it with a fork until you get a fluffy ice granita.

To make the lemon tapioca, place tapioca maltodextrin in a bowl and drizzle in lemon oil, working them together with your hands until soft and powdery. Set aside.

To make the lemon jelly, gently heat limoncello and liquid glucose together in a saucepan. Soak gelatine in some cold water, squeeze off the water and then add it into the hot limoncello, stirring to dissolve. Strain the mixture into a mould and leave to set in the fridge. Once firm, remove the jelly and cut into small cubes.

To assemble, spread a tablespoon of lemon curd on the centre of four plates, and add a few cubes of lemon jelly to the curd. Place a scoop of sorbet in the middle, then crumble the lime meringue, milk wafer and lemon tapioca over. Top with verjus granita, chrysanthemum petals, lemon thyme and a tiny amount of yuzu flakes.

TIP

Fromage blanc culture can be sourced from your local cheesemaker or specialty food store.

EMMA METTRICK & PAUL HOWELLS
THE LITTLE BISTRO

WHITE ONION, APPLE & CIDER SOUP
SEAFOOD CASSOULET WITH AKAROA SALMON

Akaroa is a beautiful village at the end of a winding, amazingly scenic road with great local produce & cool artisan producers right here on the peninsula. I love what we do — it's done with integrity, it's what we love, it's providing for our son in a fab community... & we're having fun!

We have chosen to use Akaroa Salmon — it's local, sustainable, antibiotic free & tastes great. And the white onion soup... love it!

Emma x

The Little Bistro

taes - sat nights
dinner from 5:30pm
(closed sunday & monday)
ph # 304 7311

the little bistro

rustic european inspired, locally sourced food

66... a bistro is a small

Akaroa

WHITE ONION, APPLE & CIDER SOUP

Servings: 4 | Prep Time: 5 mins | Cook Time: 1¼ hours | Skill Level: 1 (Easy)

INGREDIENTS

6 white onions
250 g butter
3 cloves garlic
3 Granny Smith apples
2 vegetable stock cubes
salt and white pepper
2 tbsp caster sugar
330 ml good-quality cider
600 ml milk

METHOD

Slice onions finely. Melt butter gently in a large pan over a medium heat, add onions and sweat off slowly until soft. Chop and add garlic and cook for a further 5 minutes.

Peel and core apples, then slice finely and add to the onion mixture. Crumble in the stock cubes, add a good pinch of salt and pepper and add the sugar. Continue cooking for a further 5 minutes.

Finally, add cider and milk. Cook on a low heat for a further 45 minutes – the mixture will reduce and thicken. Let it cool for 10 minutes before blending in a food processor. A hand blender can also be used. Taste, and season with salt and pepper to your liking.

SEAFOOD CASSOULET WITH AKAROA SALMON

Servings: 4 | Prep Time: 10 mins | Cook Time: 45 mins | Skill Level: 2 (Moderate)

INGREDIENTS

½ tsp saffron threads
100 ml warm water
2 red capsicums
2 small red onions
3 cloves garlic
3 spring onions
olive oil
1 tsp ground cumin
¼ tsp turmeric
1 tsp smoked sweet
  paprika powder
250 g Puy lentils
250 ml fish stock
800 g tinned chopped
  tomatoes
1 glass red wine
4 green-lipped mussels
4 pieces Akaroa Salmon
  (180–200 g each)
butter, for cooking
1 small bag marinara mix
handful of fresh herbs,
  e.g. flat-leaf parsley,
  chive and dill
1 lemon

METHOD

Soak saffron in warm water for 30 minutes. Finely chop capsicums, onions, garlic and spring onions. Pre-heat the oven to 200°C.

For the cassoulet base, add a good glug of olive oil to a medium-sized stockpot. Add capsicums, onions, garlic and spring onions. Gently cook until soft. Now add all the spices apart from the saffron, then the lentils, and cook for a further 5 minutes – the spices should be well incorporated and give off a rich aroma.

Next add all the wet ingredients, including the saffron and water. Cook on a low heat, stirring frequently, until the liquid has reduced markedly and the lentils are firm to the bite. Set aside.

In a separate, smaller, pot bring 2 litres of water to the boil. Clean and scrape green-lipped mussels, add to water and cook until they open. Cool under running cold water and set aside. Discard any mussels that don't open.

In a separate frying pan, cook salmon skin-side down in a little butter and olive oil for 3 minutes per side. Place fillets in the oven and cook for a further 5 minutes.

While the salmon is cooking, put the cassoulet base back on a medium heat and add the marinara mix plus the cooked mussels. Cook for another 3–4 minutes until piping hot. Add herbs of your choice and a good squeeze of lemon juice.

Spoon the cassoulet into a large bowl and top with the salmon. Serve garnished with chargrilled lemon, aïoli of your choice, and hunks of fresh sour-dough bread.

TIPS

Mount Cook salmon is also good, and so is Campbell's fish stock. Marinara mix is available at most supermarkets.

JULIE LE CLERC

SYRIAN FATTOUSH SALAD
CREAMY SESAME CHICKEN
FRENCH VANILLA & BERRY MINI CAKES

These recipes are very close to my heart, as they represent both my mother's Syrian heritage and my father's French ancestry. It wasn't until a few years ago – in an attempt to piece together my own history – that I connected with my Syrian extended family for the very first time. When I arrived in Damascus, my great Aunts Nabiha and Hind were so overjoyed that I had reunited the families they rallied together for days to cook and celebrate! Now when I cook these recipes at home, I am taken back to all those feelings of generosity, warmth, flavours and family. I believe, no matter where you are from, feeding people really is the most wonderful way to show love.

Julie

Westmere,
Auckland

SYRIAN FATTOUSH SALAD

Servings: 4 | Prep Time: 10 mins | Cook Time: 10–15 mins | Skill Level: 1 (Easy)

INGREDIENTS

2 large rounds stale pita bread
olive oil
2 small Lebanese cucumbers
8 medium-sized ripe tomatoes
1 small red onion
4–5 radishes
⅓ cup chopped fresh parsley
⅓ cup chopped fresh coriander

3 tbsp chopped fresh mint
1 tbsp sumac (optional)

Lemon dressing
1 clove garlic, finely crushed
juice of 1 lemon
3–4 tbsp pomegranate molasses
⅓ cup extra virgin olive oil

(DF) (GF) (V)

METHOD

Break bread into bite-sized pieces, drizzle with a little oil and toss well to coat. Bake for 10–15 minutes in an oven pre-heated to 180°C, tossing once or twice, until golden. Alternatively, toast in a large frying pan, turning often until crisp and golden. Remove to cool.

Dice cucumbers, tomatoes and onion and thinly slice radishes. Combine in a bowl with herbs and season well with salt and freshly ground black pepper.

Blend dressing ingredients together. The dressing needs to taste fairly sharp and lemony – adjust with extra lemon juice if necessary. Pour dressing over salad ingredients and toss well to coat.

Finally, toss pita pieces through (don't dress too far in advance, or the bread will turn soggy). Sprinkle with sumac, if available.

TIPS

Sumac is a sour-tasting, ground, red-berry spice, available in specialist food stores and some supermarkets. Don't worry if you can't find it: the salad will still be delicious.

If pomegranate molasses isn't available, then substitute with more lemon juice.

CREAMY SESAME CHICKEN

Servings: 4 | Prep Time: 5 mins | Cook Time: 20–25 mins | Skill Level: 1 (Easy)

INGREDIENTS

¼ cup tahini (sesame
  seed paste)
2 cloves garlic, crushed
1 cup thick, plain, Greek-
  style yoghurt
4 skinless chicken
  breasts
olive oil
3 tbsp sesame seeds

(GF)

METHOD

Place tahini, garlic and yoghurt in a bowl, season with salt and freshly ground black pepper and stir to combine. Line a low-sided oven pan with baking paper, as this makes cleaning up easier.

Trim excess fat off chicken breasts, season with salt and pepper and place in oven pan. Spread a thick layer of tahini–yoghurt topping over chicken, drizzle with a little oil and sprinkle with sesame seeds.

Allow chicken to come to room temperature while the oven pre-heats to 190°C. Bake for 20–25 minutes, depending on size of chicken breasts, or until chicken is cooked through. Serve with Fattoush salad (see above).

FRENCH VANILLA & BERRY MINI CAKES

Makes: 12 | Prep Time: 10 mins | Cook Time: 20–25 mins | Skill Level: 1 (Easy)

INGREDIENTS

1½ cups icing sugar
½ cup plain flour
1 cup fine
   desiccated coconut
175 g butter
6 egg whites
1 tsp vanilla extract
1½ cups berries
   (fresh or frozen)
extra icing sugar, to dust

METHOD

Pre-heat the oven to 190°C. Grease 12 individual patty pan or muffin tins, of ½ cup capacity.

Sift icing sugar and flour into a mixing bowl and add coconut. Melt butter and lightly beat egg whites with a pinch of salt. Add butter, egg whites and vanilla to the mixing bowl and stir well to combine – expect the mixture to be quite runny.

Spoon mixture into prepared tins to fill by two-thirds. Top each mini cake with a few berries, pressing these into the surface.

Bake for 25 minutes or until well browned on the outside and cooked in the middle when tested – a skewer inserted into the centre of one mini cake should come out clean.

Remove to stand in tins for 5 minutes before turning out onto a cooling rack. Dust with icing sugar and serve with whipped cream or yoghurt on the side, if desired.

These mini cakes are lovely enjoyed with a nice cup of tea or coffee, but can also double as dessert.

TIPS

The berries can be raspberries, blueberries, blackberries, or a mixture.

If you prefer, substitute the same quantity of ground almonds for the coconut.

JACOB BROWN
THE LARDER

VENISON WELLINGTON
WITH KALE
CREPES
CHOCOLATE MOUSSE
COFFEE GRANITA

There is a real sense of community here in Miramar. Our kids go to the local school and we have Weta just down the road. We get a lot of regulars here at The Larder which we love.

One of the first things Sarah and I did when we first took over the building was cut a massive hole in the kitchen wall so we could connect with our customers. It's great to see friends walk past with their kids and be able to wave and say "Hi". I also think people appreciate seeing where their food comes from.

The only time it gets a bit awkward is when there is a queue of six people – and you go to say "Hi" to one of them – and six people say "Hi" and wave back! It's been really nice because over time many customers have become friends.

Jacob

Miramar, Wellington

VENISON WELLINGTON WITH KALE

Servings: 8 | Prep Time: 1 hour | Cook Time: 15 mins | Skill Level: 2 (Moderate)

INGREDIENTS

2 rashers streaky bacon
6 Portobello mushrooms
1 brown onion
1 clove garlic
1 tbsp butter
1.2 kg venison loin,
  trimmed and silver
  skin removed
20 ml vegetable oil
3 tbsp Dijon mustard
8 crêpes (see below)
square of puff pastry
  (45 cm x 45 cm)
4 egg yolks
2 tbsp cream
2 bunches fresh curly kale
butter, for cooking

METHOD

Cut bacon into 2 cm squares, de-stalk and slice mushrooms and thinly slice onion. Chop garlic. Sauté bacon in butter, over a medium heat, until golden brown. Add onion and cook until soft. Add garlic and mushrooms, and cook until the liquid from the mushrooms has evaporated. Season with salt and pepper and set to one side.

Season venison with salt and pepper, then sear in oil in a heavy-based pan, over a high heat, to seal in the juices and caramelise the venison. Brush venison with Dijon mustard.

Spread crêpes out with them overlapping, to form a large mat. Place mushroom mix along the centre. Place Dijon-coated venison on top of the mushroom mix, and wrap the crêpes around the venison.

Mix 2 egg yolks, brush puff pastry with egg yolk and place wrapped venison fillet in the centre. Roll the puff pastry over the venison fillet to fully encase it, pushing down on each side of the pastry to seal the venison inside the pastry. Glaze with egg wash made by combining remaining egg yolks with cream. Place the parcel on a baking tray lined with baking paper. (These steps can be done up to 24 hours in advance.)

When ready to cook, pre-heat the oven to 200°C and cook until the Wellington is golden brown, approx. 12–15 minutes. Leave to rest on a rack for 10 minutes, then slice with a sharp knife.

While the venison is resting, chop kale and gently sauté with a little butter, salt and pepper until wilted but still with a little bit of crunch. Serve venison on top of curly kale.

CRÊPES

Makes: 8 | Prep Time: 5 mins plus resting | Cook Time: 30 mins | Skill Level: 1 (Easy)

INGREDIENTS

60 g plain flour
pinch of salt
50 g caster sugar
60 ml cream
1 egg
160 ml milk
15 ml melted butter
oil, for cooking

METHOD

Combine flour, salt and sugar in a bowl. In a separate bowl, beat together cream, egg and milk. Add this to the flour mixture, stirring with the whisk to combine. Leave the crêpe mix to sit for 1 hour, then add melted butter.

Heat a non-stick pan over medium heat. Lightly season pan with oil, then ladle in just enough batter to thinly coat the pan, tilting it to produce a uniformly thin crêpe. Cook over a moderate heat until bubbles appear on the surface of the crêpe. Gently flip the crêpe over and cook the other side until a pale golden colour. Remove the crêpe from the pan and repeat the process until all the crêpe batter has been used.

TIPS

Crêpes are delicious served with citrus yoghurt and fresh berries, or if you want something savoury try Gruyère and shavings of ham from the leg.

CHOCOLATE MOUSSE

Servings: 10 | Prep Time: 25 mins plus chilling | Skill Level: 2 (Moderate)

INGREDIENTS

300 g dark chocolate (70%)
5 egg yolks
2 eggs
250 g caster sugar
80 ml water
500 ml cream

METHOD

Melt chocolate in a double boiler or a heatproof bowl set over a pan of simmering water. Remove and allow to cool.

Beat egg yolks and eggs in an electric mixer until thick. As the mixture is rising in volume, combine sugar and water in a small saucepan and bring to the boil until it reaches the thread stage (120°C.) Carefully pour the boiling sugar mixture down the side of the bowl and beat at high speed for 10 minutes.

In a stainless-steel bowl, beat cream until soft peaks form. Fold melted chocolate into egg and sugar mix, then fold whipped cream into chocolate/egg mix until fully combined. Refrigerate in a suitable container for at least 2 hours or until set.

Serve with coffee granita (see below).

TIP

To check thread stage without a thermometer, drop a little syrup into a glass of cold water – it should form a liquid thread that does not ball up.

COFFEE GRANITA

Servings: 6 | Prep Time: 5 mins plus freezing | Cook Time: 5 mins | Skill Level: 1 (Easy)

INGREDIENTS

1 litre weak black espresso coffee
about ½ cup caster sugar

METHOD

Add sugar to the coffee, to your taste. Pour liquid into a shallow metal tray and place in freezer. When it has just started to freeze, scrape with a fork to create granita flakes, and return to the freezer. Repeat scraping a few more times during freezing and again just before serving.

Birkenhead,
Auckland

SOPHIE GRAY
DESTITUTE GOURMET

BAPS
HOT CROSS BUNS

Every family has traditions for special occasions. My Mum made floury Scottish baps every year on Christmas Eve to have as part of Christmas Day Breakfast. She died when I was 23 and I took over making them. Fortunately they are easy even for a beginner bread maker.

Baps are tender white rolls that smell and taste fantastic.

Hot Cross buns are very much part of our culture. They are fragrant and spicy and very evocative. I make them every Easter. Placing them in a circle symbolizes God's unending love.

Both these recipes are easy, inexpensive and delicious. Enjoy!

Sophie

BAPS

Makes: 12 | Prep Time: about 1¼ hours | Cook Time: 15 mins | Skill Level: 2 (Moderate)

INGREDIENTS

50 g butter
450 g plain or high-grade flour
1½ tsp sugar
1 sachet of instant
   yeast (7 g)
1 tsp salt
125 ml hot water
125 ml cold milk

METHOD

In a large bowl, rub butter into flour with your fingertips and then stir in sugar, yeast and salt. Combine hot water and cold milk in a bowl so that the liquid is lukewarm. Test by holding your little finger in the liquid and counting to 10 – it should feel warm, not hot or cold.

Stir the liquid into the dry mixture, then turn out onto a floured surface and knead until smooth and elastic, adding more flour if needed to prevent sticking. Place dough in a greased bowl and cover with greased plastic wrap. Leave in a warm place to rise for about 40 minutes. Alternatively, microwave on low power for 1 minute, rest and repeat.

When dough is doubled in size, knead it again lightly, then form it into 12 round rolls. Place rolls on a floured oven tray. With a floury index finger, press each roll very firmly in the middle, making a deep dimple. Sift a light dusting of flour over the baps and set aside to double in size while the oven heats to 200°C.

Bake for 15 minutes until pale golden, and hollow-sounding when tapped on the bottom. Serve warm with butter and marmalade or jam for breakfast, or fill for lunches, or dunk in soups.

HOT CROSS BUNS

Makes: 24 | Prep Time: 1½–1¾ hours | Cook Time: 20 mins | Skill Level: 2 (Moderate)

INGREDIENTS

1½ cups warm water
¼ cup sweetened condensed milk
2 tbsp dried yeast granules
   or 1½ sachets of instant yeast
5 cups plain or high-grade flour
3 tsp mixed spice
3 tsp ground cinnamon
½ tsp salt
1 cup currants or raisins
½ cup mixed peel
50 g butter, softened
2 eggs

Crosses
1 cup plain flour
1 tsp baking powder
2 tbsp butter
about ½ cup water

Sugar glaze
3 tbsp sugar dissolved in ⅓ cup
   warm water

METHOD

Blend water and condensed milk together. If using granulated yeast, sprinkle it on and stir in, then set aside for about 10 minutes until it is frothy-looking. Sift flour, spices and salt into a large bowl. If using instant yeast, add it to the dry ingredients.

Mix in the dried fruit and peel, then make a hole in the centre. Pour in the milk mixture along with the butter and eggs. Stir until combined, then turn out onto a floured surface and knead it lightly. The dough can be quite wet, so add extra flour as you knead until the dough is smooth and springy.

Put dough in a greased bowl and cover with greased plastic wrap. Leave in a warm place until dough doubles in size; this should take around 40 minutes.

Punch the dough down, then give it another quick knead. Divide into 24 portions and roll into balls. Place buns in a circle on a greased oven tray and cover with the greased plastic wrap from before. Leave them for around half an hour or until doubled in size.

Pre-heat the oven to 200°C. In a small bowl, blend the ingredients for the crosses, using sufficient water to make a mixture soft enough to be piped. If you haven't got a piping bag, put the mixture in a plastic bag, snip a tiny bit off the corner and squeeze the mix through. Make crosses with the mixture on the top of each bun.

Bake for 15 minutes, then brush with sugar glaze and return to the oven for a further 5 minutes or until they look cooked.

RUTH PETTITT &
CAROL WHITFORD
COLENSO CAFÉ

BAKED APPLE
CHEESECAKE TART
CHOCOLATE FUDGE SLICE

I first met Carol when she moved to the farm down the road thirty-eight years ago. I quickly discovered what a great cook she was (she can make three cakes while I'm still looking at the recipe!). So when Andy and I started Colenso Café twenty-five years ago, Carol came on board to run the kitchen and even after working together all these years we are still great friends.

Both of these recipes have been on our menu since day one. I chose the chocolate fudge slice because it is such a kiwi favourite and Carol chose the apple tart because she would always make it for me on my birthday even before we had the café. It has been wonderful working together all these years.

Ruth

Whenuakite,
Coromandel

BAKED APPLE CHEESECAKE TART

Servings: 12 | Prep Time: 50 mins including chilling | Cook Time: 20 mins | Skill Level: 1 (Easy)

INGREDIENTS

Pastry
130 g butter
75 g sugar
1 egg
½ cup self-raising flour
1¼ cups plain flour

Filling
5 apples
zest of 1 lemon
½ cup sultanas

Topping
175 g cream cheese
45 g sugar
1 tsp vanilla essence
3 eggs
½ cup cream
1 tbsp cornflour

METHOD

Pre-heat the oven to 150°C fan-bake. For the pastry, cream butter and sugar together. Add egg and beat in, then mix in flours. Press into a 30 cm springform tin and chill in the fridge for 20 minutes.

For the filling, slice apples thinly and arrange over the pastry, overlapping them onto each other. Sprinkle lemon zest and sultanas evenly over.

For the topping, soften cream cheese, add sugar, vanilla, eggs, cream and cornflour and whizz in a food processor until combined. Pour over apples. Bake for approx. 20 minutes until a light golden brown.

CHOCOLATE FUDGE SLICE

Servings: 36 | Prep Time: 15 mins plus cooling | Skill Level: 1 (Easy)

INGREDIENTS

4 packets vanilla
  wine biscuits
1 cup sultanas
500 g butter
2 cups sugar
2 tsp vanilla essence
1 cup good-quality
  cocoa
5 eggs, lightly beaten

METHOD

Crush biscuits in a food processor, or with a rolling pin, and place in a large bowl. Add sultanas and mix.

Dice butter and place in a medium-sized saucepan. Partially melt butter, then remove from the heat and add sugar, vanilla, cocoa and eggs. Stir until combined and butter is fully melted. Pour into crushed biscuits and mix well. Turn into a 24 cm square cake tin, press down firmly and leave to cool in the fridge. Cut into 36 squares. Store in the fridge in an airtight container – it makes enough to feed many!

TIPS

The chocolate should look smooth and glossy; do not overcook it. Nuts may also be added.

Auckland Central

PLEASE ORDER HERE

PETER WASHER
THE WHITE LADY

THE WHITE LADY BURGER

My family has owned and operated The White Lady since 1948 – thats over 65 years – parking mostly on Shortland Street but now on Commerce in Auckland's C.B.D. catering to the need for a munch in the wee small hours

My Pop claimed he had never missed a night and I certainly haven't missed one either.

We have always taken pride in providing a decent meal – Simple flavours and quality ingredients.

I love making people happy.

Peter

THE WHITE LADY BURGER

Servings: 12 | Prep Time: 15 mins | Skill Level: 1 (Easy)

INGREDIENTS

Meat patty mix (enough for 12 patties)
1 kg minced beef
70 g fresh breadcrumbs
1 egg
2–3 tsp salt
1 tsp pepper

For each burger
1 white bread bun
50 g slice of
  colby cheese
plenty of butter
Wattie's tomato sauce
iceberg lettuce leaves
2 slices ripe tomato
120 g minced beef
  patty mixture
caramelised sliced
  onions
1 egg
100 g Scotch fillet
1–2 rashers of bacon
slice of pineapple

METHOD

Start with love and respect – love of the 'cooking magic' and respect for the customer. The better the ingredients, the better the burger. Select well.

This is a challenge in the kitchen, so probably best attempted on the barbie. Both halves of the bun must be toasted, with the colby cheese melted onto the top bun. Use a brush to soak the bottom bun in melted butter (try not to clarify it) – we soak it in with a 4-inch paintbrush.

Next the tomato sauce – 'It must be Wattie's!' – and be generous on the bottom but just pop a dab on the cheese.

Lettuce … everything seems to be called 'iceberg' these days, but you want crispy inner lettuce leaves to give crunch, but not too much. It's a knack that comes with practice. We use fresh iceberg lettuce folded no more or less than four layers thick. Add two slices of ripe tomato, no ends.

Then the stack – prepared on the grill/barbie. The mince for the patty is mixed in the cart, traditionally with eggs, breadcrumbs, salt and pepper. It's rolled into 120 g meatballs and chilled for no longer than two days in the fridge, then squashed with the aid of a trowel and spatula. Grill on the hotplate, flipping just once. Don't move the meat around – have a system.

Then comes the onions, heavily sautéed in a little butter (not too much). Our onions are sautéed in batches throughout the night and are reheated if necessary. Next on the stack is a not-overly-done fried egg. You don't want it runny, but equally you don't want rubber. Eggs cook fast.

On top of that, medium/well-done Scotch fillet. It needs to be juicy enough, but you don't need juices running out. Then a decent rasher or two of proper bacon (with rind and fat), topped with a well-cooked (caramelised) slice of pineapple. Pineapple is a slow cooker – butter it and put it down with the patty. We use commercial pineapple, but you could use a thin slice of the real thing.

Best served half out of the bag.

TIPS

The key to a great burger is having it all ready at the same time – which takes practice. Get your onions sautéeing, then pop the patty, pineapple and steak on the hotplate. Then the bacon and the egg when you judge it's time, and have everything else sliced and washed ready to go. You know when you get it right!

HESTER GUY
HG CATERING

PASSIONFRUIT
MELTING MOMENTS
CHICKEN, GRAPE
& ALMOND SALAD

My philosophy is to create food that speaks for itself, that's honest, that's prepared carefully and where the flavour of every ingredient is important. I also love the friendships associated with food and the humour and joy that comes with it. Whenever I make food for anyone, be it at my bakery or at home, I always watch people's eyes when they eat. If their eyes light up, then I know I have exceeded their expectations.

- Rose.

Shannon

PASSIONFRUIT MELTING MOMENTS

Makes: about 25 | Prep Time: 20 mins | Cook Time: 15 mins plus cooling | Skill Level: 1 (Easy)

INGREDIENTS

250 g butter, softened
1 tsp vanilla extract
80 g soft icing sugar
250 g plain flour
75 g cornflour
4 passionfruit

Butter cream
100 g butter, softened
110 g soft icing sugar

METHOD

Pre-heat the oven to 150°C (140°C if fan-baked). Line three baking trays with baking paper.

Beat butter, vanilla and sifted icing sugar with an electric mixer until pale. Stir in the combined sifted flours in two batches. Remove pulp from passionfruit – reserve 1 tablespoon of pulp for the butter cream and stir the rest into the mixture.

With lightly floured hands, roll the equivalent of 2 level teaspoons of mixture into balls and place about 3 cm apart on oven trays. Dip a fork into a little extra flour and press biscuits lightly.

Bake for about 15 minutes or until biscuits are a pale straw colour (the secret is to cook the biscuits in a slow oven so they barely colour). Stand biscuits on the trays for 5 minutes, then transfer to wire racks to cool.

To make the butter cream, beat butter and sifted icing sugar in a small bowl with an electric mixer, until pale and fluffy. Beat in reserved passionfruit pulp. Sandwich biscuits together with a teaspoon of passionfruit butter cream. Dust with a little extra sifted icing sugar, if desired. Store, well covered, in the fridge.

CHICKEN, GRAPE & ALMOND SALAD

Servings: 12 | Prep Time: 20 mins | Skill Level: 2 (Moderate)

INGREDIENTS

Mayonnaise
2 egg yolks
1 clove garlic (optional)
½ tbsp mild mustard
½ tsp salt
¼ tsp freshly ground
  black pepper
1 tbsp lemon juice
zest of 1 lemon
250 ml grapeseed oil
1–2 tbsp finely snipped
  fresh chives

Salad
6 cooked boneless,
  skinless chicken breasts
4–6 stalks of celery
300 g grapes (either
  green or red)
3 spring onions
3–4 tbsp slivered
  almonds

METHOD

Place egg yolks, garlic, mustard, salt and pepper, and lemon juice and zest in a food processor and process together. With food processor running, very slowly drizzle the oil through the feed tube. Gradually the yolks will combine with the oil to form a thick, rich, buttery mayonnaise. If by any chance your mayonnaise curdles, start again by creaming an additional egg yolk very well and slowly dripping into the curdled egg yolk/oil mixture with a teaspoon, by hand, until you are certain the oil has started to combine with the yolk base. Remember, you are trying to combine two fats together, i.e. egg yolks and oil, and they do not normally like each other – that is why the oil must be combined with the egg yolk mixture very slowly initially until you are certain that an emulsion has formed and the mixture has not curdled.

Taste-test mayo for seasoning, adding extra lemon juice if necessary. The mayo can be thinned with boiling water or a couple of tablespoons of plain yoghurt if too thick. Add chives and stir in. Store in the refrigerator for up to a week.

Slice chicken against the grain, on a diagonal. Remove the coarse string from the back of the celery then slice in thin diagonal strips. Halve grapes and remove the seeds. Slice spring onions thinly. Lightly toast almonds in the oven.

To assemble, place half the sliced chicken on a large platter, spoon mayo over, sprinkle with celery, grapes and spring onions, then repeat. Garnish salad with almonds.

(DF) (GF)

As in many Kiwi households, meatloaf was a staple when I was growing up. I remember the horrible smell of sausage meat and tomato sauce wafting through the house – I absolutely hated it and remember being force-fed it! Dishes like that inspired me to want to cook and become a chef (sorry Mum!). So, I thought I'd make a NICE meatloaf by taking the classic Edmonds recipe and sprucing it up a bit. Meatloaf needs a chutney or relish to add interest, and my beetroot relish really is as 'Kiwi As'.

– Des

Freemans Bay,
Auckland

MEATLOAF

Servings: 6 | Prep Time: 15–20 mins | Cook Time: 1 hour | Skill Level: 1 (Easy)

INGREDIENTS

500 g prime beef mince
250 g sausage meat
250 g firm chorizo, diced
1 onion, finely chopped
2 cloves garlic, minced
2 rashers bacon, sliced
oil, for cooking
½ cup grated carrot
½ cup grated zucchini

½ cup grated celeriac
½ cup chopped fresh flat-leaf parsley
2 tbsp wholegrain mustard
2 eggs, beaten
1 tsp Worcestershire sauce
1 cup panko breadcrumbs
1 tbsp freshly picked thyme leaves
50 g butter, melted

METHOD

Pre-heat the oven to 180°C. Combine mince, sausage and chorizo and set aside. In a saucepan over a low heat, gently cook onion, garlic and bacon together with a dash of cooking oil. Add to the meat mix.

Squeeze excess moisture from the grated vegetables and add to the mix. Add parsley, mustard, eggs, Worcestershire sauce and some salt and pepper. Mix until well combined, and pack into a loaf tin or terrine mould. Cover with tinfoil and bake for 30 minutes.

Combine breadcrumbs, thyme and butter together. Remove tinfoil from meatloaf and top with the breadcrumb mix, pressing down slightly. Continue baking for another 30 minutes, or until the juices run clear when tested with a skewer. For a crunchier topping, broil under the grill for a few minutes. Allow to cool slightly before tucking in.

Best served with beetroot relish (see below) and a bitter-leaf salad of witlof, radicchio, arugula (rocket) and baby cos, seasoned and dressed with olive oil and lemon juice.

BEETROOT RELISH

Makes: 1 kg | Prep Time: 10 mins | Cook Time: up to 1 hour | Skill Level: 1 (Easy)

INGREDIENTS

1 kg fresh beetroot,
  julienned
350 g sliced onion
60 ml balsamic vinegar
60 ml malt vinegar
150 g white sugar
pinch of dried thyme
25 ml canola oil

METHOD

Put all of the ingredients into a saucepan and simmer gently, stirring from time to time to ensure the mixture doesn't catch on the bottom. Cook until the excess moisture has evaporated but the beetroot retains some tenderness. Season to taste with sea salt and freshly ground black pepper. Cool and refrigerate – this relish keeps very well in the fridge and is always better if made a few days in advance.

TIP

Use juicy beetroot for best results. If your beets seem a little dry, add a dash of water to the pan before cooking – otherwise the beets will not be sufficiently cooked by the time the moisture evaporates.

DAVID GRIFFITHS
MISTER D

GINGER MARINATED CHICKEN WITH WILTED SPINACH & RED CAPSICUM
MOONSHINE BIFF

This ginger chicken dish was the first recipe that I ever had published so it's pretty special. I remember at the time I was working at Bonaparte's in Auckland city. That place was like walking into another world: marble floors, glass pillars, Billy Farnell on the Liberace piano, flambéed pepper steaks, theatre and high drama daily. For a boy from Sandringham, it was all pretty crazy. I was wowed, amazed and hooked. The path was set and I haven't looked back since.

I was experimenting with staff dinners one day and tossed the ginger chicken together; the manager got a taste: "Gee, this is good." By the end of the day, after a little refining and side-stepping the Head Chef's ego, it ended up on the menu — I was pretty proud of that moment.

Here we have the dish photographed on a Bonaparte's plate: kept as a memento, a tribute to my time at a truly iconic New Zealand establishment.

David

Napier

GINGER MARINATED CHICKEN WITH WILTED SPINACH & RED CAPSICUM

Servings: 2–4 | Prep Time: 10 mins plus marinating | Cook Time: 10–15 mins
Skill Level: 1 (Easy)

INGREDIENTS

2 poussins (young chickens, 450–500 g each), spatchcocked
olive oil
2 red capsicums
10 g peeled fresh ginger, cut into fine strips
15 g sesame oil
2 generous handfuls picked washed spinach
50 g soy sauce
50 g butter

Marinade
½ cinnamon quill
1 star anise
50 g fresh ginger, sliced
50 g soy sauce
30 g sesame oil
70 ml Frantoio olive oil
25 g liquid honey
zest of 1 large orange

METHOD

For the marinade, lightly toast cinnamon quill and star anise in a hot oven (210°C) for 30 seconds. Mix together all marinade ingredients and massage into poussins, then leave in the fridge for at least 2 hours, but no more than 3. If you plan to finish the birds in the oven, pre-heat it to 165°C.

To a hot barbecue grill or moderate-to-hot pan, add a little olive oil and then the poussins, skin-side down, until lightly caramelised. Watch carefully — they will turn black quickly. Turn birds over and place in the oven, or lower the barbecue lid and reduce the temperature to 165°C (or drop to just two flames on the lowest setting). Cook for 10–15 minutes until well cooked through; I prefer a little pink on the bone.

Meanwhile, blacken capsicum over a naked flame. Place in a bowl and cover for 5 minutes, then rub the skin off, de-seed and tear into strips.

Five minutes before the birds are ready, heat 50 grams of olive oil in a large frying pan and toast ginger until fragrant. Add sesame oil and spinach, and turn until wilted. Add capsicum and soy sauce and stir butter in, adding a little salt if required.

To serve, arrange spinach and capsicum on hot plates. Place poussins on top and drizzle with cooking juices.

MOONSHINE BIFF (MARSHMALLOW)

Servings: 16–20 | Prep Time: 20 mins plus chilling | Skill Level: 1 (Easy)

INGREDIENTS

450 g sugar
450 g water
4 tbsp powdered gelatine
240 g icing sugar
3 capfuls rum
2 tsp vanilla paste
50 g desiccated coconut

METHOD

Bring sugar, water and gelatine to the boil in a pot and let simmer for 8 minutes. Place in the bowl of an electric mixer and whisk on high for 3 minutes. Add icing sugar, rum and vanilla and whisk on high for another 5 minutes, until light and fluffy.

Place in a lightly greased tray to required thickness and allow to set for 2–4 hours in the fridge.

Place coconut on a roasting tray under a medium-hot oven grill for 30 seconds at a time, stirring repeatedly until golden. Watch it like a hawk — coconut will burn quickly if unattended. Allow to cool, then cut biff into cubes or rectangles and coat with coconut.

Blenheim

GARDEN

ROBYN MARTIN

BELGIUM BISCUITS
ANZAC BISCUITS

Necessity became the mother of invention for me as I tried to meet the demands of being a dedicated mother and my job as Food Editor of the New Zealand Woman's Weekly.

Melt-in-the-pot baking became my crusade to make life easier for all those who liked to have home baking in their tins but were short on time to make this happen.

There is no creaming the butter & sugar in my baking repertoire so I have changed these recipes for the Kiwi classics Anzac & Belgium Biscuits to my melt-in-the-pot method. That makes them quick & easy to make with success assured, providing you measure the ingredients accurately.

BELGIUM BISCUITS

Makes: 14 | Prep Time: 25 mins plus cooling | Cook Time: 12—15 mins | Skill Level: 1 (Easy)

INGREDIENTS

125 g butter
¼ cup brown sugar
1 egg
1¾ cups plain flour
1 tsp baking powder
1 tsp ground cinnamon
1 tsp ground ginger
1 tsp mixed spice
1 tsp cocoa
about ½ cup
  raspberry jam

Icing
1 cup icing sugar
2 drops pink food
  colouring
hot water

Coloured sugar
1 tbsp sugar
1 drop pink food
  colouring

METHOD

Pre-heat the oven to 180°C. Grease an oven tray or line with baking paper.

Melt butter in a saucepan large enough to hold all the ingredients. Remove from the heat and mix in sugar and egg, beating with a wooden spoon until well combined. Sift flour, baking powder, spices and cocoa into the saucepan and mix until combined.

Roll dough out between two sheets of baking paper to 3 mm thick. Using a 6 cm biscuit cutter, cut out rounds. Carefully lift the rounds and place on oven tray. Bring the dough scraps together and repeat the rolling and cutting. Bake for 12—15 minutes or until lightly golden, removing to a rack to cool.

Sift icing sugar into a bowl, then add food colouring and enough hot water to make a spreadable icing. Mix sugar and food colouring together in a separate small bowl.

When biscuits are cold, ice half of them and sprinkle with coloured sugar. Place 1 tablespoon of raspberry jam in the centre of the baking-tray side of the remaining biscuits. Top with an iced biscuit.

ANZAC BISCUITS

Makes: 28 | Prep Time: 10 mins | Cook Time: 10—12 mins | Skill Level: 1 (Easy)

INGREDIENTS

125 g butter
¼ cup golden syrup
½ tsp baking soda
1 tbsp hot water
½ cup plain flour
½ cup sugar
1 cup desiccated
  coconut
1 cup rolled oats

METHOD

Pre-heat the oven to 180°C.

Melt butter and golden syrup in a saucepan large enough to hold all the ingredients. Remove from the heat. Dissolve baking soda in hot water and mix into the melted ingredients. Mix flour, sugar, coconut and oats together until combined. Mix into the butter mixture until well combined.

Using a measuring tablespoon, take spoonfuls of the mixture and place on an oven tray lined with baking paper. Press with a fork to flatten – allow room for spreading.

Bake for 10—12 minutes or until golden. Leave on the oven tray to cool and firm up before moving to a cooling rack.

KATE FAY
CIBO

LAMB SAUSAGE ROLL
WITH MINTED PEA PURÉE
RASPBERRY LAMINGTONS

This is a big year for us as we celebrate Cibo's 20th anniversary; it takes a great team to make it to this point. In the spirit of celebration, I've updated classic birthday party food from my childhood. The pink lamington was always my favourite when I'd peer through the bakery window. For this version, I've added white chocolate and freeze-dried raspberries. I've taken the lamb sausage from finger food to the plate with a fresh pea salad, pea purée and mint jelly (the base of which I stole from an old Aunt Daisy cookbook!): a nod to the past whilst celebrating the future!

Kate.

Parnell,
Auckland

LAMB SAUSAGE ROLL WITH MINTED PEA PURÉE

Servings: 4 | Prep Time: 50 mins | Cook Time: 3¼ hours plus overnight
Skill Level: 2 (Moderate)

INGREDIENTS

Sausage rolls
olive oil, for frying
500 g lamb neck fillets
2 tbsp butter
1 medium-sized onion, roughly chopped
½ head garlic, cloves separated
1 small carrot, roughly chopped
1 stick of celery, roughly chopped
½ leek, roughly chopped
2 sprigs fresh thyme
1 sprig fresh rosemary
about 1 litre beef stock
12 sheets of filo pastry
melted butter, for brushing

Pea purée
2 cups frozen baby peas
50 g butter
¼ small brown onion, finely diced
2 cloves garlic, crushed
¼ cup cream
fresh mint leaves
3 tbsp olive oil

Mint jelly
225 g sugar
½ cup white wine
½ cup water
3 cups fresh mint leaves
½ onion, sliced
5 cloves garlic
agar for setting

METHOD

Pre-heat the oven to 170°C and prepare vegetables. Heat a frying pan to moderate heat and add olive oil, then sear lamb all over, until caramelised a deep golden brown. Remove from pan and place in a casserole dish. Add butter to the pan, then onion, garlic and vegetables and cook until coloured and caramelised. Add this mixture to the lamb, add herbs, and season well with salt and black pepper. Cover with beef stock, then cover with a lid or tinfoil and place in the oven for 3 hours until lamb is tender. Cool. Remove lamb from the liquid and shred the meat. Strain the stock, and process 1 cup of the braised vegetables in a blender, then mix these with the meat. Season the mix again, and add extra herbs to taste. Roll into a sausage shape and chill in the fridge overnight.

Next day, pre-heat the oven to 160°C. Divide meat sausage into 12. Brush a sheet of filo with melted butter and fold it in half. Brush again with butter and fold into a strip a third of the width. Place a cylinder of meat at one end and roll the strip up, sealing the end with butter. Repeat. Place rolls on a baking sheet lined with baking paper and bake for 15 minutes, until golden brown.

For the pea purée, cook peas in boiling water for 2–3 minutes, until tender. Drain. Melt butter in a frying pan over medium heat. Add onion and garlic and cook for 2–3 minutes until softened. Add peas, then cream, and bring to the boil. Stir for 1 minute or until heated through. Remove from the heat and add mint leaves. Process until smooth, then add olive oil and season to taste with salt and pepper. Pass the mix through a fine sieve and serve on sausage rolls.

For the mint jelly, bring all ingredients except agar to the boil and simmer for about 10 minutes, then set aside to cool and infuse for 2 hours. Strain, and measure the liquid. Add 2 grams agar for every 100 ml of liquid and bring back up to the boil. Simmer for 5–8 minutes, until all the agar is incorporated. Strain again and place in the fridge to set. To serve, blend until smooth and place in a squeeze bottle.

You may wish to add a pea salad of cooked peas, fresh pea leaves and tendrils and blanched sugarsnap peas, tossed with olive oil and shredded fresh mint.

RASPBERRY LAMINGTONS

Servings: 6 | Prep Time: 30 mins | Cook Time: 35 mins | Skill Level: 2 (Moderate)

INGREDIENTS

Milk sponge
butter, for greasing
1 cup plain flour, plus extra for dusting
1 tsp baking powder
pinch of salt
3 eggs, separated
140 g sugar
65 ml milk
½ tsp vanilla extract

Coconut crisps
50 g desiccated coconut
200 g caster sugar
20 g plain flour
100 g cream

Raspberry icing
125 g Valrhona Ivoire white chocolate
20 g butter
250 g icing sugar
½ cup milk
2 tbsp raspberry powder

To finish
1 cup desiccated coconut
whipped cream, for serving
a few fresh raspberries

METHOD

Pre-heat the oven to 180°C. Butter and flour a 16 cm x 26 cm sponge tin.

Sift flour, baking powder and salt into a bowl and set aside. Whisk egg whites in an electric mixer until frothy and then gradually add sugar, continuing to whisk until you have a stiff meringue. Add egg yolks, one at a time, and whisk until combined.

Fold milk and the flour mixture alternately into the egg mixture, then fold vanilla in. Pour into the prepared tin, then bake for 20–25 minutes or until the cake springs back when lightly pressed. Allow to cool, then cut into 12 small squares.

Leave the oven at 180°C for the coconut crisps. Line a baking tray with baking paper. Combine coconut, sugar and flour in a food processor. With the motor running, slowly pour cream in until it is incorporated.

Spread very thin strips of the coconut mixture on the baking paper (or spread all over the baking paper to create a single large biscuit), then bake for 8–10 minutes until golden and crisp. Cool on a wire rack. If you have baked a single sheet of biscuit, break it into smaller pieces.

For the icing, place chocolate and butter in a heatproof bowl over a saucepan of simmering water. Heat, stirring, until melted and smooth. Remove bowl from the heat and stir in icing sugar, milk and raspberry powder, then whisk until smooth and combined.

Place the desiccated coconut on a plate. Dip sponge squares in icing to coat, then roll in coconut. Serve baby lamingtons with whipped cream, whole raspberries and coconut crisps.

JULIANS BERRY FARM

BERRY JAM
BERRY COULIS
FRENCH TOAST

As soon as we open our doors every October people start piling in to get their first taste of summer. The berry season is a short intense season so we need lots of extra hands on deck. We have a lot of university students, high school students and backpackers working here.

When they first turn up I like to show them another workers hands covered in berry juice and scratches from the berry vines. The contrast with their clean hands makes me laugh.

One of my favourite parts of my job is the pastoral element that goes with it. I am interested in their futures and hope Julians Berry Farm and Cafe can make a positive contribution to their lives.

Paul.

Whakatane

BERRY JAM

Makes: 7 x 300 ml jars | Cook Time: 40 mins | Skill Level: 1 (Easy)

INGREDIENTS

1.5 kg fresh or
frozen raspberries,
boysenberries, Ranui
berries, loganberries,
tayberries or
blackberries

1.5 kg sugar

METHOD

Place a couple of small plates in the fridge to chill. Wash seven 300 ml jars, rinse and place in a warm oven (100°C) to sterilise while you are making the jam, or for about 20 minutes. Sterilise lids by placing in a bowl and covering with boiling water. After a few minutes, tip into a colander and shake off all the water.

Bring berries to the boil in a large preserving pan or saucepan. Then add sugar and bring to a rapid boil. Boil rapidly for about 15 minutes. KEEP WATCHING.

Check that it's setting by placing a small amount of jam on a cold plate and returning it to the fridge for 2 minutes. Take it out and tip the plate on its side. If jam is ready, a wrinkling or skin will form on its surface. Keep testing until this happens, then bottle into sterilised jars and seal with lids while still hot.

BERRY COULIS

Makes: about 1.2 litres | Cook Time: 30 mins | Skill Level: 1 (Easy)

INGREDIENTS

1 kg frozen berries

500 g sugar

1 small cinnamon quill

2 cm x 1 cm piece
each of lemon and
orange peel

METHOD

Place all ingredients in a large saucepan and bring to the boil. Boil for 10 minutes, remove and discard peel and cinnamon, then purée in a heatproof blender or food processor until creamy. Bring back to the boil for 5 minutes. Can be bottled while hot, but serve cooled.

Will keep for 3 months in the fridge, or can be frozen.

FRENCH TOAST

Servings: 4 | Prep Time: 5 mins | Cook Time: 8 mins | Skill Level: 1 (Easy)

INGREDIENTS

2 eggs
140 ml cream
4 tsp sugar
a few drops vanilla essence
pinch of ground cinnamon
2 baguettes
2 bananas
a few knobs of butter
8 rashers streaky bacon
6 tbsp berry coulis
6 tbsp maple syrup
whipped cream and
fresh berries, to serve

METHOD

In a large bowl, mix eggs, cream, 2 teaspoons sugar, vanilla and cinnamon. Slice each baguette into six pieces and soak in egg mixture for 1 minute. Pre-heat the oven to 100°C.

Slice bananas in half lengthways, then halve into shorter lengths and sprinkle with remaining sugar. In a pre-heated frying pan, fry the baguette in a little butter, then place in the warm oven while frying the bacon and bananas. Bananas should be just caramelised so they still hold their shape.

To serve, dress plates with a swirl each of berry coulis and maple syrup. Build layers from three slices of baguette, two rashers of bacon and two slices of banana per serve. Drizzle with maple syrup and berry coulis, add a dollop of freshly whipped cream and garnish with fresh berries.

SHAUN CLOUSTON
LOGAN BROWN

STICKY BEEF PANCAKES
ORANGE CAKE
POHUTUKAWA HONEY
ROASTED STONE FRUITS

I grew up in Northland where it was just me and my Mum and we didn't have a lot. An early memory is getting up early, making toast and putting it on the tray along with jam and marmite. I'd take it to Mum in bed - I've always enjoyed that sort of thing.

I love to cook and it comes from the heart. Cooking at home, cooking for my family, cooking for our friends is really important to me. I like to try out new dishes at home, test them out on the people I trust before integrating them into the menu, so in a way Logan Brown is an extension of myself. - Shaun

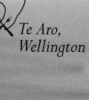

Te Aro,
Wellington

STICKY BEEF PANCAKES

Servings: 6 | Prep Time: 50 mins | Cook Time: 2½ hours | Skill Level: 2 (Moderate)

INGREDIENTS

Ribs
1.2 kg lean beef ribs
oil
120 g hoisin sauce
50 g fresh ginger, sliced
10 cloves garlic
6 star anise
5 cloves
1 tsp Szechuan peppercorns
150 ml full-hopped beer
150 ml mirin
90 ml soy sauce
200 ml chicken stock

Pancakes
30 g duck fat or lard
½ cup plain flour
pinch of salt
hot water

Assembling and serving
1 cup reduced braising liquid
½ cup bean sprouts
¼ cup cucumber, sliced
¼ cup radish, sliced
6 fresh basil leaves
6 fresh mint leaves
8 fresh coriander leaves, sliced
½ shallot, finely sliced
¼ large red chilli, seeds removed and finely sliced
a few drops of toasted sesame oil
2 tbsp toasted peanuts, chopped

METHOD

Pre-heat the oven to 165°C. Sear beef ribs with a little oil in a large non-stick pan and colour evenly. Place the ribs in an ovenproof dish.

Heat hoisin sauce, aromatic spices and liquids together and pour over beef ribs. Cover the dish and place in the oven. Slowly braise until tender, approx. 2½ hours. Allow the beef ribs to fully cool in the liquid.

Remove the braised beef ribs after cooling and reduce the braising liquid in a pot down to 1 cup of liquid.

For the pancakes, place duck fat, flour and salt into a bowl. Add a little hot water and gently mix to form a soft dough. Cover and rest for 10 minutes.

Dust a work surface with a little flour. Divide the dough into small balls and roll out thinly. Cook in a dry pan on both sides until lightly coloured.

To assemble and serve, turn the oven up to 200°C. Remove bones from beef ribs and cut the meat into six even portions. Place on a non-stick ovenproof tray. Brush the reduced braising liquid over the rib meat and place in the hot oven for 5 minutes. Repeat the process until the ribs have a sticky glaze. This should take 15 minutes in total.

Place bean sprouts, cucumber, radish, herbs, shallot and chilli together in a bowl. Dress with toasted sesame oil and mix.

Place the sticky ribs onto the warm pancakes and then place salad on top of this. Sprinkle toasted peanuts evenly over the top. Serve to your guests and enjoy.

ORANGE CAKE

Servings: 6 | Prep Time: 15 mins | Cook Time: 2¾ hours | Skill Level: 2 (Moderate)

INGREDIENTS

2 oranges
6 eggs
225 g sugar
225 g ground almonds
1 tsp baking powder

METHOD

Boil whole oranges for 2 hours. Remove from the pot, cool a little, then purée and sieve. Grease and line a 20 cm round cake tin.

Pre-heat the oven to 150°C. Lightly whisk eggs and sugar together, then whisk in puréed oranges, almonds and baking powder. Pour mix into the cake tin. Bake for about 35–40 minutes, or until a skewer inserted into the cake comes out clean.

Let the cake sit for about 10 minutes before turning out of the tin and serving with a good dollop of Greek unsweetened organic yoghurt. Also delicious with some warm roasted stone fruit (see below) with a little syrup drizzled over.

POHUTUKAWA HONEY ROASTED STONE FRUITS

Servings: 6 | Prep Time: 15 mins | Cook Time: 12–15 mins | Skill Level: 1 (Easy)

INGREDIENTS

200 g sugar
400 ml water
50 g pohutukawa honey
2 tbsp brandy
6 golden peaches, white
  nectarines or apricots

METHOD

Pre-heat the oven to 190°C. Gently heat together sugar, water, honey and brandy in a saucepan over a low heat, until sugar and honey are dissolved. Bring to the boil, and then remove from the heat.

Halve the stone fruit and remove the stones. Place fruit, flat side up, in an ovenproof dish and evenly cover with the pohutukawa honey syrup. Place in the oven to bake, basting the fruit with the syrup every 5 minutes or so. Bake until fruit is soft but still holding its shape and just beginning to colour. The time will vary depending on the ripeness of the fruit, but should be approx. 12–15 minutes.

TIP

This keeps well in the fridge – warm it gently before serving.

BRENTON LOW
À DECO

ROASTED FLOUNDER
WITH SUMMER VEGETABLES
TIRAMISU

My family is one of the original families that came to Northland and I was born and grew up in Whangarei. My grandparents owned a Hereford Stud and we kids spent a fair bit of time out on the farm. When they were busy haymaking I'd help my grandmother make lemon and Barley water and massive big cakes for the haymakers' lunch and roasts or toad in the hole for dinner. It was on the cards I would end up being a chef, it's what I've always wanted to do.

When we started 'à Deco we lived out the back in the garage. Sunday was our day off but we'd have people knock on the window and I'd be sitting watching T.V. in my undies shouting out "we're not open"!! Nowadays we live near Tutukaka, we love it. A great day is: up early and have breakfast with my wife and little fella then off to the beach for a surf or to walk the dog — family time is precious — then it's off to work. This is our version of paradise ☺

Cheers Brenton

Whangarei

ROASTED FLOUNDER WITH SUMMER VEGETABLES

Servings: 4 | Prep Time: 15 mins | Cook Time: 10 mins | Skill Level: 2 (Moderate)

INGREDIENTS

4 handfuls of seasonal
  vegetables

2 fresh corn cobs

12 small new potatoes

2 lemons

1 medium-sized tomato

4 super-fresh flounder

1 tbsp vegetable oil

3 tbsp butter

1 tbsp capers

1 tbsp roughly chopped
  fresh parsley

METHOD

Prepare vegetables as appropriate. Cut corn kernels off cobs. Blanch corn in salted boiling water, quickly to retain its nutrients, then pre-cook vegetables and new potatoes until just done. Set aside.

Peel 1 lemon and slice rounds out of it, reserving the other for juice. Mark a cross in the top of the tomato with a sharp knife, blanch briefly in boiling water and remove the skin and seeds. Cut the flesh into a dice.

Heat a heavy-bottomed frying pan on a medium heat. Clean flounder and pat dry, season with salt, then add oil to the pan and fry flounder, dark side down first (for better presentation), for 3 minutes. Turn and fry for another 3 minutes until just cooked, then season with salt. They will keep cooking on the way to the table.

Place flounder on four warmed plates, then work quickly – add butter to the hot frying pan and let it sizzle away until it starts to go light brown, then add the juice of the remaining lemon, the lemon slices, capers, tomato, corn kernels and parsley. Meanwhile, reheat potatoes and vegetables and place around the flounder, then spoon the brown butter and lemon sauce over the fish and you are good to go!

TIRAMISU

Servings: 10 | Prep Time: 15 mins | Skill Level: 1 (Easy)

INGREDIENTS

1 egg

2 egg yolks

100 g sugar

1 kg mascarpone

4 shots espresso

3 tbsp good-quality
  coffee granules

1 tbsp dark rum

1 tbsp brandy

200 g packet sponge
  finger biscuits

2 tsp honey

½ tsp arrowroot or
  cornflour

2 tsp cold water

1 jar bottled stone fruit
  (plums, peaches or
  cherries)

1 tub of caramel
  ice cream

10 g cocoa powder

METHOD

Place egg, yolks and sugar in a metal bowl over a pot of simmering water and whisk, making sure not to scramble the eggs. When this sabayon has reached the ribbon stage (i.e. it will hold its shape when drizzled on top of the mixture), cool and then fold in a third of the mascarpone, then add the rest and whisk until it is a whipped cream consistency (but not over-whipped).

Combine 2 shots of espresso with coffee granules, ½ cup of hot water, together with the rum and brandy. Spray a terrine mould or suitable dish with vegetable oil, then line with a double thickness of plastic wrap. Start to layer up the tiramisu: dip sponge fingers in coffee mixture and place in the mould, then cover with the mascarpone mix. Repeat until the mould is full, making sure to push down each layer firmly. Chill for 5–6 hours.

Combine remaining 2 shots of espresso with honey and bring to a simmer. Mix arrowroot or cornflour to a slurry with water and add to the coffee and honey, whisking until mixture thickens slightly. Strain and cool.

To serve, lift the terrine out of the mould and onto a board. Place some honeyed espresso in the centre of the plates. Slice the tiramisu and lay portions, cut side up, on the syrup, add a little fruit and a ball of ice cream, then dust with cocoa.

SARAH & MARTIN ASPINWALL
CANTERBURY CHEESEMONGERS

ROUGH PUFF
FLAKY PASTRY
MINCE & CHEESE PIES
ECCLES CAKES

The best thing about our rough-puff pastry is that it tastes lovely, and you can use it for anything. We've used it for both the Eccles cakes and mince and cheese pies. This is the same recipe we use in the shop and it's one of those things where the more you do, the easier it gets. If you have a spare Sunday afternoon, make a whole heap and freeze it. We have made Eccles cakes ever since we opened and they go really well with chunks of cheese for morning tea or dessert – the savoury and sweet make a wonderful combination. As for the mince and cheese pies, we use quality meat from our local butcher and proper cheese. The cheese is key; you need a good, flavourful mix and a generous amount; ours contain Barry's Bay cheddar, Meyer Gouda and Taleggio from Italy – glorious!

Martin and Sarah

Christchurch
Central

ROUGH PUFF FLAKY PASTRY

Makes: 1200 g | Prep Time: 2 hours | Skill Level: 2—3 (More challenging but easier with practice)

INGREDIENTS

240 g plain flour
240 g high-grade flour
½ tsp salt
480 g butter (cold but
  not straight from
  the fridge)
240 g cold water

METHOD

Sift flours and salt together into a mixing bowl and rub in 140 grams of butter until the mixture resembles fine breadcrumbs. Add cold water and stir to form a shaggy dough. Use your hands to push the dough into a ball, then squash this onto a lightly floured work surface and roll into a rectangle approx. 20 cm x 30 cm.

Divide the rest of the butter into 8 cubes and flatten each piece between your palms. Place 4 pieces to cover the middle third of the dough and fold one of the ends over to seal. Cover this with the remaining butter and stretch the last third of dough over to seal.

Rotate pastry so that the short sides are at the top and bottom and roll this out into a rectangle approx. 28 cm x 44 cm. Use a dough scraper or palette knife to help push the pastry into shape. Fold the short ends over to meet in the middle, then fold again as if closing a book. Rotate clockwise so that short ends are at top and bottom. This is your first turn.

Repeat this rolling and folding two more times; you may need to chill the dough in the fridge for 30 minutes after each turn, to keep it cool and not sticky. Be gentle with your rolling out and remember to sprinkle a little flour on your work surface and rolling pin each time.

Do one final turn, but instead of folding your dough into a book shape, mentally divide it into three, folding the top down to cover the middle third and the bottom up to cover that. Your finished flaky pastry should measure approx. 15 cm x 30 cm and will have had four turns.

One recipe of pastry will be enough for eight Eccles cakes plus four mince and cheese pies.

TIPS

Using a mix of flours gives good texture (both light and crisp), but either flour will work on its own. A food processor can be used to combine the flour and butter at the 'rub-in' stage.

On a hot day, leave the pastry to cool in the fridge for longer between turns.

The pastry can be made in advance; store finished pastry for a couple of days in the fridge or a month in the freezer.

MINCE & CHEESE PIES

Servings: 4 | Prep Time: 90 mins including cooling | Cook Time: 30 mins
Skill Level: 2 (Moderate)

INGREDIENTS

Filling base
½ small onion
1 small carrot
½ small stick of celery
2 tsp olive oil
200 g good-quality
   beef mince
200 g skirt or
   chuck steak, chopped

Seasonings
1 bay leaf
½ tsp smoked paprika
1 tsp chopped fresh thyme
zest of 1 lemon, chopped
2 cloves garlic, crushed
   and chopped
salt and pepper to taste

Sauce
2 grated tomatoes
   (skins discarded)
2 tsp tomato purée
2 tsp Worcestershire sauce

Pies
600 g rough puff flaky
   pastry, chilled
80 g mature cheddar, grated
80 g vintage gouda, grated
80 g taleggio, cut into 4 slices

METHOD

Finely chop onion, carrot and celery. Heat oil in a medium-sized saucepan and fry vegetables until soft (4–5 minutes). Add meats and cook until brown and any moisture has evaporated. Add seasonings and cook for a further 2–3 minutes.

Next, add sauce ingredients and simmer gently with the lid on for 15 minutes, then take the lid off and cook for a further 15 minutes until the filling is fairly dry. Allow this to cool for 30 minutes.

Divide your pastry into four, then divide each one of these into a large half and a small half. Sprinkle a little flour on your work surface and roll out the larger pieces into rectangles approx. 15 cm x 12 cm x 4 mm thick. Use these to line oval pie tins (size 13 cm x 10 cm x 3 cm deep). Roll the tops out to approx. 15 cm x 10 cm.

Place 20 grams (a good pinch) of cheddar cheese in the bottom of each pastry case, followed by a quarter of the filling. Top each with 20 grams of gouda and a slice of taleggio. Mix egg and milk to make egg wash. Brush pastry rims with egg wash and cover with the tops. Crimp the edges to seal them and use a knife to trim off excess pastry. Pierce through the top to make a steam hole, brush with egg wash and chill for 15 minutes. Pre-heat the oven to 180–190°C.

Bake for 30 minutes.

TIPS

Always allow your pies to cool a little before eating, to get the best flavour. They are also lovely cold, and seem to become cheesier. Remember, the Taleggio must be proper Taleggio!

The pies can be prepared in advance and kept for 24 hours in the fridge before baking.

ECCLES CAKES

Makes: 8 | Prep Time: 45 mins | Cook Time: 20–30 mins | Skill Level: 2 (Moderate)

INGREDIENTS

250 g currants
100 g caster sugar
40 g butter, melted
1 level tsp freshly
   ground nutmeg
1 level tsp
   ground ginger
1 level tsp allspice
600 g rough puff flaky
   pastry, chilled
1 egg
a little milk

METHOD

In a bowl, mix together currants, 70 grams of sugar, butter and spices. Let them sit for at least 15 minutes for the flavours to combine.

Divide your pastry into eight equal pieces, and on a floured surface roll each into a 12 cm square (approx.). Mix egg with milk to make egg wash, and brush this on the outer edges of each square. Place a tablespoonful of currant mixture in the centre of each square. Gather up the edges and crimp together to form a cross-shaped seal.

Turn your Eccles cakes over and gently round the ends so they become more of an oval shape. Place them on a baking sheet lined with baking paper, brush with egg wash and sprinkle with remaining caster sugar. Use some scissors to make three small cuts on top to let the steam out when cooking.

Chill for a minimum of 15 minutes in the fridge or a cool place, to allow time for the pastry to relax. Meanwhile, pre-heat the oven to 180–190°C. Bake for 20–30 minutes and remove to a rack to cool.

TIP

Best eaten when just cool with a chunk of Lancashire or Wensleydale cheese.

JULIE BIUSO

LUCA'S WINTER CHICKEN
STEAMED DATE PUDDING
HOMEMADE VANILLA CUSTARD

My son Luca really loves good food, and one of his favourites is this winter chicken dish. It's French and has all the great things that French housewives back in the 60's had access to: plump flavoursome chickens, bacon, shallots, garlic, herbs and red wine. It sounds simple but the flavour is sensational and the smell of the chicken browning in the butter is wonderful.

My mum was a good cook, a great baker and really good at desserts; her steamed puddings were legendary because they were so light. This is an old-fashioned kind of dessert which takes me straight back to her kitchen.

- Julie

Northcote Point,
Auckland

LUCA'S WINTER CHICKEN

Servings: 4 | Prep Time: 45 mins | Cook Time: 1 hour | Skill Level: 2 (Moderate)

INGREDIENTS

1 x size 12 free-range
   corn-fed chicken

1 tbsp olive oil

1 tbsp butter

2 tbsp brandy

350 g shallots, peeled

12 cloves garlic, peeled
   and halved

150 g free-range thickly
   sliced smoky bacon

2 fresh bay leaves

1 tbsp chopped
   fresh thyme

½ cup red wine

1 tbsp chopped fresh
   parsley, for garnish

Beurre manié

2 tsp soft butter

1¾ tsp plain flour

METHOD

Rinse chicken thoroughly, including inside cavity; drain, then pat dry with paper towels. Season chicken cavity with salt. Tie chicken legs together with string and loop the string around the parson's nose, so that the cavity is closed, then take it round the back of the chicken, bring it back to the parson's nose and tie it in a tight bow.

Pre-heat the oven to 190°C. Heat a heavy-based casserole dish over a fairly low heat and add oil and butter. When butter has melted, put in chicken, breast-side down. Brown gently for 5 minutes, then turn it over and brown the underside.

Gently warm brandy in a small frying pan, ignite it and pour it flaming over the chicken. Gently shake casserole dish once or twice, until flames subside. Transfer chicken to a plate.

Increase heat under casserole dish, add shallots and garlic and brown well. Transfer these to a second plate. Chop bacon into strips, add to casserole dish and cook until crisp, stirring often.

Return chicken to casserole dish, sprinkle with half a teaspoon salt, grind over plenty of black pepper and add bay leaves, thyme and wine. Bubble up, then cover casserole dish with a lid and transfer to the oven. Cook for 45 minutes, then add shallots and garlic. Cook for 15 minutes more, or until chicken is thoroughly cooked, then remove casserole from the oven.

Transfer chicken to a heated serving plate (carve it into joints if you prefer) and set casserole dish over a medium heat.

To make the beurre manié, blend butter and flour with a knife on a flat plate. Whisk this into bubbling juices in the casserole dish, a little at a time. Stir for 1 minute as juices thicken. Taste for seasoning and turn off heat.

Spoon gravy over chicken and arrange shallots and garlic around the sides. Sprinkle with parsley and serve. Good accompaniments are grilled mushrooms and parsnip mash – cook parsnips until tender, then whip with hot cream.

TIPS

Take your time browning the chicken – slowly does it – to develop wonderful nutty, buttery flavours without burning the butter (allow about 20 minutes).

If the juices have evaporated after cooking, add chicken stock; or, if too thick after whisking in the beurre manié, thin with chicken stock or hot water.

STEAMED DATE PUDDING

Servings: 8+ | Prep Time: 30 mins | Cook Time: 1½ hours | Skill Level: 1 (Easy)

INGREDIENTS

butter, for greasing
120 g self-raising flour
pinch of salt
½ tsp mixed spice
90 g unsalted butter
30 g fresh white
  breadcrumbs
3 tbsp soft brown sugar
170 g fresh dates,
  pitted and chopped
finely grated zest of
  1 lemon
2 medium-sized (size 6)
  free-range eggs
1 tbsp golden syrup
2 tbsp milk, at room
  temperature

METHOD

Before starting, ensure that butter, eggs and milk are at room temperature.

Grease a 5-cup (1¼-litre) china pudding basin with butter. Prepare a paper covering by folding a large piece of greaseproof paper in half and making a 2 cm pleat at the folded edge. Open paper out and grease it with butter, then fold pleat back in, with the rest of the paper lying open like a book.

Sift flour, salt and mixed spice into a bowl. Roughly chop butter and rub into dry ingredients with two round-bladed knives or a pastry blender, then stir in breadcrumbs, sugar, dates and lemon zest.

Whisk eggs with golden syrup and milk, then tip into the other ingredients. Mix with a wooden spoon until smooth.

Turn mixture into buttered basin, then cover with paper butter-side down and tie securely with string. Transfer pudding to a large, deep (rather than wide) saucepan with a trivet or put a small, clean cloth under the basin to stop it clattering during cooking. Fill pan with hot water to come about one-third of the way up the basin, and cover with a tight-fitting lid. Bring water to the boil, then turn heat to the lowest setting and gently steam the pudding for 1½ hours. Top up with boiling water from a kettle if water runs low.

When ready, remove pudding basin from pan, snip off string and remove paper. Cover basin with a serving plate, invert and leave for 10 minutes to drop, then remove basin. Serve pudding with hot vanilla custard (see below).

HOMEMADE VANILLA CUSTARD

Servings: 6 | Prep Time: 2 mins | Cook Time: 15 mins | Skill Level: 1–2 (Easy–Moderate)

INGREDIENTS

300 ml whole milk
½ vanilla pod
3 medium-sized (size 6)
  free-range egg yolks,
  at room temperature
1 level tsp arrowroot
2 tbsp caster sugar
extra caster sugar, for
  sprinkling (optional)

(GF)

METHOD

Put milk in a small saucepan. Scrape in seeds from vanilla pod and add the pod too. Heat gently until warm (not hot), then remove from heat and leave to infuse for 10 minutes.

Beat egg yolks, arrowroot and sugar together in a small bowl with a wooden spoon for 2–3 minutes until creamy and smooth. Blend in milk. Clean the saucepan, then return mixture to pan over a low-to-medium heat. Stir constantly with a wooden spoon until custard thickens and coats the back of the spoon. On no account let it reach boiling point, or it will curdle.

Remove vanilla pod (it can be washed, dried and reused), then pour custard into a bowl and serve hot, or sprinkle with caster sugar, cool then cover and refrigerate.

BEVAN SMITH
RIVERSTONE KITCHEN

PORK RILLETTE
MT COOK SALMON WITH
ASIAN SALAD GREENS
NAHM JIM

It's a fantastic feeling putting food on the plate that is so fresh, locally sourced and seasonally inspired. Here at Riverstone, we grab as much as possible in our extensive vegetable gardens and orchards and support local growers who share our ideals about good produce. Our salmon comes in from the hydro canals at Mt Cook about ninety minutes away, and our free-range pork is even closer, just fifteen minutes away in Waimate. It feels great to support the local players who have such stunning, diverse products and are just so passionate about what they do. They are part of what makes this country so great and why we love living here!

Bevan

Oamaru

PORK RILLETTE

Servings: 4 | Prep Time: 10 mins | Cook Time: 2½ hours plus cooling | Skill Level: 1 (Easy)

INGREDIENTS

800 g pork shoulder, skin on

1½ tsp fennel seeds, roasted

good pinch of chilli flakes

1 tsp flaky sea salt

2 cloves garlic, peeled

50 ml olive oil

1 cup finely chopped fresh parsley

¾ cup finely chopped gherkins

½ cup capers, rinsed well and finely chopped

1 small red onion, finely chopped

METHOD

Pre-heat the oven to 200°C. Score pork skin with a sharp knife and place in an ovenproof dish.

In a mortar and pestle, crush fennel seeds, chilli flakes and salt. Add garlic and grind to a fine paste. Add olive oil and muddle with the pestle to combine. Rub the mixture into the skin and flesh of the pork, and roast for 30 minutes.

Remove meat from the oven and reduce heat to 160°C. Add half a cup of water to the pork and cover with tinfoil. Return meat to the oven for a further 2 hours or until the pork falls apart easily. Allow to cool completely, still covered with tinfoil.

Once cool, remove skin and any excess fatty bits, saving cooking juices and liquid fat. Shred pork with your fingers and place in a stainless-steel bowl. Add cooking juices and half the liquid pork fat. Add parsley, gherkins, capers and red onion and mix together well. Adjust seasoning and press into sterilised jars or an airtight container. Tip the remaining liquid fat onto the top of the pork rillette to seal it.

Rillette will keep for several weeks if not exposed to the air. Serve with baby gherkins, salad greens and toasted ciabatta.

TIP

The key to the flavour and the keeping ability of rillette is the liberal use of the rendered pork fat from the cooking process being added back to the shredded pork. Do not be shy. If you think you do not have enough, add a little melted duck fat. Delicious!

MT COOK SALMON WITH ASIAN SALAD GREENS

Servings: 4 | Prep Time: 12 mins | Cook Time: 5 mins | Skill Level: 1 (Easy)

INGREDIENTS

½ small red onion

6 spring onions

½ telegraph cucumber

2 green chillies

2 cups basil leaves

4 cups coriander leaves

1 cup mint leaves

¼ cup Vietnamese mint leaves (optional)

2 cups finely sliced white cabbage

¼ cup finely sliced chives

petals from 2 calendula flowers (optional)

1 x 700 g piece salmon fillet

40 ml canola or peanut oil

½ cup deep-fried shallots

¾ cup Nahm Jim (see below)

METHOD

Finely slice both types of onion and the cucumber. Halve chillies, remove seeds and slice into fine strips. Prepare the other salad ingredients and set aside.

Pin-bone salmon, remove skin and cut into four pieces. Season with a little salt and pepper and sear for 2 minutes in a very hot non-stick frying pan with the oil. Reduce heat slightly, turn salmon over and cook for a further minute or until medium-rare to medium. Remove from pan and rest.

Place salad ingredients and half the shallots in a large bowl. Add half the Nahm Jim and gently toss together. Divide half the salad between four plates and place salmon on top. Finish with remaining salad greens, shallots and Nahm Jim. Serve immediately.

TIPS

Have all your salad ingredients and Nahm Jim ready beforehand. And don't overcook the salmon!

Crispy deep-fried shallots are widely available from most Asian food stores.

NAHM JIM

Makes: 1¼ cup | Prep Time: 5 mins | Skill Level: 1 (Easy)

INGREDIENTS

½ tsp dried chilli flakes

2 cloves garlic, peeled

1 tsp salt

½ cup light palm sugar

½ cup lime juice

3–4 tsp fish sauce

DF

METHOD

Place chilli, garlic and salt in a mortar and pestle and grind to a smooth paste. Add palm sugar and grind into paste until smooth. Add lime juice and fish sauce and muddle together.

Keeps for one week in the fridge in an airtight container.

TIP

If you don't have any limes use lemons instead, and don't be afraid to use plenty of fish sauce – it makes the Nahm Jim really come alive.

LISA SCHOLZ
SAGGIO DI VINO

SPAGHETTI AGLIO E OLIO
PANNA COTTA

I came to New Zealand from Europe at a time when there were many food scandals over there, but in Christchurch I found clear skies, ski fields, beaches and endless opportunities.

The recipe for Spaghetti aglio e olio is an old favourite of mine and it is easy to produce. The panna cotta is also very easy to make and you can use whatever fruits are in season. I prefer a traditional panna cotta with berries in summer. For both recipes, do make sure you use fresh and best-quality ingredients; I think that's really important.

Lisa

Christchurch
Central

SPAGHETTI AGLIO E OLIO

Servings: 4 | Prep Time: 10 mins | Cook Time: 15 mins | Skill Level: 1 (Easy)

INGREDIENTS

500 g spaghetti

200 ml extra virgin olive oil

10 gloves garlic, peeled,
  coarsely minced

3 hot red chillies, seeds
  removed, finely chopped

3 tbsp finely chopped
  fresh parsley

grated parmesan,
  for serving

METHOD

Cook spaghetti in salted water until al dente, approx. 10 minutes. Meanwhile, prepare the other ingredients. Drain spaghetti, reserving 2 tablespoons of the pasta water.

Heat oil gently in a large skillet or wok. Add garlic and sauté until it turns lightly golden. Add chilli and parsley. Add pasta and reserved pasta water. Toss to coat the pasta evenly.

Season with freshly ground pepper and sea salt and serve immediately with the parmesan.

TIPS

For best results use fresh, good-quality ingredients. I like Rustichella spaghetti.

Avoid burning the garlic: heat the oil to a moderate temperature, then take the skillet off the heat as soon as the garlic has reached the desired golden hue and quickly add the chilli and parsley.

PANNA COTTA

Servings: 4 | Prep Time: 15 mins | Cook Time: 10 mins plus 2–3 hours to set
Skill Level: 1 (Easy)

INGREDIENTS

3 gelatine leaves

1 vanilla pod

500 ml cream

60 ml milk

25 g sugar

3 gelatine leaves

seasonal berries,
  for serving

Coulis

175 g sugar

175 ml water

splash crème de cassis
  or cherry liqueur

175 g raspberries,
  fresh or frozen

METHOD

Soak gelatine in a little cold water until soft. Split vanilla pod lengthwise and scoop out the seeds.

Place cream, milk, vanilla pod and seeds and sugar into a pan and bring to a simmer. Remove vanilla pod and discard. Squeeze the water out of the gelatine leaves, then add to the pan and take off the heat. Stir until gelatine has dissolved.

Divide the mixture among four ramekins and leave to cool. Place in the fridge for at least 1 hour, preferably 2–3, until set.

For the coulis, place sugar, water and liqueur in a pan and bring to the boil. Reduce the heat and simmer until sugar has dissolved. Take the pan off the heat and add raspberries. Using a hand blender, blend the sauce until smooth, then pass through a sieve into a bowl.

To serve, turn each panna cotta out onto a serving plate. Spoon coulis over and serve with your favourite seasonal berries.

Parnell,
Auckland

TONY ASTLE
ANTOINE'S

CHICKEN, LEEK
& MUSHROOM PIE

I came from a big family and I'd volunteer to cook so I didn't have to mow the lawns or go to church. Sunday was my big day to cook the roast for all the family coming over. I loved doing that. It made my week.!!

The Edmonds cookery book was my bible and I think I baked every single cake and biscuit from it! When we opened Antoine's in 1973, the first item we put on the menu was chicken, leek and mushroom pie and it's still there 40 years later. It's the most decadent thing you can have – plenty of cream, booze and butter. If you're on a diet, Don't Touch It!

– Tony

CHICKEN, LEEK & MUSHROOM PIE

Servings: 6 | Prep Time: 45 mins plus overnight| Cook Time: 1 hour
Skill Level: 2 (Moderate)

INGREDIENTS

*Leek and
    mushroom mix*
100 g butter
2 large onions
4 large leeks
125 g shiitake
    mushroom caps
150 g oyster (phoenix
    tail) mushrooms
150 g Swiss brown
    mushrooms
250 ml Madeira or
    medium sherry
750 ml cream
2 tbsp chopped fresh
    tarragon or sage
3 cloves garlic, chopped

Chicken filling
1 large free-range
    chicken
2 large onions
4 whole cloves
3 large carrots
4 bay leaves
½ tbsp salt
6 peppercorns
250 ml fresh,
    well-flavoured
    chicken stock

To assemble
butter and flour,
    for pie dish
about 200 g puff pastry
beaten egg, to wash

METHOD

Melt butter in a large saucepan or heavy-based pot. Finely chop onions and leeks (not too much of the green part) and add to pan. Slowly sweat, not allowing them to brown (approx. 2 minutes). Slice and add all the mushrooms and cook for a further 5 minutes, stirring frequently.

Add Madeira or sherry, then cream. Stir well, then add herbs and garlic. Bring to a simmer and cook for approx. 25 minutes over a low heat, being careful not to let the mixture catch on the bottom of the pan. When the mixture has reduced by about a quarter, add salt and freshly ground black or white pepper to taste. Remove from the heat and allow to cool to room temperature before refrigerating. This mixture is best made the day before it is required.

To make filling, place chicken in a large pot. Stud onions with cloves and roughly slice carrots, then add to chicken together with bay leaves, salt and peppercorns. Cover the chicken completely with water. Bring to a boil over a high heat, then turn down and simmer for 25 minutes.

Remove chicken from heat, cover and cool in the cooking liquid. When at room temperature, remove chicken from pot and place in a non-corrosive container. Add stock, making sure to cover completely. Refrigerate until required.

To assemble the pie, grease a pie dish well with butter and dust with flour. Divide pastry in two, one piece smaller than the other (for the lid), and roll out to approx. 3 mm thick. Line pie dish, letting some of the pastry overlap the rim. Refrigerate until required.

Pre-heat the oven to 180°C. Remove chicken from stock and discard skin. Remove chicken meat from bones and cut into large chunks. Mix with the cold mushroom mixture. Place into the pie crust, heaped to the top. Apply pastry lid, bringing the overlap over to seal the pie. Wash top of pie with beaten egg and bake for 1 hour, until cooked.

TIPS

Make sure you use good-quality butter puff pastry. If you have time to make your own, the rough puff pastry recipe in the Edmonds cookbook is fantastic. If making pastry, make sure the butter is cold from the fridge and be sure to be as quick as possible when making.

When cooking chicken, do not overcook. Follow the recipe! Definitely make the pie mixture the day before; it's best cold from the fridge when making the pie.

Serve with a fresh green salad, tossed with buffalo mozzarella.

JUDITH TABRON
SOUL

SMOKED KAHAWAI WITH SPANISH CHICKPEA, GREEN BEAN & POTATO SALAD
ROAST HĀPUKU WITH SUMAC & LEMON CRUMBS
GOAT'S CHEESE MASH

My passion for fish stems from fishing with my family when we were kids. I've always loved to be out on the water and I remember Dad putting all 5 kids in his new tinnie, launching it at Westhaven and taking us across the harbour to the beach — except he forgot to put the bung in the bottom and nearly drowned the lot of us.

Given we have this amazing harbour and everywhere you go you can see water, it seems to me a natural thing that Auckland's food should be focused on fish – Judith

Viaduct Basin, Auckland

SMOKED KAHAWAI WITH SPANISH CHICKPEA, GREEN BEAN & POTATO SALAD

Servings: 6 | Prep Time: 20 mins | Cook Time: 10 mins | Skill Level: 1 (Easy)

INGREDIENTS

300 g smoked kahawai

2 bunches of fresh green beans (approx. 150 g)

1 medium-sized red onion (approx. 100 g)

2 large tomatoes

100 g pitted whole green olives

200 g cooked chickpeas

½ cup fresh parsley leaves

½ cup fresh mint leaves

2 large waxy potatoes

100 ml extra virgin olive oil

60 ml sherry vinegar

METHOD

Pick kahawai flesh off the bones and chop roughly. Trim green beans and blanch in boiling water for 2 minutes. Refresh in cold water and cut into 3 cm pieces. Finely slice onion. De-seed tomatoes and dice very small.

Combine kahawai, beans, onion, tomatoes, olives, chickpeas, parsley and mint in a large salad bowl.

Peel potatoes and trim off the ends and sides. Cut into neat 1 cm cubes – or roughly chickpea size. Steam for 10 minutes, or until they are tender. Do not overcook or they will go mushy in the salad. When potatoes are ready, season them with salt and pepper, pour olive oil and sherry vinegar over them and stir gently.

To assemble, tip potatoes and dressing into the salad mixture. Toss gently and serve immediately after adjusting seasoning.

TIPS

Serve this Spanish-inspired salad as a light lunch dish with plenty of crusty bread or as part of a shared lunch.

Alternatively, leave out the kahawai and serve with a barbecued spatchcocked chicken.

You can use drained chickpeas from a can if you wish.

ROAST HĀPUKU WITH SUMAC & LEMON CRUMBS

Servings: 6 | Prep Time: 15 mins | Cook Time: 15–20 mins | Skill Level: 1 (Easy)

INGREDIENTS

6 x 180 g hāpuku fillets
¼ cup ground sumac
¼ cup fennel seeds,
  roasted and crushed
zest of 2 lemons
2 cups fresh breadcrumbs
2 tbsp olive oil
2 tbsp Dijon mustard

Garnish
6–8 Brussels sprouts
oil, for frying
fresh watercress or pea
  shoots (optional)

METHOD

The hāpuku needs to be seared in a frying pan and then finished in the oven (on fan-grill to brown the crumbs). Heat the oven to 220°C fan-grill. Mix sumac, fennel seeds and lemon zest with breadcrumbs.

Heat a large frying pan and add olive oil. When hot, add hāpuku fillets and quickly sear on both sides. (This process is only to seal the outside of the fish, not to cook it.) Remove from the pan and place on a baking tray. Season with salt and pepper.

Brush each piece of hāpuku with Dijon mustard, then pack ½ cm of breadcrumb mix on top of each piece of fish. Place the tray of fish high in the oven under the grill for 10 minutes, or until the crumbs turn golden brown. If the hāpuku is very thick, after the 10 minutes turn the grill off and leave in the hot oven for a further 5 minutes.

For the garnish, peel off the Brussels sprout leaves (reserving the hearts for another use). Heat a little oil and fry the leaves until crisp. Drain on paper towels before serving. Garnish with watercress or pea shoots if wished. Hāpuku is great with goat's cheese mash (see below).

TIPS

Hāpuku is a great dish for a dinner party due to its size and thickness. All six portions will fit in one large frying pan, which rarely happens if cooking fish like snapper.

I also love serving roasted vine tomatoes as an accompaniment to this dish. Either place three small ones on each plate or serve as a dish on the side.

GOAT'S CHEESE MASH

Servings: 6 | Prep Time: 10 mins | Cook Time: 20 mins | Skill Level: 1 (Easy)

INGREDIENTS

800 g Agria potatoes
60 ml extra virgin olive oil
100 g butter
100 ml cream
100 g goat's feta cheese
2 tbsp finely chopped
  fresh chives

METHOD

Peel potatoes and cut into equal sizes. Place in a large pot and cover with cold, salted water. Bring to the boil and simmer for 15–20 minutes or until potatoes are just cooked and not mushy. As they are cooking, place olive oil, butter and cream in another pot. Bring to the boil, then simmer and reduce by one-third. Keep warm.

When potatoes are cooked, drain, then put back in the pot and allow them to dry over the heat for approx. 1 minute. Mash by either pushing them through a sieve or using a masher. Pour the cream mix over and beat in with a wooden spoon. Adjust seasoning with salt and pepper. Roughly crumble goat's cheese into the mash and mix well, then add chives.

Whenever I'm travelling overseas it's always the little back-street restaurants that you normally can't find that are my favourites. I bring back menus and sit down with my chefs and muddle some recipes around to suit the local ingredients available here in Taranaki. This Moroccan chicken is one such dish and, with the new craze for 'Gluten-free' dishes, it's perfect! and if you take the chicken out, it can be vegetarian as well. - M

Kerry

TERRY PARKES
TABLE @ NICE HOTEL

MOROCCAN RUBBED
FREE-RANGE CHICKEN

ISRAELI COUSCOUS WITH
ROASTED VEGETABLES

SALSA VERDE

New Plymouth

MOROCCAN RUBBED FREE-RANGE CHICKEN

Servings: 4 | Prep Time: 5 mins plus overnight | Cook Time: 30 mins | Skill Level: 1 (Easy)

INGREDIENTS

4 free-range chicken breasts

Marinade
2 tbsp Moroccan spice
1 tsp harissa paste
100 ml avocado oil
pinch of paprika
juice of 2 lemons
handful of fresh chopped mint

METHOD

Combine all marinade ingredients in a bowl and season with salt and pepper to taste. Place chicken breasts in marinade and leave in the fridge overnight.

Pre-heat the oven to 200°C. Place chicken in a roasting pan and roast for 30 minutes, then remove and slice on an angle into three. Serve with Israeli couscous and salsa verde (see below).

ISRAELI COUSCOUS WITH ROASTED VEGETABLES

Servings: 4 | Prep Time: 20 mins | Cook Time: 30 mins | Skill Level: 1 (Easy)

INGREDIENTS

250 g pumpkin
250 g kūmara
2 carrots
¼ cup diced capsicum
1 tsp crushed garlic
¼ cup fresh thyme leaves
100 ml olive oil
1 cup cooked Israeli couscous
pinch of saffron
½ cup grated parmesan cheese
½ cup egg mayonnaise
¼ cup chopped spring onions

METHOD

Pre-heat the oven to 200°C. Dice pumpkin, kūmara, carrots and capsicum. Place in a roasting pan with garlic, thyme and olive oil and roast for 30 minutes.

Cook couscous according to packet instructions, then add saffron and toss with roasted vegetables and parmesan. Fold in egg mayo and spring onions and add salt and pepper to taste.

TIPS

Use dry herbs if fresh are not available, and use pre-cooked couscous to save on time.

SALSA VERDE

Servings: 4 | Prep Time: 5 mins | Skill Level: 1 (Easy)

INGREDIENTS

handful of fresh basil leaves
½ cup grated parmesan cheese
handful of fresh parsley
5–6 anchovies (optional)
1 tbsp capers
100 ml olive oil
handful of fresh spinach

METHOD

Place all salsa verde ingredients in a blender, adding salt and pepper to taste, and pulse until well mixed but not too smooth.

Leave the anchovies out for a vegetarian option.

THE KERR FAMILY
CURLY TREE WHITEBAIT COMPANY

WESTLAND-STYLE
WHITEBAIT FRITTERS

My Grandma Dulcie used to say "the only thing you put into a good whitebait pattie is more whitebait".

Since being a kid, I've absolutely loved whitebaiting here at Haast — the place has a raw, elemental beauty that takes root in your soul and doesn't let go.

Our family's story started here with my great-grandparents, Sam and Sarah May, and it continues with our own two boys, five whitebaiting generations later.

There are plenty of tasty ways to enjoy whitebait — at our place, we reckon all you need is a good piece of bread and butter, a drop of mint sauce or a squeeze of lemon, then let Dulcie's advice take care of the rest.!

— Tony

Haast

WESTLAND-STYLE WHITEBAIT FRITTERS

Servings: 2—4 | Prep Time: 5 mins | Cook Time: 4 mins | Skill Level: 1 (Easy)

INGREDIENTS

500 g South Westland
  whitebait, fresh
  or frozen
1 large or 2 small eggs
rice bran oil spray,
  or a couple of
  knobs of butter
white bread, to serve
juice of 1 lemon
mint sauce

METHOD

If using frozen whitebait, let it thaw overnight in the fridge, then drain. Fresh whitebait – only in season, remember! – is best, of course.

Beat or whisk egg in a medium-to-large bowl. Mix lightly with whitebait and season with salt and pepper to taste (you could also use smoked garlic salt as an option).

Heat a hotplate or frying pan to medium-to-hot heat. Spray with oil or add butter. Scoop whitebait mixture onto oil/butter, to whatever size you wish. Cook until golden underneath, then flip over and cook the other side.

Serve while still hot – traditionally on white bread, spread with a fat layer of butter, with lemon juice and mint sauce (an essential item in the West Coast cupboard!) on top. Fold in half and get stuck in.

TIPS

Mo's number one tip: Regardless of the order you put ingredients together in… you have to think nice thoughts while you make them – they just taste better.

A variation is to separate the eggs and discard the yolks, then whisk whites until stiff, fold in whitebait and cook as before. The patties are lighter with more whitebait flavour (this always gets Grandma's approval). If you add lemon juice to either mixture before cooking, it firms the fish.

SIR DES BRITTEN

FAIL-SAFE ASIAN
SALMON WITH SMASHED
POTATOES & SLOW-
ROASTED TOMATOES

I have made this fail-safe salmon dish for friends + family many, many times over the years. Everyone loves it so much I've given away the recipe countless times! Guests would think I had spent all day in the kitchen but, in reality, it is so simple.

You can have great fun with it + even vary the toppings. Don't be worried that the Salmon will be undercooked and raise the heat any higher; it will turn out beautifully, I promise!

Oh yes, with the Smashed Potatoes, use floury Agria or similar variety.
You have fun + Enjoy!
Des

Island Bay,
Wellington

FAIL-SAFE ASIAN SALMON WITH SMASHED POTATOES & SLOW-ROASTED TOMATOES

Servings: 4 | Prep Time: 15 mins plus cooling | Cook Time: 1 hour 10 mins
Skill Level: 1 (Easy)

INGREDIENTS

Potatoes
4 medium-sized Agria
  potatoes
olive oil
basil pesto (optional)

Salmon
2 thick centre cuts of
  salmon fillet
4 tbsp Dijon mustard
2 tbsp hoisin sauce
2 tbsp oyster sauce
2 tbsp runny honey
2 tbsp light soy sauce
2–4 tbsp dry sherry
  (optional)

Tomatoes
4 medium-sized
  ripe tomatoes
a little oil spray
  or olive oil
dried oregano

METHOD

Pre-heat the oven to 225°C.

Par-boil potatoes (skin on) until slightly undercooked. Cool. (You can pre-do this.) Cut deeply into the flesh in a criss-cross form, then with your thumbs and index fingers squeeze the potatoes so they open up like a flower. Make a small well in the exposed flesh. Top up with olive oil, dribbling a little over the sides. Bake in a shallow baking dish for approx. 35–40 minutes or until brown and crisp.

Turn the oven down to 100°C (fan-forced) or 110°C (regular).

Place salmon in an ovenproof serving dish. Spread mustard on each fillet, then dribble the next three ingredients over. Sprinkle the light soy and sherry (if using) around the dish. This can also be done way ahead of time.

Simply cut a criss-cross through the skin of the tomatoes and coat with an oil spray or a smidgeon of olive oil. Add a dash of salt and a pinch of dried oregano (or another herb that takes your fancy). Place in the same serving dish as the salmon.

Place dressed salmon and tomatoes in the 100°C or 110°C oven for 30 minutes. Remove, turn the oven temperature up, and return potatoes to the oven to warm for a few minutes.

Serve with a dollop of pesto on top of the potatoes if wished.

TIP

All of the ingredients for dressing the salmon are variable. The more condiments, the more delicious the sauce.

ANDREW & JULIA CLARKE
VICTORIA STREET BISTRO

BEEF BOURGUIGNON WITH ROASTED ASPARAGUS, BABY CARROTS & POTATO MASH
TOMATILLO CLAFOUTIS

Jules and I met while working together at the Balcony Restaurant just up the road. I was in the kitchen working as as sous chef while Jules was a DM out the front. I'm a pretty shy person and Jules is the complete opposite! She enjoyed teasing me relentlessly. Her favourite thing to do was call out 'Hello, my lover!' every time she walked through the kitchen, knowing that I would go bright red every time. It obviously worked nowadays we're not only Andy and Jules the chef and waitress but Andy and Jules the husband and wife. We love having a restaurant in hamilton with wonderful customers who are open to trying anything and who let me cook whatever I want.

Andy & Jules

Hamilton

BEEF BOURGUIGNON WITH ROASTED ASPARAGUS, BABY CARROTS & POTATO MASH

Servings: 6 | Prep Time: 40 mins | Cook Time: 4 hours plus marinating | Skill Level: 2 (Moderate)

INGREDIENTS

Beef bourguignon
6 beef cheeks (around 250 g each)
500 ml port
300 ml red wine
oil, for browning
1 leek
2 sticks celery
1 carrot
2 onions
6 cloves garlic, crushed
2 tbsp chopped fresh thyme
3 bay leaves
500 ml beef stock

Garnish
12 rashers streaky bacon
12 button mushrooms
12 baby onions (or shallots)
oil, for browning

Vegetables
500 g baby carrots
oil, for roasting
2 tbsp honey
about 350 g butter
1 kg Agria potatoes
2 tbsp salt
about 100 ml milk
12 spears asparagus

METHOD

Trim excess sinew from cheeks. Place in a deep dish, cover with port and wine and leave to marinate for 12–24 hours.

Pre-heat the oven to 150°C.

Remove and dry cheeks, reserving the liquid, and season well with salt and pepper. Brown cheeks in a hot pan with a little oil; remove and place in a casserole dish. Roughly chop leek, celery, carrot and onions, and brown in the same pan. Add browned vegetables to the casserole dish, along with garlic, thyme, bay leaves and reserved marinade, and add in the beef stock.

Cover and place in the oven for 3½–4 hours, until cheeks are tender. Once the meat is cooked, gently remove them from the dish, strain the braising liquid into a saucepan and reduce over a medium-high heat for a nice, rich sauce. Cheeks can be added back in to reheat, but will fall apart if boiled too hard.

For the garnish, place bacon, mushrooms and baby onions (or shallots) on a tray with a little oil drizzled over the top, and seasoning. Cover and place in the oven with the cheeks about 40 minutes before serving.

Add carrots to a hot pan with a little oil to give them some colour, then bake uncovered at 150°C for around 15 minutes. When they are done, season and stir butter and honey through to finish.

Peel and quarter potatoes and place in a saucepan. Cover with cold water, add salt and bring to the boil, simmering until soft. Drain well and mash with a masher or potato ricer. While still hot, dice 300 g butter and whisk in, and add enough milk to get a nice smooth consistency. Season well with salt and white pepper.

Sauté asparagus in a pan with a little butter until tender.

TIPS

To save a little on cook time, bring braising liquid to the boil before it goes into the oven. The beef cheeks should be super-tender when done. If they are not starting to feel tender after 3 hours, turn the heat up a bit, to about 165–170°C, for 30 minutes.

There is no such thing as too much butter in mashed potatoes!

TAMARILLO CLAFOUTIS

Servings: 6 | Prep Time: 15 mins | Cook Time: 20 mins | Skill Level: 1 (Easy)

INGREDIENTS

50 g butter, melted
8 tamarillos

Clafoutis batter
50 g ground almonds
pinch of salt
1 tbsp plain flour
1 vanilla bean,
 seeds only
100 g caster sugar
2 eggs plus 3 yolks
250 ml cream
60 g sliced almonds
icing sugar, for dusting
150 g good-quality
 white chocolate,
 melted
ice cream

METHOD

Pre-heat the oven to 160°C. Brush six ramekins, about 10 cm in diameter and 4 cm deep, with melted butter. Please note that the image opposite is a serving for two.

Cut tamarillos in half and scoop flesh out in one piece with a spoon. Cut in half again and place in the bottom of the ramekins.

For the batter, mix together ground almonds, salt, flour, vanilla seeds and sugar. Add eggs and yolks, and mix well. Lastly, add cream and stir until combined.

Pour batter over fruit, filling to about 1 cm from the top of each ramekin, then sprinkle with sliced almonds. Bake for around 20 minutes, until golden and still slightly wobbly.

Serve hot from the oven with a good dusting of icing sugar, a drizzle of melted white chocolate and a big scoop of ice cream.

TIPS

This batter is easy to make in a food processor, but don't blend it too much once the cream is added as it can split.

Feijoas, poached rhubarb or fresh figs also work really well as a substitute for tamarillos.

DEAN BRETTSCHNEIDER

PLAITED SCONES
DELUXE CHOCOLATE CAKE

I think baking is one of the hottest trends in the world right now because a whole new generation wants to bake the way their grandmothers used to.

As a Rangiora boy, I was always interested in food. My grandmother was a North Canterbury farmer's wife so there was always something interesting happening in the kitchen.

Baking took my interest and I went on to do an apprenticeship at Rangiora Bakery where I discovered baking is actually quite technical and I got a passion for that.

I always say to people, if you are interested in baking, start with scones because they are so basic. Perfect your scones and then move on to chocolate cake!

- Dean

Rangiora

PLAITED SCONES

Makes: 2 (1 sweet, 1 savoury) | Prep Time: 25 mins plus standing | Cook Time: 30–35 mins
Skill Level: 2 (Moderate)

INGREDIENTS

Sweet filling
100 g dates,
  pitted and chopped
25 ml dark rum
25 g butter, softened
1 tsp ground cinnamon

Savoury filling
75 g tasty cheese, grated
½ small egg (from below)
15 g red onion,
  finely chopped
1 clove garlic, crushed
15 g finely chopped
  red capsicum
15 g finely chopped green
  capsicum
2 tbsp chopped fresh parsley
20 g sun-dried tomatoes,
  finely chopped
30 g olives, chopped
½ tsp smoked
  ground paprika
salt and pepper to taste

Scone dough
400 g plain flour
20 g caster sugar
25 g baking powder
good pinch of salt
70 g butter, softened
1½ eggs (use other
  half above)
200 ml milk
1 tbsp water
additional flour, for dusting

METHOD

Sweet filling – mix all ingredients together in a bowl, ensuring that the dates are broken down a little; cover and set aside for a few hours or overnight, then mix again. You will notice the dates will break up easier as they soften, so the longer the soaking time the better.

Savoury filling – mix all ingredients together in a bowl to form a rough, spreadable paste. Cover and set aside until required.

Pre-heat the oven to 190–200°C.

Sift flour, sugar, baking powder and salt into a large mixing bowl. Add butter and rub in, using your fingertips and thumbs, to form coarse crumbs. Whisk 1 egg and the milk together and pour into the dry ingredients. Using a wooden spoon, mix together to form a soft dough. Tip dough onto a floured surface and knead for 10–20 seconds – don't over-knead or the dough will become too elastic.

Cut dough into two equal pieces and shape into squares. Using a rolling pin, roll out each dough piece on a floured surface to a 25 cm square.

Whisk the ½ egg and water together to make an egg wash.

Evenly spread one dough square with the sweet filling and the other with the savoury filling, leaving about 1 cm free along one edge of each. Brush egg wash along that edge.

Working towards the edge painted with egg wash, firmly roll up each dough sheet to achieve a Swiss roll or log shape. Using a large chef's knife or dough scraper, make a single lengthways cut along the middle of each log, right the way through.

For each log, take one strand in each hand, with the cut side of each strand facing towards you, and twist the strands around each other. Press the ends firmly together to make sure they do not unwind during the baking process. Place the twists on a baking tray lined with baking paper, keeping them well apart so they don't join together during baking. Brush the twists with the remaining egg wash and allow them to rest for 10 minutes.

Bake for 30–35 minutes. Halfway through the baking time, turn the tray to ensure an even colour. Remove from the oven and transfer to a cooling rack.

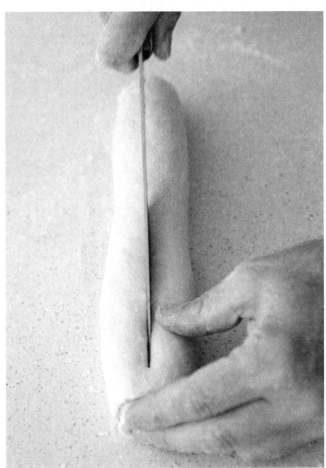

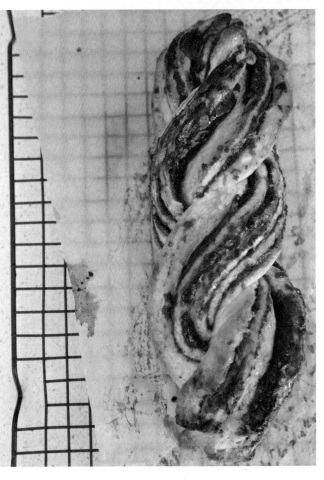

DELUXE CHOCOLATE CAKE

Servings: 8 | Prep Time: 25 mins | Cook Time: 45 mins plus standing
Skill Level: 2 (Moderate)

INGREDIENTS

Chocolate cake
160 g milk
¾ tsp cream of tartar
80 g oil
2 small eggs
1 tsp vanilla extract
180 g plain flour
70 g cocoa powder
290 g caster sugar
1 tsp baking soda
½ tsp baking powder
100 g hot water

*Ganache filling
and coating*
150 ml fresh cream
300 g chocolate, finely
chopped

Decoration
1 large packet
Maltesers
icing sugar, for dusting

METHOD

Pre-heat the oven to 180°C. Butter and flour a 20 cm round, high-sided cake tin.

Place milk and cream of tartar in a small glass; stir and set aside for 5 minutes. In a bowl, place oil, eggs and vanilla extract, and stir to combine.

Sift flour, cocoa, sugar, baking soda and baking powder into a large bowl. Add the milk/cream of tartar solution to the oil, egg and vanilla mixture and stir, then add to the dry ingredients. Using a hand beater, mix to combine, then slowly add hot water and mix well until you have a smooth batter.

Pour the mixture into the prepared tin and bake for approx. 45 minutes, until a cake skewer comes out clean when inserted. Cool for 15 minutes in the tin, then remove and cool completely on a wire rack. Once cool, wrap in plastic wrap and keep overnight for best results and finish it the following day.

To make the ganache, place cream in a saucepan and gently bring to the boil. Remove from the heat and add chocolate. Stir, using a wooden spoon, until chocolate has melted. Cool a little, then beat with the wooden spoon until ganache filling has begun to thicken slightly.

Unwrap the cake from the day before and rub the palm of your hand on the cake's edges to remove any loose crumbs. Place the cake on the work surface, then use a palette knife held vertically to coat the outside sides of the cake with the ganache, ensuring that there is an even coating all round.

Now, holding the palette knife horizontally, spread a layer of ganache on the top surface of the cake, making sure that you have an even coating. Use the palette knife to lift the cake up and gently place it on a large, flat serving plate.

While the ganache is still fresh, arrange the Maltesers around the top surface of the cake and lightly dust the top with icing sugar.

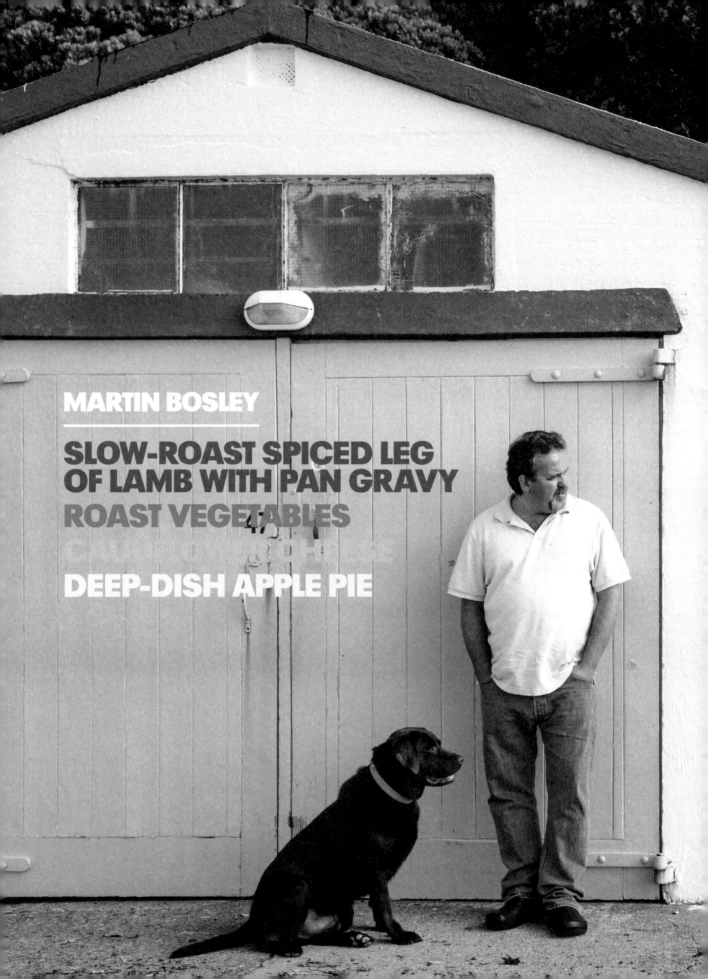

MARTIN BOSLEY

**SLOW-ROAST SPICED LEG
OF LAMB WITH PAN GRAVY
ROAST VEGETABLES
CAULIFLOWER CHEESE**

DEEP-DISH APPLE PIE

As far back as I can remember, Sunday was a day with my parents pottering around the kitchen before sitting around the table for the Sunday roast with their friends. Now I find myself continuing that same tradition with my own daughter. It's amazing the sort of conversations that happen around a roast meal. To get everyone started I carve the meat, then let guests help themselves from there. There is no fancy presentation. Sometimes the dish the lamb and veges are cooked in goes on the table and you get amongst it all and make it your own by adding mint sauce, mustard or radish - that sort of thing. It's "pass me this", "pass me that". Barriers get broken down, people lose their inhibitions and they just feel good - Martin

Oriental Bay,
Wellington

SLOW-ROAST SPICED LEG OF LAMB WITH PAN GRAVY

Servings: 8 | Prep Time: 15 mins | Cook Time: 3 hours 35 mins | Skill Level: 1 (Easy)

INGREDIENTS

4 cloves garlic

1 tsp ground cumin

1 tsp ground coriander

pinch of sweet paprika

2 tsp fresh rosemary leaves

juice of 2 lemons

3 tbsp olive oil

1 leg of lamb, boned (about 2.5 kg)

200 ml chicken stock

METHOD

Pre-heat the oven to 160°C. Peel and finely chop garlic and mix in a bowl with cumin, coriander, paprika, rosemary, lemon juice and olive oil. Season with salt and ground black pepper. It should resemble a thick paste.

Massage the leg of lamb with the spice rub, spreading it over the skin and into the flesh. Leave at room temperature while the oven heats up. Place the lamb into the oven and roast for 35 minutes. Pour in 2 cups of water, baste the lamb with the liquid, and continue roasting for a further 3 hours, basting the lamb every half hour. Add more water if the juices evaporate too much.

Remove from the oven and rest the meat in a suitable place while you make the gravy. Pour off the top layer of oil from the cooking juices, then put the roasting pan over a medium heat, pour in the stock and bring to a simmer. Using a wooden spoon, scrape the caramelised meat juices into the sauce. Season with salt and pepper if required, then strain into a sauce boat.

Serve with roasted vegetables, cauliflower cheese and minted peas.

TIPS

Ask your butcher to bone a leg of lamb and tie it up, leaving the shank bone attached.

The spices introduce a wintry depth of flavour, adding an earthy warmth.

ROAST VEGETABLES

Servings: 8 | Prep Time: 15 mins | Cook Time: 45 mins | Skill Level: 1 (Easy)

INGREDIENTS

400 g pumpkin
300 g kūmara
200 g young carrots
  or parsnips
250 g potatoes
a good splash of olive oil
2 lemons
2 tbsp chopped fresh
  parsley (optional)

METHOD

Pre-heat the oven to 200°C. Cut pumpkin into chunks, peel and chop kūmara, and peel carrots or parsnips. Give potatoes a good scrub and cut into wedges.

Steam all the vegetables separately for 15 minutes – place a saucepan of shallow water over the heat and bring to the boil, then place vegetables in a steaming basket over the water and cover with a lid. Alternatively, cook vegetables in the microwave – place on a plate with a splash of water, cover with plastic wrap and microwave on high until just tender (be careful not to overcook).

Toss vegetables gently in olive oil and tip into different parts of a roasting dish, or toss them all together. Squeeze the juice from the lemons over the top and season with salt and pepper. Roast for 30 minutes. Serve vegetables spooned around the lamb and sprinkled with chopped parsley, if wished.

CAULIFLOWER CHEESE

Servings: 8 | Prep Time: 40 mins | Cook Time: 25 mins | Skill Level: 1 (Easy)

INGREDIENTS

1 cauliflower
500 ml milk
a few peppercorns
3 cloves
1 bay leaf
50 g unsalted butter
50 g plain flour
125 g grated cheddar
1–2 tbsp grated
  parmesan cheese

METHOD

Break cauliflower into florets, discarding the thick stalks. Place a saucepan of shallow water over the heat and bring to a boil. Place cauliflower in a steaming basket over the water and cover with a lid. Steam until tender, then arrange in a shallow baking dish. Pre-heat the oven to 180°C.

Heat milk in a saucepan with peppercorns, cloves and bay leaf. Allow to infuse for 15 minutes, then strain into a jug. Clean the saucepan and melt butter and flour together, stirring until it thickens. Whisk in the strained milk, bring to the boil and add the grated cheddar. Simmer for 15 minutes.

Pour sauce over cauliflower, scatter parmesan over and bake for 25 minutes until you have a golden-brown crust.

DEEP-DISH APPLE PIE

Servings: 8 | Prep Time: 15 mins plus resting | Cook Time: 1 hour | Skill Level: 1 (Easy)

INGREDIENTS

250 g plain flour
pinch of salt
80 g unsalted butter, cold
80 g beef lard, cold
ice-cold water
1.2 kg cooking apples
sugar, to taste
a little milk
caster sugar, for
  sprinkling
whipped cream

METHOD

Put flour in a mixing bowl with a good-sized pinch of salt. Cut butter and lard into chunks and rub into flour with your thumbs and forefingers. Add a little ice water to bring the mixture to a smooth but firm dough. Cover with a tea towel and rest in the fridge for 30 minutes.

Pre-heat the oven to 200°C. Peel, core and quarter apples, cutting them into thick chunks. You want them to retain some shape rather than all turning to a purée as the pie cooks. Place apple in a pie dish and sprinkle with enough sugar to relieve some of the tartness of the apples – a rough guide is 1 tablespoon per apple. Toss the apples in the sugar.

Roll out pastry to fit the top of the pie dish. Wet the rim of the dish and lower pastry gently over the top of the apples, pressing the edge firmly to the rim of the dish. Crimp it with your thumb and forefinger or use the prongs of a fork. Cut away any excess pastry that may be hanging over the edge of the dish and use it to make a simple decoration for the top of the pie.

Cut two or three slits in the centre of the pastry to allow any steam to escape, brush with milk and sprinkle with caster sugar. Bake for 1 hour, until the pastry is crisp and golden, covering if necessary with tinfoil if it looks like it may burn.

You could serve custard with this but, for me, tradition dictates cream. Serve the pie hot and the cream will melt right through it.

Kaikoura

ROD & JOHNNY CLARK
NINS BIN

CRAYFISH ON THE BBQ

MY DAD STARTED NINS BIN IN 1977. ORIGINALLY THE CARAVAN WAS PARKED BY THE WATER DURING THE DAY AND WE USED TO TOW IT HOME EACH NIGHT, UNTIL IT GOT A BIT RUSTY AND WE HAD TO LEAVE IT HERE. IT GOES TO SHOW, IF YOU LEAVE AN EYESORE LONG ENOUGH, IT BECOMES AN ICON! MY SONS ARE NOW THE THIRD GENERATION OF FISHERMEN IN OUR FAMILY IN NEW ZEALAND. MY GRANDFATHER WAS A LOBSTER FISHERMAN IN SCOTLAND AND HIS FATHER COULDN'T SELL FISH BECAUSE OF THEIR ABUNDANCE AND RESORTED TO A CHIP SHOP.

THERE ARE HEAPS OF WAYS TO COOK CRAYFISH BUT I RECOMMEND GIVING THE AVERAGE-SIZED CRAY ABOUT 10 MINUTES ON A GALLOPING BOIL, UP FROM COLD. THE SECRET IS TO DUNK IT IN COLD WATER STRAIGHT AFTERWARDS SO IT DOESN'T GO RUBBERY AND STOPS COOKING. ENSURE YOU DROWN CRAYFISH FIRST OR ALL THE LEGS FALL OFF AND THE WATER WILL BOIL THROUGH THE BODY AND WASH FLAVOUR OUT.

ROD

CRAYFISH ON THE BBQ

Servings: 2 | Prep Time: 20 mins | Cook Time: 15 mins | Skill Level: 1 (Easy)

INGREDIENTS

2 live crayfish
4 cloves garlic
6 tbsp butter

METHOD

This is one of my favourite simple ways to cook crayfish if boiled cray is getting boring.

Drown crays in fresh water for around 15 minutes.

Split crays by putting a big serrated knife in between their teeth and cutting down the body and through the centre of the tail, then break the rest so that there are two halves. Take the poo tube and gut bag out, but leave the mustard in.

Place crays on barbecue on a low heat, with the shell side towards the flames. Put the main heat on the body as this takes longer to cook.

Crush garlic, mix with butter and add into body of crays, with the cray mustard, and brush down the tail. Stir garlic butter and cray mustard regularly. Do not turn the cray over.

Once meat goes white, the cray is ready — about 15 minutes for an average-sized cray.

Serve with a lettuce salad with Highlander condensed milk and vinegar dressing. Dip the tail into the body, and enjoy.

SIMON GAULT

MUSSEL FRITTERS
ROAST CHICKEN,
MASH & SLAW

I have early memories of my Dad going snorkelling around the wharf and rocks at Paihia, looking for mussels. We'd take them home, steam them open on the BBQ and then eat them, just like that. Green-lipped mussels are New Zealand seafood heroes and by adding a touch of cheese, pulling all those tough bits out and not overcooking them, you end up with a fritter that says New Zealand, says unique and says damned good.

Simon

Drury

MUSSEL FRITTERS

Servings: 4–6 | Prep Time: 30 mins | Cook Time: 20 mins | Skill Level: 2 (Moderate)

INGREDIENTS

600 g mussel meat (about 3½ kg fresh mussels)
100 ml white wine
100 g mascarpone
zest of 1 lemon
20 ml lemon juice
250 g parmesan cheese
160 g finely chopped onion
2 cups flour
2 tsp salt
2 tsp baking powder
½ tsp freshly ground black pepper
4 eggs
1 cup milk
50 ml extra virgin olive oil
2 tbsp capers
100 ml canola oil
fresh pea tendrils to garnish

METHOD

Clean mussels thoroughly and place them in a saucepan with wine. Cover and bring to a simmer. With a spoon, rotate mussels in the wine. As the shells open, remove them from the saucepan and allow to cool. Discard any mussels that don't open. To de-beard your mussels, pull the threads down towards the pointy end of the shell, discarding the brown foot and any muscle attached to the shell. Remove mussel meat from the shells, then remove tongues and the main (round) muscle. Cut mussels into halves or thirds depending on size.

In a small bowl, mix mascarpone, lemon zest and juice together and set aside until required. Grate parmesan and chop onion.

Put flour, salt, baking powder and pepper in a bowl and mix together. Add eggs and milk to create a thick batter, and then add parmesan, onion and mussel meat. Mix through the batter.

In a non-stick pan, heat a splash of olive oil until hot and add a generous spoonful of batter for each fritter. Cook until golden brown on both sides and firm to the touch. Repeat until all the batter is cooked. Keep warm or reheat in a microwave before serving.

If capers are salted, soak in water for about 10 minutes. Heat canola oil until it shimmers and fry capers until crispy. Remove and drain on paper towels. Place fritters on a board draped with baking paper, and serve with a heaped tablespoonful of mascarpone and sprinkled with fried capers. Garnish with pea tendrils.

ROAST CHICKEN, MASH & SLAW

Servings: 4 | Prep Time: 45 mins | Cook Time: 1 hour | Skill Level: 1 (Easy)

INGREDIENTS

1 size 18 chicken

40 g Italian seasoning (mine's perfect)

Mash

1 kg Agria potatoes

50 g butter, cubed

70 ml hot milk

70 ml hot cream

pinch of ground nutmeg

1 tbsp chopped fresh parsley or chives

¼ tbsp white truffle oil (optional)

Madeira sauce

150 ml Madeira

150 ml water

1 tbsp beef stock concentrate

2 tsp cornflour

1 tbsp butter

cracked pepper, to taste

Slaw

¾ cup good-quality mayonnaise

1 medium-sized clove of garlic, minced

½ head green cabbage

¼ head red cabbage

¼ cup roasted salted peanuts

1 tbsp chopped fresh parsley

2 tbsp aged balsamic vinegar

METHOD

Pre-heat the oven to 180°C. Remove excess fat from the neck and bottom cavity of the chicken, then remove wing tips by chopping through the outermost joint with a sharp knife. Using your fingers, loosen the skin around the breast and thighs, then massage some of the Italian seasoning under the skin. Liberally season the cavities too, as well as the inside and outside of the chicken.

Place chicken, breast side up, on a roasting tray and cook in the oven for about 1 hour – the internal temperature should reach 65°C or the juices should run clear when the thickest part of the thigh is pierced with a skewer. Allow chicken to rest for a good 10 minutes in a warm place.

Peel and roughly chop potatoes. Place in a saucepan, cover with cold salted water and bring to the boil. Simmer until just past tender. Drain and pass through a potato ricer, or mash. Add butter to the hot milk and cream. Return mashed potato to the heat and add milk, cream and butter, stirring until the mixture is smooth and creamy – not all the liquid may be needed, depending on how starchy the potatoes are. Add nutmeg and chopped herbs and season to taste with salt and pepper. If you decide on the luxury of truffle oil, add it just before serving, with a final whisk.

To make sauce, heat a saucepan and pour in the Madeira, bring to the boil and reduce by half. In a bowl, mix water with beef stock and cornflour. Pour mixture into the pan and stir while bringing back to the boil, then whisk butter in, remove from the heat and finish with cracked pepper. Set aside.

For the slaw, mix mayonnaise with minced garlic and set aside. Remove the dry outer leaves of both cabbage halves and discard. Cut cabbage in half again, then slice thinly. Place in a large mixing bowl with peanuts, parsley and balsamic vinegar. Add enough of the mayonnaise to coat the slaw, and season with salt and pepper to taste. Mix well.

To assemble, place cooked chicken on a chopping board and insert a large chef's knife into the bird, cutting along the inside of the backbone all the way to the neck. Remove backbone by chopping along either side. Place the resulting chicken halves on the board, skin-side up, and cut diagonally, separating breast and thigh. Transfer chicken pieces to a baking tray and reheat in the oven for 5 minutes. Heat mash in a saucepan or the microwave and spoon onto warmed plates. Stack a breast or a leg on each serving of mash. Arrange the slaw on the plate, next to the mash. Bring the Madeira sauce to the boil, and then pour over and around the chicken and mash. Serve and enjoy.

Mrs CLARK'S
est 1891
CAFE
Ph (03) 234 8600
OPEN From 8am Seven Days

Mrs CLARK'S
est 1891
CAFE

Riverton

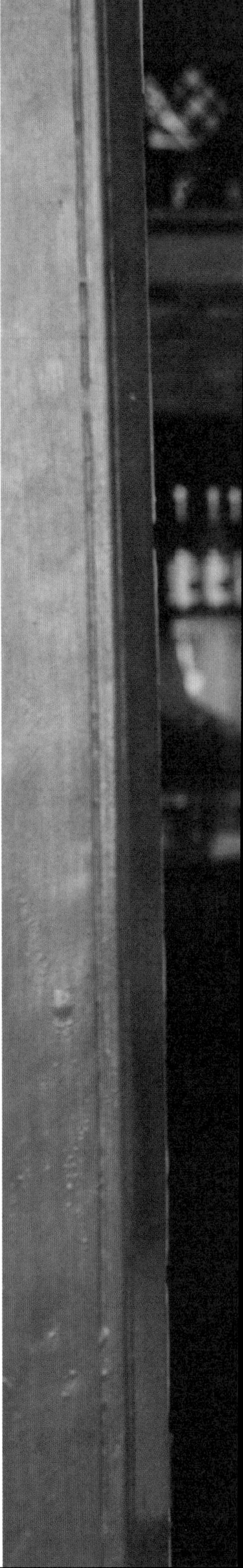

CAZNA & PAT GILDER
MRS CLARK'S CAFE

BLACK DORIS PLUM
& ALMOND TORTE
GINGERBREAD

Way down South here, we get our fair share of wild, wet & woolly days, and this Gingerbread is the ultimate in comfort food. Here @ the Cafe we toast a fat slab in the sandwich grill and smother it in caramel sauce and real butter. I swear, even the staunchest ginger hater will be converted, I see it every day! Oh the joys....

I ♡ this plum & almond Torte. It has the look of an old-school tea cake & can be whipped up very quickly — AND it's GLUTEN FREE! Just about any fruit can be used - fresh or tinned, cherries, tamarillos, gooseberries - best served with a dollop of natural yoghurt - healthy even!

— Cazna

BLACK DORIS PLUM & ALMOND TORTE

Servings: 6 | Prep Time: 10 mins | Cook Time: 40 mins | Skill Level: 1 (Easy)

INGREDIENTS

3 black doris plums
8 egg whites
2 cups ground almonds
¾ cup icing sugar, sifted
50 g butter, melted

METHOD

Pre-heat the oven to 170°C. Grease and line a 20 cm round cake tin.

Cut plums in half and remove the stones. Whisk egg whites until soft peaks form. Add almonds, icing sugar and butter and fold until combined. Add half the batter to the tin, and place your halved plums on top. Then top with the rest of the batter. *BANG!* Done… It's best not to let the wet mix sit around, so work quickly and bake straight away.

Bake for 40 minutes, until your touch springs back. Serve warm with natural yoghurt, and toasted flaked almonds and icing sugar for prettiness. *ENJOY!*

GINGERBREAD

Servings: 8 | Prep Time: 15 mins | Cook Time: 45 mins | Skill Level: 1 (Easy)

INGREDIENTS

50 g butter
1 tbsp each of
  molasses, treacle
  & golden syrup
2 eggs
1 cup yoghurt
1 cup milk
1 tsp vanilla essence
3 cups plain flour
2 tsp baking powder
1 tbsp ground ginger
1 tsp mixed spice
good pinch of sea salt
½ cup brown sugar

METHOD

Pre-heat the oven to 165°C. Line and grease a loaf tin (23 cm x 13 cm x 7 cm deep).

Melt butter in a largish pan, then add molasses, treacle and golden syrup and melt together. Add eggs, yoghurt, milk and vanilla. Beat together until smooth as.

Sift flour, baking powder, spices and salt together, then add sugar. Make a well in the dry ingredients and pour in all the wet mix – beat furiously until smooth and yummy. Resist eating the mix, and pour it into the loaf tin. Bake for 45 minutes, cool in the tin, then slice, eat and enjoy.

TIP

To make 'easy as' caramel sauce, put 1 cup brown sugar and 1 cup cream in a microwave-safe jug, heat on high for 2 minutes, stir, then heat for another 2 minutes. Cool to let it thicken up.

DAME ALISON HOLST

PAVLOVA
PIKELETS

My mother was a wonderful cook and I started cooking by helping her out in the kitchen.

I have always loved teaching people to cook and encouraging them to produce interesting, tasty and varied meals without spending too much time and money. Cooking is not scary!

I'm not a great pavlova maker but anyone can make this easy recipe. Everything goes into the bowl, you whip it up and then it goes into the oven.

Pikelets are another simple, inexpensive food. They don't take very long to make, and everyone likes them.

Alison

Orewa

PAVLOVA

Servings: 8 | Prep Time: 20 mins | Cook Time: 1¼ hours | Skill Level: 1 (Easy)

INGREDIENTS

1 cup caster sugar
2 tsp cornflour
¼ tsp salt
1 tsp wine vinegar
½ tsp vanilla essence
½ cup (3–4) egg whites

METHOD

Pre-heat the oven to 100°C. Carefully measure sugar, cornflour and salt into a clean, dry bowl with no traces of fat. Stir together.

Add vinegar and vanilla, then measure and add egg whites, taking care to get absolutely no yolk in the mixture. Beat with an electric mixer at high speed for about 15 minutes, until a thick, non-gritty meringue forms. When you lift out the mixer blades, the peaks should stand up stiffly, or just bend over at their tips.

Cover a baking sheet with baking paper, then pile the mixture onto this into a round shape about 25 cm across. Bake for 1 hour, then turn oven off and leave for 15 minutes longer. Take out of oven after this time.

Leave unwrapped, in a cool place, for up to two days. To serve, top with whipped cream. Decorate traditionally with strawberries, kiwifruit or passionfruit or use other fruit. Drizzle chocolate topping over strawberries if desired.

TIPS

Because ovens vary, cooking times may need slight changes. Pavlovas with a space below the crust and a compacted middle have been cooked too long. If centres are not completely set, cook a little longer next time. Fan-bake for the first 10 minutes if you have this option. If fan-baking for the whole time, lower the temperature by about 10°C.

PIKELETS

Servings: 4 | Prep Time: 4 mins | Cook Time: 15–20 mins | Skill Level: 1 (Easy)

INGREDIENTS

1 rounded tbsp
  golden syrup
25 g butter
1 tbsp sugar
½ cup milk
1 large egg
1 cup self-raising flour

METHOD

Heat a frying pan. (Use a high heat setting if the frying pan is electric.) Dip an ordinary tablespoon in hot water and use to measure the golden syrup into a bowl. Add butter and warm to soften both (microwaving is easiest), then mix in sugar, milk and egg. Sprinkle or sieve flour over the top, then mix in briefly with a whisk or beater just until smooth.

Rub the surface of the hot frying pan with a little butter on a paper towel. Drop dessertspoon or tablespoon lots of mixture into the pan, pouring mixture off the tip of the spoon. If the mixture is too thick and doesn't spread easily, add a little extra milk to it.

Turn pikelets over as soon as bubbles begin to burst on the surface. (Turn heat up if the cooked sides are not brown enough OR turn heat down if they brown too much by the time the first bubbles burst.) Cook the second side until the centres spring back when touched with your finger.

Cook in batches until all the batter is used. Keep cooked pikelets warm between the folds of a clean tea towel. Serve soon after making – spread with butter and jam, top butter with hundreds and thousands for small children, or 'dress them up' with whipped cream, jam and fresh berries. Yum!

JOSE CARLOS DE LA MACORRA
MEXICAN SPECIALITIES

VEGETABLE SOPES
CRISPY CHICKEN TACOS
GUACAMOLE

Mexicans have been cooking with a huge variety of local ingredients for thousands of years. Most of these Flavours are new to New Zealanders today and what a special moment we find ourselves in. What a Great! event where we all are taking part "as creators" of the "Kiwi-Mexican" cuisine.

Food is just the side dish, the main course is sharing the celebration of something "Greater"; this gives meaning and soul to all of our food.

And why not take someone to the park, hold hands, walk around the cathedral, kiss kiss and along the way enjoy a couple of sopes and tacos.

JOSE

Ellerslie,
Auckland

VEGETABLE SOPES

Servings: 3 | Prep Time: 25 mins | Skill Level: 1 (Easy)

INGREDIENTS

500 g masa harina (maize flour)
pinch of salt
1 cup water
¼ onion
1 clove garlic
100 g mushrooms
oil, for cooking
pinch of epazote
1 chile guajillo
200 g re-fried beans
¼ lettuce, shredded
1 tomato, chopped
cream cheese, for serving
1 avocado, chopped

METHOD

You will need a tortilla press for this recipe. Place masa harina and salt in a bowl and add water slowly as required. Mix until dough is smooth and moist. Divide into small balls, approx. 2 cm. Press them in the tortilla press until each measures about 5–7 cm in diameter and 1 cm in thickness. Cook on a hot, ungreased pan for 50 seconds on each side. Pinch the sides in order to make a 'lip' which will hold ingredient fillings later. Set aside.

Finely chop onion and garlic, and chop mushrooms. Heat oil and fry onion, garlic, epazote and chile guajillo with mushrooms for 2 minutes. Set aside.

Warm re-fried beans and spread onto your sope. Add mushroom filling and garnish with lettuce, tomato, cream cheese and avocado.

TIP

Masa harina, epazote (a dried herb) and chile guajillo – as well as tortilla presses – can be found in specialist Mexican food stores.

CRISPY CHICKEN TACOS

Servings: 3 | Prep Time: 15 mins plus cooling | Cook Time: 10 mins | Skill Level: 1 (Easy)

INGREDIENTS

1 chicken breast
1 clove garlic
¼ onion
pinch of oregano
pinch of salt
2 tsp corn oil
6 corn tortillas

METHOD

Place chicken breast in a pan and add boiling water to cover it, then simmer with garlic, onion, oregano and salt until cooked. Shred chicken and set aside to cool.

Heat oil in a pan. Place a tortilla on a board and fill it with the chicken (about 1½ tablespoons). Roll the tortilla up – you should be able to roll it at least twice around. Place the rolled tortillas in the hot oil and turn around until all sides are crispy. Make sure your oil is nice and hot, and keep your tortilla tight while frying.

GUACAMOLE

Servings: 3 | Prep Time: 3 mins | Skill Level: 1 (Easy)

INGREDIENTS

1 large or medium tomato
¼ medium onion
1 fresh chilli
1 bunch of fresh coriander
3 large avocados
juice of ½ lime or small lemon
pinch of salt
1 tbsp pomegranate seeds

METHOD

Dice tomato, onion and chilli into small squares and place in a bowl. Finely chop coriander and add to bowl. Cut avocados open and remove pits, then peel. Add to bowl with lime or lemon juice and salt. Mix well, breaking up the avocado as you do so, but try not to make mashed potatoes! Garnish with pomegranate seeds.

STEPHEN BARRY
MOUNT BISTRO

SOUS VIDE SCOTCH FILLET WITH SOUTHERN SMOKED SHORT RIB
CHOCOLATE SELF-SAUCING PUDDING
PASSIONFRUIT POSSET

Here at the Mount, we are located directly opposite the caravan park, so we are always surrounded by people on holiday. Before we came here we were in Rotorua. In fact, Mum was my first head chef as my family bought a restaurant there when I was 13... you could say I've never left the kitchen since! Self-saucing chocolate spongy pud has always been one of my favourites, I've tweaked this one a little bit and made it gluten and egg free because my daughter's allergic to both. This is a dessert she can actually have and enjoy, just as I did as a kid — Stephen

Mt Maunganui

SOUS VIDE SCOTCH FILLET
WITH SOUTHERN SMOKED SHORT RIB

Servings: 4 | Prep Time: 40 mins plus overnight | Cook Time: 4 hours
Skill Level: 3 (More challenging)

INGREDIENTS

600 g beef short rib

Spice mix
1 tbsp smoked paprika
1 tsp ground cumin
½ tsp cayenne pepper
1 tsp chilli powder
½ tsp freshly ground
  black pepper
1 tbsp brown sugar
½ tsp salt

Barbecue sauce
1 tbsp vegetable oil
1 onion, finely chopped
3 cloves garlic, crushed
½ cup tomato sauce
½ cup chopped tomatoes
  (canned or fresh)
2 tbsp molasses
1 tbsp cider vinegar
½ cup water

Sous vide scotch fillet
700 g beef scotch fillet
1 tbsp spice mix
  (from above)
1 tbsp avocado oil

Béarnaise sauce
1 egg yolk
2 tbsp white wine
  vinegar, heated
175 g butter, melted
1 tbsp chopped fresh
  tarragon leaves

*Swede fondant and
  asparagus*
2 large swedes
500 g duck fat
300 g asparagus

METHOD

Place short rib in a deep casserole dish. Combine all spice mix ingredients. Reserve 1 tablespoon for the scotch fillet, and rub the rest onto the short rib then refrigerate overnight. Place short rib in a deep tray, cover with plastic wrap and use a smoke gun to pump smoke in. Repeat three times, then place covered tray in refrigerator for 30 minutes. Alternatively, hot-smoke it – line a deep tray with tinfoil, add ½ cup of mānuka chips and place a rack over. Put short rib on the rack and cover the whole tray with tinfoil. Place a burner under the tray and smoke for 10 minutes.

For the barbecue sauce, place oil, onion and garlic in a saucepan set over a low heat and stir until onion becomes translucent. Add tomato sauce, tomatoes, molasses, vinegar and water. Bring to the boil and cook for 5 minutes. With a stick blender, purée the sauce until smooth (or cool and use a standard blender).

Pre-heat the oven to 140°C. Cover short rib with barbecue sauce. Seal dish well with a close-fitting lid or a layer of baking paper and then tinfoil. Braise for 4 hours until tender.

Trim all the sinew and fat from the scotch fillet, and cut into even portions 3–4 cm thick. Rub with reserved spice mix and avocado oil. Seal meat in vacuum-pack pouches or four individual medium-sized zip-lock bags. Poach scotch fillet in a water bath at 55°C for 1 hour (see tips below). Remove scotch fillet pieces from sealed bags and sear in a hot pan to colour the steaks.

Turn the oven up to 170°C. Cut both swedes into four even pieces, place in an oven tray and cover with duck fat. Bake for 30–40 minutes until tender. Place egg yolk in a food processor, add heated vinegar and process until frothy. With the motor running slowly, add melted butter until a smooth sauce is formed. Stir tarragon in. Break woody ends off asparagus and blanch in simmering water for 3–4 minutes.

To serve, spoon some Béarnaise sauce onto the plates, and place swede and asparagus alongside. Top the swede with the scotch fillet and add a slice of short rib.

TIPS

A chilly bin and meat thermometer can make an economical water bath or sous vide cooker. Line a polystyrene chilly bin with a clean plastic rubbish bag or use a small plastic chilly bin. Fill with hot water. Use a meat or espresso thermometer to check that the temperature is 60°C before adding the meat. Allow the temperature to drop to 55°C once the meat has been added. The temperature has to be kept constant to ensure safe, accurate cooking. As the water cools, top up with hot water from the jug – check the temperature every 10 minutes.

If you like your steaks rare, hold the water bath at 50°C; 60°C will give you a medium steak.

CHOCOLATE SELF-SAUCING PUDDING

Servings: 4 | Prep Time: 10 mins | Cook Time: 15–30 mins | Skill Level: 1 (Easy)

INGREDIENTS

3 tbsp gluten-free cocoa powder

2 cups Bakels gluten-free baking mix

pinch of salt

½ cup sugar

50 g butter

⅓ cup milk

½ tsp vanilla essence

½ cup brown sugar

¼ cup white sugar

1 cup boiling water

METHOD

Pre-heat the oven to 180°C. Sieve 1 tablespoon of cocoa together with baking mix and salt, and stir sugar in. In a separate bowl, melt butter and mix with milk and vanilla. Combine the dry and wet ingredients and mix to a smooth batter.

Put into a greased dish so it comes no more than a third of the way up the sides (either deep individual muffin tins placed on an oven tray, or a single pudding bowl). Mix brown sugar, white sugar and remaining cocoa and sprinkle on top.

Just before it goes into the oven, carefully pour boiling water over a spoon onto the mixture. Bake for 15 minutes for individual puddings or 30 minutes for a single large pudding. The puddings are cooked once a skewer inserted into the centre of the pudding comes out clean. Serve straight away.

TIPS

If gluten isn't a problem, substitute ¾ cup of plain flour plus 1½ tsp baking powder for the Bakels baking mix. (You don't need as much flour to get the same texture in the pudding.)

Remember to use deep moulds for the pudding, as otherwise the mix can boil over and mess up your oven. An oven tray placed under the pudding bowl can help catch any extra mix that may escape from your dish.

PASSIONFRUIT POSSET

Servings: 4 | Prep Time: 8 mins plus chilling | Skill Level: 1 (Easy)

INGREDIENTS

250 ml cream

⅓ cup sugar

pulp of 4 passionfruit

METHOD

Put cream and sugar in a saucepan and bring to the boil, then simmer for 3 minutes.

Sieve passionfruit pulp to remove the seeds. Add passionfruit juice to hot sweetened cream and stir until well combined, then pour into small dishes and put in the fridge for a few hours until set.

TIP

Posset is a simple yet elegant creamy dessert, traditionally made with the juice of 1 lemon. It can be set in a glass or ramekin or scooped onto a plate.

SID SAHRAWAT
SIDART

BUTTER DUCK
BEETROOT RAITA
PANEER TIKKA
CHICKPEA KEBABS

While being a chef is extremely rewarding, I don't see my young daughter Zoya as much as I'd like to as I work such long hours at the restaurant. When I have a day off, one of the things we love to do together is to go foraging for herbs. Foraging suggests we go into the wild but we just pick herbs from our surroundings, I love that we can have that connection with nature together.

— Sid

Ponsonby, Auckland

BUTTER DUCK

Servings: 4–6 | Prep Time: 10 mins plus chilling | Cook Time: 1½ hours | Skill Level: 2 (Moderate)

INGREDIENTS

6 cloves garlic, finely grated
4 tsp finely grated peeled fresh ginger
4 tsp ground turmeric
2 tsp garam masala
2 tsp ground coriander
2 tsp ground cumin
1½ cups whole-milk yoghurt (not Greek)
1 tbsp kosher salt
2 tbsp tandoori masala paste
1 whole duck

3 tbsp ghee or vegetable oil
1 small onion, thinly sliced
¼ cup tomato paste
6 cardamom pods, crushed
2 dried chillies or ½ tsp crushed red pepper flakes
400 g canned whole tomatoes
2 cups cream
¾ cup chopped fresh coriander, plus sprigs for garnish
steamed basmati rice, for serving

METHOD

Combine garlic, ginger, turmeric, garam masala, coriander and cumin in a small bowl. Whisk yoghurt, salt and half of the spice mixture in a medium-sized bowl with the tandoori paste; rub all over duck and turn to coat. Cover and chill for 4–6 hours. Cover and chill remaining spice mixture.

Heat ghee or oil in a large heavy pot over medium heat. Add onion, tomato paste, cardamom and chillies, and cook, stirring often, until tomato paste has darkened and onion is soft, about 5 minutes. Add remaining half of spice mixture and cook, stirring often, until bottom of pot begins to brown, about 4 minutes.

Add tomatoes with juice, crushing them with your hands as you add them. Bring to a boil, reduce heat and simmer, stirring often and scraping up browned bits from the bottom of the pot, until sauce thickens, 8–10 minutes.

Add cream and coriander. Simmer, stirring occasionally, until sauce thickens, 30–40 minutes.

Meanwhile, pre-heat the oven to 200°C. Line a rimmed baking sheet with foil and set a wire rack on top of sheet. Arrange duck on rack, skin-side up. Cook until duck starts to blacken in spots (it will not be cooked through), about 20 minutes. Reduce oven temperature to 180°C and cook for a further 40 minutes.

Portion duck into even pieces, add to sauce, and simmer, stirring occasionally, until duck is cooked through, 8–10 minutes. Serve with rice and coriander sprigs.

TIP

The duck can be roasted a day ahead. Cover, chill, then reheat before serving. Spices can be found in any Indian grocery store.

BEETROOT RAITA

Servings: 4 | Prep Time: 5 mins | Skill Level: 1 (Easy)

INGREDIENTS

2 medium-sized beetroots
3 cups thick yoghurt
1 tsp roasted cumin powder
1 tsp red chilli powder
fresh mint leaves, for garnish

METHOD

Peel skin off beetroots. Grate beetroots using a box grater or food processor.

Whisk yoghurt in a bowl. Add beetroot, cumin, chilli and salt to taste and mix well. Garnish with mint leaves and serve.

Note: The bright, dark colour of the beetroot will bleed and change the colour of the yoghurt to dark pink.

PANEER TIKKA

Servings: 4 | Prep Time: 10 mins plus marinating | Cook Time: 15 mins | Skill Level: 2 (Moderate)

INGREDIENTS

Marinade
½ tsp lemon juice
½ tsp chilli powder
½ tsp roasted and ground cumin seeds
¾ cup fresh yoghurt
½ tbsp crushed ginger paste
½ tsp green chilli paste
1 tsp ground black pepper
½ tsp carom seeds
1 tsp ground fennel seeds
¾ tsp ground turmeric

½ tbsp ground paprika
⅓ cup besan (Bengal gram flour)
1 tsp oil
salt to taste
a few saffron strands, dissolved in 1 tbsp milk

Tikka
12 x 5 cm cubes paneer
1 tbsp oil, for cooking
1 tsp chaat masala
1 tbsp finely chopped fresh coriander

METHOD

Combine paneer and marinade in a bowl, toss gently and set aside to marinate for at least half an hour. Soak four wooden satay sticks in water. On each satay stick, arrange three pieces of paneer. Repeat with the remaining ingredients to make three more tikkas.

Heat a non-stick frying pan or griddle, and cook the tikkas on a medium flame, basting with oil, until the paneer is light brown in colour on all sides. Alternatively, grill the paneer tikkas on a tandoor or barbecue grill until light brown in colour on all sides. Serve immediately, sprinkled with chaat masala and coriander.

TIP

Chaat masala can be found in any Indian grocery store, as can the other spices, as well as besan and paneer. If paneer is bought frozen, thaw before marinating.

CHICKPEA KEBABS

Servings: 4 | Prep Time: 10 mins | Cook Time: 20 mins | Skill Level: 2 (Moderate)

INGREDIENTS

400 g canned chickpeas
1 medium-sized onion
1 fresh green chilli
1 tbsp chopped fresh mint
1 tbsp chopped fresh
  coriander leaves
1 tsp coriander powder
½ tsp red chilli powder
½ tbsp ginger paste
½ tsp garam masala
2 tbsp chickpea flour
oil, for frying
fresh mint leaves,
  for garnish

METHOD

Drain and rinse chickpeas and place in a large bowl. Mash with a wooden spoon, a blender or with your hands, making a semi-coarse mixture which is not too smooth.

Finely chop onion and chilli, and add to chickpeas with the rest of the ingredients. Mix well. Form into small, round-shaped kebabs or patties.

Shallow-fry the kebabs in medium-hot oil until crisp and browned on both sides. Garnish with mint leaves and serve hot.

TIP

Fry one kebab to check that it holds together. If the mixture is too wet and breaks, add more chickpea flour.

DIMITRIS & NIKOS MERENTITIS
DIMITRIS GREEK FOOD

LAMB SOUVLAKI WITH PITA
BAKLAVA

I CAME TO NEW ZEALAND FROM KARDITSA, GREECE, IN 1984, AND STARTED "DIMITRIS GREEK FOOD". SHORTLY AFTERWARDS, I FOUND THAT I NEEDED HELP SO I CALLED MY BROTHER NIKOS AND HE FOLLOWED ME DOWN HERE —

AFTER THE 2011 EARTHQUAKES, IT WAS TOUGH FOR US, SAME AS FOR EVERYONE IN CANTERBURY. OUR SHOP WAS DEEMED UNSAFE AND LATER DEMOLISHED. BUT AFTER A SMALL BREAK, WE CAME BACK WITH OUR CARAVAN.
EVEN AFTER EVERYTHING THAT HAS HAPPENED, WE WOULD NEVER LEAVE CHRISTCHURCH — OUR FAMILY AND FRIENDS ARE HERE!!
AND WE HAVE THE BEST CUSTOMERS THAT RESPECT OUR HARD WORK, AND HEALTHY FOOD —

IF THE CUSTOMERS ARE HAPPY — WE ARE HAPPY —

DIMITRIS — NIKOS.

— ΚΑΛΗΜΕΡΑ ΣΕ ΟΛΟΥΣ —

Christchurch
Central

LAMB SOUVLAKI WITH PITA

Servings: 4 | Prep Time: 10–15 mins | Cook Time: 10–20 mins | Skill Level: 1 (Easy)

INGREDIENTS

1 kg diced leg of lamb
1 finely chopped tomato
salt, to taste
freshly ground black
  pepper, to taste
oregano, to taste
¼ cup olive oil

Tzatziki sauce
1 telegraph cucumber
500 ml Greek yoghurt
4–5 cloves garlic
¼ cup olive oil

To serve
4 pita breads
chopped lettuce
2 ripe tomatoes, chopped

METHOD

Place lamb, tomato, salt, pepper, oregano and oil in a bowl and combine. Leave to marinate. Thread meat onto wooden skewers that have been soaked in water. Cook meat on a hot grill, to your liking – between 10 and 20 minutes.

To prepare the tzatziki sauce, grate cucumber, and drain. Mix with yoghurt and crushed garlic. Pour olive oil over and mix, then season to taste with salt.

Lightly oil pita bread and grill until hot and golden, about 2 minutes.

Either serve meat and pita bread on a plate with salad ingredients and tzatziki, or remove meat from skewers and wrap into the pita with the salad ingredients and tzatziki.

TIP

Squeeze fresh lemon juice over the cooked meat for a bit of zing.

BAKLAVA

Makes: 30–45 | Prep Time: 25 mins | Cook Time: 20–25 mins | Skill Level: 2 (Moderate)

INGREDIENTS

1 cup shelled pistachios
2 cups almonds
2 cups walnuts
1½ cups sugar
1½ tbsp ground cinnamon
1 packet filo pastry (375 g)
melted butter, for layering
whole cloves

Syrup
2 cups sugar
2 cups water
zest and juice of
  2 lemons
2–3 cinnamon quills
1 heaped tbsp whole
  ground cloves

METHOD

Pre-heat the oven to 180°C, regular bake not fan-bake.

Place pistachios, almonds, walnuts, sugar and cinnamon in a large food processor and process into a fine crumb.

Brush two to three sheets of filo with butter and layer them. On the top layer of filo apply a thin layer of melted butter, then add a layer of nut crumb mixture over the first two-thirds of the filo. Beginning at the nut-covered end, roll the filo tightly up into a cylinder and place on a baking tray. Repeat until all the nut mixture is used.

Cut the cylinders into your desired length, and place a whole clove at the centre of every piece. Place the tray into the middle of your oven and cook until golden, about 20 minutes.

While the baklava is cooking, prepare the syrup. Place all ingredients in a saucepan and simmer over a medium heat for about 10 minutes.

When the baklava is ready, pour the warm syrup over it while it is still hot. Spoon any excess syrup over the baklava until all the syrup is absorbed.

TIPS

Sprinkle the cut ends of your baklava with water to prevent it drying out too quickly during the baking process.

Prick the baklava with a fork, before baking, to help the syrup seep into the baklava.

MARANUI CAFE

SCRAMBLED TOFU
TOASTED MUESLI

Being here in Lyall Bay above the Maranui
Surfclub and right on the Ocean is truly amazing.
On beautiful days we get pods of dolphins and
in stormy weather we get kite surfers &
windsurfers - it can be carnage out there!
This place is just magic, we're so lucky
We nearly lost everything in 2009, when we
got a call in the middle of the night to
say the café was ablaze with flames pouring
out the windows. It was pretty grim.
After 10 months & a huge amount of community
support & goodwill, we managed to rebuild &
reopen. We're lucky & take nothing for granted.

Katie, Matt & Bronwyn

Lyall Bay,
Wellington

SCRAMBLED TOFU

Servings: 4 | Prep Time: 10 mins | Cook Time: 10 mins | Skill Level: 1 (Easy)

INGREDIENTS

1 carrot, peeled
1 red onion
1 stick of celery
1 zucchini
½ red capsicum
2 cloves garlic

1 thumb-sized piece peeled
  fresh ginger
500 g tofu
½ bunch of fresh coriander
  (with stalks)
1 tbsp vegetable oil

1 tbsp sesame oil
1 tbsp ground turmeric
1 tbsp ground cumin
1 tbsp ground coriander
3 tbsp tamari sauce

(DF) (GF) (V)

METHOD

Neatly dice carrot, red onion, celery, zucchini and capsicum. Finely grate garlic and ginger. Drain any liquid off tofu, then rinse and crumble. Finely slice coriander stalks. Chop coriander leaves and set aside.

Heat both oils in a deep frying pan and add all your diced vegetables. Stir continuously on a low heat until tender. Add garlic, ginger and coriander stalks and stir for another minute. Add your dry spices and stir to coat. Add tofu, and stir for another 2–3 minutes until tofu is well coated with spices.

Remove from the heat, stir in chopped coriander leaves and the tamari. Taste, and add more tamari if desired. Serve on your favourite whole-grain toast, topped with lots of avocado and garnished with sesame seeds.

TOASTED MUESLI

Servings: 6 | Prep Time: 20 mins | Cook Time: 20 mins | Skill Level: 1 (Easy)

INGREDIENTS

5 cups rolled oats
2 cups shredded coconut
1 cup hazelnuts
1 cup cashew nuts
½ cup linseed
¼ cup chia seeds
1 cup sunflower seeds

½ cup sesame seeds
½ cup pumpkin seeds
½ cup honey
½ cup vegetable oil
2 tbsp vanilla essence
zest of 1 lemon
zest of 1 orange

All the following fruit is dried:
1 cup chopped apricots
½ cup cranberries
½ cup chopped dates
½ cup diced pitted prunes
½ cup sliced dried figs
½ cup raisins

 (DF)

METHOD

Pre-heat the oven to 150°C. In a large bowl, combine all grains, nuts and seeds. Mix well to combine. To a saucepan set over a low heat, add honey, oil and vanilla and stir until melted together – make sure it does not boil. Pour this over the grains, nuts and seeds mix. Mix well, making sure everything is really well and evenly coated.

Put in a large baking dish and place in the oven. You will need to check every couple of minutes and stir, until the mixture is evenly toasted and golden brown. This will take approximately 15–20 minutes.

Remove from the oven, and add dried fruit and zest while toasted mixture is still hot. Stir well and leave to cool. Serve with freshly chopped seasonal fruit and yoghurt.

ALLYSON GOFTON

COUNTRY FIG BREAD
LAMB & PORK
CASSOULET

Stepping off the work-a-day wheel for one year to take our children to France, has been a true family Adventure, and no more so than in the discovery of foods of a very rural southwest France. Here, where little villages have nestled for centuries in the hidden valleys of the Hautes-Pyrénées, is a unique cuisine unchanged by time. Quality raw ingredients cooked simply, allowing the flavour of the ingredients to shine, are free of unnecessary garnishes, dashes, drizzles or dustings. It's been a year-long culinary sabbatical filled with joy. Here I share two recipes: Fig Bread, a favourite of the boulangeries (artisan bakeries) of the area, and my Lamb Cassoulet, a Kiwi twist on the renowned dish of southwest France.

Enjoy

Allyson

Meadowbank,
Auckland

COUNTRY FIG BREAD

Makes: 1 loaf | Prep Time: 2½–3 hours | Cook Time: 35 mins | Skill Level: 2 (Moderate)

INGREDIENTS

1½ cups tepid water
450 g high-grade flour
50 g rye flour
1 good tsp salt
 (this is essential)
1 tbsp sugar – brown or white
1 generous tbsp active dried
 yeast mixture
8–10 moist, dried figs
 (not glacéd), roughly chopped

METHOD

If making in a bread machine, use powdered yeast rather than granules. Put water, flours, salt, sugar and yeast into the working bowl of the bread machine in the right order for your machine, and set the machine to a regular standard bake cycle. Allow the machine to do the work for you. Do check, once the machine gets going, that there is the right amount of liquid or flour. I'm constantly opening the lid of my bread machine – at the beginning – to make sure the dough texture is correct, and I add more or less liquid or flour as needed. However, once the dough begins to prove for baking, avoid opening the lid as the shock of cold air will frighten the dough and it will collapse somewhat.

Meanwhile, roughly chop the figs. Add the figs just prior to the end of the initial kneading phase (some machines beep at this point). You could also add them at the beginning, as long as you don't mind the dried fruit being well mashed – I quite like it this way, especially if I am going to use the bread for toasting, as large chunks of fig do tend to burn in the toaster.

If you plan to make it by hand, first dissolve the yeast granules in the warm water. Stir the yeast into the water and set aside until the mixture turns slightly porridge-like and has formed frothy bubbles on top.

Sift the flour, salt and sugar onto a work surface – make sure you have a large, clean space to work on. Spread the flour out, making a very large circle in the centre. Into this, pour all the frothy water. Make sure there are no gaps in the flour walls, lest you have an unexpected flood. Using the fingertips on one hand only, and keeping the free hand clean, stir the flour into the well. Once all the flour is added, bring the dough together with both hands and knead well until the bread is soft and spongy. Knead in the diced figs.

Cover and rest dough for 45–60 minutes, or until well risen. Turn out onto a floured surface, deflate gently, then shape and place on a greased baking tray or in a well-greased large loaf tin (12 cm x 26 cm).

Some fig slices arranged on top add a nice finish, but it is optional. Leave in a warm place for about 45 minutes to rise until doubled in bulk. Pre-heat the oven to 200°C.

Bake for 25–35 minutes, depending on size and shape. The bread will be cooked when tapping it underneath makes a hollow sound. Once cooked, cool on a wire rack. It's delicious served warm with jambon and soft cheese.

LAMB & PORK CASSOULET

Servings: 6 | Prep Time: 1 hour plus overnight | Cook Time: 2–2½ hours | Skill Level: 1 (Easy)

INGREDIENTS

2–3 slices pork belly

1 tbsp flaky salt (less if finely milled)

500 g dried haricot beans

6 cups good-quality chicken or light lamb stock

1 bouquet garni

4–6 cloves garlic

1.2 kg lamb, cut into large chunky pieces

6 duck or lamb sausages

100 g duck fat or unsalted butter

2 onions, peeled and diced

1 carrot, diced

2 tbsp tomato paste

2 tomatoes, blanched and diced

large piece of pork skin (optional; ask your butcher)

½ cup fresh white breadcrumbs

METHOD

Begin the day before. Rub flaky salt into pork slices and place in a container in the fridge overnight. Soak beans in plenty of cold water overnight. The next day, wash off the salt and drain the beans.

Put beans, stock and bouquet garni into a large flameproof casserole dish, and simmer gently for 1 hour or until almost tender. Pre-heat the oven to 150°C.

Dice pork. Crush, peel and mash garlic to a paste with a little salt. Brown pork, lamb and whole sausages well in the melted duck fat/butter and set aside. Add onion, carrot and garlic to the residue of fat and brown lightly without burning. Stir in the tomato paste and tomatoes, scraping the bottom of the pan to remove any sediment – adding a little stock from the beans will help here.

Stir the tomato and onion mixture and the meats into the bean casserole, arranging the pieces of meat evenly among the beans. If you have it, place the piece of pork skin on top. Scatter the breadcrumbs over.

Bake for 1½ hours, or until the meat and beans are tender.

In past times, duck fat would have been added, a little at a time, through a hole cracked in the crumb crust. The fat softened the beans, gave flavour and, eventually rising to the top, covered the dish. When cold, it set hard and preserved the food under the crust.

MICHAEL MEREDITH
MEREDITH'S

RAW FISH & COCONUT SALAD
FA'ALIFU TARO & CORNED BEEF

I spent my early childhood in the Islands, which gave me a respect for ingredients and the experience of working with raw materials. I came to New Zealand as a teenager and was exposed to the diversity of New Zealand culture. All these things, along with travelling, are reflected in the way I cook.

I grew up eating raw fish, along with corned beef and taro, as a Sunday tradition with extended family. Back home, corned beef comes in a tin with a lot of fat but, in this recipe, I've dehydrated it in the oven, taking out lots of the fat and giving it a crispy texture. It's not so traditional but really delicious.

Michael

Balmoral,
Auckland

OKA I'A
RAW FISH & COCONUT SALAD

Servings: 4 | Prep Time: 45 mins | Skill Level: 1 (Easy)

INGREDIENTS

300 g raw fish (tuna, mahi mahi or tarakihi)
200 g cucumber
100 g spring onions
150 g green coconut flesh
2 cups of fresh coconut cream
lemon juice to taste

salt to taste
1 red or green chilli
3 medium tomatoes
½ cup chopped coriander leaves

(DF) (GF)

METHOD

Cut fish into 2 cm chunks, chop cucumber into large dice, slice spring onions and dice coconut. Place in a non-metallic bowl.

In another bowl, make the dressing. Mix coconut cream, lemon juice and salt. Finely chop chilli and mix in. Pour onto the fish and gently mix. Adjust seasoning and also make up and add more dressing if you want.

Chop tomatoes and stir in. Let it sit for 20 minutes in the fridge before eating. Lightly mix chopped coriander in before serving.

FA'ALIFU TARO & CORNED BEEF

Servings: 4 | Prep Time: 10 mins | Cook Time: 2–3 hours | Skill Level: 1 (Easy)

INGREDIENTS

450 g canned
  corned beef
2 medium-sized firm
  and heavy taro
1 onion
500 g silverbeet
dash of oil
pinch of curry powder
400 ml fresh coconut
  cream
100 ml coconut water

(DF) (GF)

METHOD

Remove corned beef from can and spread it out on a baking tray with a silicone liner. Dry slowly in the oven at 80°C for 2–3 hours.

Peel taro and cut into pieces. Place in plenty of lightly salted water and bring to the boil. Cook until the taro root is fully done – it should be soft but not falling apart. Drain water off and keep taro warm.

Thinly slice onion and chop silverbeet. Heat oil and lightly sweat onion without colouring it, then add curry powder and cook for a few minutes to release the aroma.

Add coconut cream and bring to a light boil. If gravy is too thick, adjust with coconut water. Add silverbeet and then the cooked taro. Stir to coat the taro pieces with coconut cream.

Check seasoning before serving, then sprinkle some dried corned beef on top and serve.

TIP

Depending on what's in season, you can use green bananas, breadfruit or yams in this dish instead of the taro.

one piece of

or
FRENCH FRIES

- If Scoop $2.20

SNAPPER

$3.50

7. 50

Can't

LEE GRAHAM
MANGONUI FISH SHOP

FISH & CHIPS
BATTERED MUSSELS

ABOUT FIVE YEARS AGO WHEN MY WIFE AND I WERE
WORKING OVERSEAS AND WERE BOTH A LITTLE BIT
HOMESICK, WE HEARD THAT THE ICONIC MANGONUI
FISH SHOP WAS UP FOR SALE. WE THOUGHT - WHAT
A GREAT OPPORTUNITY, NOT ONLY TO COME HOME, BUT
TO CONTINUE A LEGACY THAT BEGAN IN THE 1940s.

WE SOURCE OUR FISH FROM THE LOCAL WHARF
BECAUSE WE HAVE THE FRESHEST FISH IN NEW ZEALAND
RIGHT AT OUR BACK DOOR. WHEN OUR CUSTOMERS
WALK IN, THEY SEEM GENUINELY EXCITED TO BE HERE.
WHETHER THEY ARE KIWIS OR VISITORS FROM OVERSEAS
WHO HAVE HEARD ABOUT US, THERE'S ALWAYS A
REAL BUZZ, WHICH WE LOVE.

-LEE

Mussel $1.80 EA   Seafood Stick $2.00 EA

ecide? Try the **FISHERMAN'S CATCH** meal

Mangonui

FISH & CHIPS

Servings: 4 | Prep Time: 25 mins | Cook Time: 20 mins | Skill Level: 1 (Easy)

INGREDIENTS

2 tsp baking powder

250 g high-ratio flour (cake flour)

350 ml cold water

4 large Agria potatoes

premium frying shortening made from natural beef and lamb

4 pieces (100 g each) firm white fish such as snapper, gurnard or tarakihi

METHOD

90 minutes before service – in a large mixing bowl, combine baking powder thoroughly with 200 g flour. Slowly add water while stirring with a whisk. Keep whisking until you have a smooth mix without lumps. Set aside to stand.

60 minutes before service – peel potatoes and cut into chunky chips. Parboil in boiling salted water for 4–5 minutes, until half cooked, then strain into a colander. Leave to steam dry in the colander until ready to cook your fish.

30 minutes before service – pre-heat the shortening in your fryer to 180°C. Use a deep, heavy cast-iron frying pan if you do not own a deep-fryer. Do not fill the fryer more than halfway to the top, to ensure that hot fat does not overflow during cooking. Remember, safety first!

20 minutes before service – pre-heat the oven to 150°C. Coat fish in the 50 grams of flour you had put aside. Place floured fish into batter. Using a pair of metal tongs, lift each piece of fish out of the batter, shaking off any excess batter, and carefully place into the hot fat. After 1 minute, turn fryer down to 170°C. Continue to cook fish for about 8–10 minutes, until golden brown and crispy on the edges. Remove using clean metal tongs, place on a baking tray and then in the oven to keep the fish crispy and warm while you finish off the chips.

10 minutes before service – turn fryer back up to 180°C and slowly add the par-boiled chips to the hot fat, using clean metal tongs. Fry for about 2–3 minutes until golden, then remove and place on the baking tray with the fish. Season with table salt or sea salt if available. Serve with your favourite salads and sauces.

BATTERED MUSSELS

Servings: 4 | Prep Time: 20 mins | Cook Time: 3 mins | Skill Level: 1 (Easy)

INGREDIENTS

5 g baking powder

250 g high-ratio flour (cake flour)

350 ml cold water

premium frying shortening made from natural beef and lamb

16–24 pre-shelled New Zealand green-lipped mussels

METHOD

60 minutes before service – prepare the batter as for fish and chips (above). Set aside to stand.

20 minutes before service – pre-heat the shortening in your fryer to 180°C (see safety notes above!).

10 minutes before service – coat mussels in the 50 grams of flour you had put aside. Place floured mussels into batter. Using a pair of metal tongs, lift each mussel out of the batter, shaking off any excess batter off, and carefully place into the hot fat. Cook for about 3 minutes until golden brown and crispy on the edges, then remove using a slotted metal spoon and place on a baking tray lined with paper towels. If you are not ready to serve straight away, place tray in the oven, set to 150°C, to keep the mussels crispy and warm. Season with table salt or sea salt if available.

Serve with your fish and chip meal, or on a frilly green lettuce leaf with aïoli (garlic mayonnaise) on the side for a tasty snack.

ANNABELLE WHITE

FLORENTINES
SHORTBREAD

One of my favourite things to do on a Sunday afternoon is to get together
with my great mate Rodney Greaves; we've been cooking together
for over twenty years! We call each other the Hudson & Halls
of cooking because we inspire each other with recipes and share ideas,
but we are not gay and we don't fight! I tend to read
large sections of cookbooks out loud to him. How the poor
devil puts up with it, I don't know!

Annabelle a.k.a. The Cuddly Cook.

Waiwera

FLORENTINES

Makes: 22 | Prep Time: 40 mins | Cook Time: 20–25 mins | Skill Level: 1 (Easy)

INGREDIENTS

70 g butter

75 g sugar
(about ⅓ cup)

1½ tbsp crème fraîche

25 g mixed peel

50 g currants or
sultanas

110 g sliced almonds

10 glacé cherries

1 cup chocolate buttons

METHOD

Spray silicone muffin pans (7 cm wide) with oil and heat the oven to 180°C.

Melt butter in a medium-sized pot, add sugar and stir in. Once this is dissolved, add the rest of the ingredients except the glacé cherries and chocolate. With your beloved wooden spoon, stir well for a few minutes to make sure all the ingredients are well coated with the butter and sugar mix.

Remove from the heat and use a dessertspoon to divide the mix between the muffin pans. (About 1 heaped dessertspoon per pan will work.) Rip cherries into thirds and place on top of mixture. Let it cool slightly, and then push it down with clean hands to ensure an even spread all around the muffin pans. Bake for 20–25 minutes, or until a good golden brown. Cool completely in the pans.

Once florentines are cool, melt chocolate in a stainless-steel bowl set over a saucepan of simmering water (make sure the bowl is not touching the water). Place a spoonful of chocolate in the centre of each florentine and smooth it out using the back of the spoon in a circular motion.

Cool until chocolate is set, and store in an airtight container in the fridge. If they soften slightly, they make a delicious, easy dessert with a scoop of vanilla ice cream.

TIPS

You really need silicone muffin pans for this recipe – it doesn't really work with conventional bakeware. On sale, recently a set cost me $9, so a good investment.

This recipe also needs scales – and a set of digital scales is a super investment for any baker.

SHORTBREAD

Makes: 28–30 | Prep Time: 40 mins including chilling | Cook Time: 15–20 mins | Skill Level: 1 (Easy)

INGREDIENTS

300 g butter,
slightly softened

1 cup icing sugar

3 cups plain flour

METHOD

Cream butter and sugar together. Mix in flour. Form the mixture into a long sausage (30 cm x 4.5 cm), cover in plastic wrap and place in the fridge for 20 minutes.

Pre-heat the oven to 160°C fan-bake or 180°C regular bake. Unwrap shortbread dough and cut into slices about 1 cm thick. Place on a lightly greased baking tray.

Prick with a fork and bake for 15–20 minutes. Make sure there is some colour on the shortbread for maximum flavour. Store in an airtight container. If for any reason air does get in and the shortbread 'softens', you can re-bake it for a few minutes to refresh it and make it firmer again.

TIPS

Placing the dough in the fridge is important. If pressed for time, you can freeze the dough at this stage and bake it off later.

KEVIN HOPGOOD
HOPGOOD'S

MUSHROOM RISOTTO CAKES WITH CRISPY EGG & ASPARAGUS SALAD
BAKED VANILLA CHEESECAKE WITH STRAWBERRIES

We came to New Zealand to bring up our boys away from the madness of London. For me, Kiwi food is fresh, honest food, cooked in a simple way and enjoyed in a relaxed enviroment - It's unpretentious. We are lucky in Nelson to have so many small-scale, high quality producers of food and wine right on our back doorstep. Whether it's asparagus, mushrooms, strawberries or Saffron - I just love knowing where my ingredients come from and I still get excited when they come into season. Both of my recipes, the risotto cake and the cheesecake, can be made if you get organised and have everything in kit form, ready to go.

Cheers Kev

good's
RESTAURANT & BAR

Nelson

MUSHROOM RISOTTO CAKES
WITH CRISPY EGG & ASPARAGUS SALAD

Servings: 4 | Prep Time: 1¼ hours | Cook Time: 20–25 mins | Skill Level: 2 (Moderate)

INGREDIENTS

Risotto cakes
20 g dried porcini mushrooms
1.2 litres chicken or vegetable stock
40 ml olive oil
1 onion, finely diced
2 cloves garlic, finely chopped
½ tsp chopped fresh thyme
300 g mixed portobello and
  button mushrooms, sliced
350 g Arborio rice
170 ml dry white wine
2 tbsp chopped fresh Italian parsley
30 g butter, diced, at room temperature
1 tbsp mascarpone or crème fraîche
½ cup freshly grated parmesan cheese
½ cup plain flour
½ cup rice flour

Crispy egg and asparagus salad
16 asparagus spears
60 ml extra virgin olive oil
½ lemon
4 large portobello mushrooms
4 small cubes butter
a few thyme leaves
large handful of baby fresh watercress
40 g fresh parmesan cheese shavings
20 ml vincotto
oil, for deep-frying
4 soft-boiled eggs, cooled
a little flour
1 egg, lightly beaten
panko breadcrumbs, to coat

METHOD

Soak the porcini mushrooms in boiling water for 15 minutes, then drain well and dice. While porcini are soaking, bring stock to a light simmer and prepare remaining risotto cake ingredients.

In a separate large, heavy-based saucepan, heat 20 ml of olive oil. Add onion, garlic and thyme and sauté gently for 5 minutes, until softened. Add porcini, portobello and button mushrooms and fry for 2–3 minutes, until browned. Stir in rice, coating it in the oil. Add wine and simmer, stirring, until the liquid has been absorbed.

Add a ladleful of stock and simmer, stirring again, until the liquid has been absorbed. Continue adding the stock in this way, until all the liquid has been absorbed and the rice is tender and creamy.

Stir in parsley, diced butter, mascarpone/crème fraîche and parmesan. Season to taste with salt and pepper. Transfer to a shallow tray and spread out thinly, to cool the risotto down quickly. Once cool, place in the fridge to set. (Alternatively, you could serve the hot risotto just as it is! Use leftovers for cakes.)

Once thoroughly cold and set, take out of the fridge and shape into burger-shaped patties/cakes. Mix flour and rice flour together and use to dust the risotto cakes, then pan-fry in remaining olive oil until golden and crispy and hot in the middle. Season with salt and pepper.

Pre-heat a grill plate and turn the oven to 180°C. Lightly peel asparagus, season and splash with extra virgin olive oil. Griddle until nicely 'bar-marked', re-season and squeeze a few drops of lemon juice over. Clean portobellos, place a butter cube inside each with a few thyme leaves, season and bake for 7–10 minutes. Cool slightly and slice. Make a warm salad of asparagus, portobellos, watercress and parmesan, dressed with vincotto and remaining 40 ml extra virgin olive oil.

In a deep-fryer, heat oil to 180°C. Coat soft-boiled eggs in flour, then beaten egg, then roll in breadcrumbs and deep-fry until golden brown. Serve risotto cakes on salad with a crispy egg to the side.

BAKED VANILLA CHEESECAKE WITH STRAWBERRIES

Servings: 8 | Prep Time: 10–15 mins | Cook Time: 1 hour 25 mins plus cooling
Skill Level: 1 (Easy)

INGREDIENTS

Base
1 pack Digestive biscuits
35 g melted butter

Filling
1 vanilla bean
180 g sugar
500 g cream cheese,
  at room temperature
5 eggs
250 g cream
juice and zest of 1 lemon

Topping
50 g sour cream
20 g cream
15 g icing sugar

To serve
100g sugar
100 ml water
300 g strawberries
a little caster or icing sugar
a squeeze of lemon juice

METHOD

Pre-heat the oven to 150°C. Line a 25 cm square baking tin with baking paper.

Place Digestive biscuits in a food processor and blend to a fine crumb. Drizzle in the melted butter and combine. Spoon biscuit mix into the base of the tin, spread it out evenly and press it down. Bake for 15 minutes or until golden. Set aside to cool.

Turn the oven down to 110°C. Split vanilla bean down the middle and scrape out seeds. Combine with all remaining filling ingredients and whisk thoroughly until smooth. Pour on top of the cooled base and bake for 60–70 minutes or until just set. The cheesecake should still be slightly wobbly when you take it out of the oven; you want the residual heat to finish the cooking to achieve the right texture. Leave the cheesecake to cool.

Whisk all topping ingredients together, then pour over cheesecake. Smooth it over, then place in the fridge to chill and thoroughly set.

Place sugar and water in a small saucepan and bring to the boil, stirring, until the sugar has dissolved. Cool. Slice 5 strawberries and brush with syrup, place on baking paper in a dehydrator and dry until crisp. (If you don't have a dehydrator, dust the slices with caster sugar instead.) Purée the remaining strawberries with sugar/icing sugar and lemon juice to taste.

To serve, carefully take the cheesecake out of the baking tin, cut slices with a hot knife and garnish with strawberry slices. Serve with purée (and extra strawberries, if wished).

LAURENT LOUDEAC
HIPPOPOTAMUS

MACARONI CHEESE
FRESH FRUIT & LEMON
JELLY TRIFLE

Who doesn't love Macaroni cheese?
It's simple and fast to make, delicious, cheap
and a great filler for kids and teenagers —
something my son, Jeremy, down at Otago
University, can cook for his flatmate.
I've put a Frenchman twist to it by adding
Kikorangi blue cheese, spinach and ham to
give that kiwi classic an extra oomph.
  The fruit trifle is both an English and a
kiwi classic, but this recipe is a modern
take w fresh fruit, coconut whipped cream
and meringue, for extra crunch. It is light,
refreshing and gluten free: the perfect end
to a meal ... especially after my macaroni
cheese.
I hope you enjoy them both.
Bon Appetit.
Laurent

Te Aro,
Wellington

MACARONI CHEESE

Servings: 4 | Prep Time: 25 mins | Cook Time: 25–30 mins | Skill Level: 1 (Easy)

INGREDIENTS

250 g macaroni
100 g butter
100 g plain flour
500 ml milk
100 g Kikorangi cheese
100 g ham, chopped
  (optional)
50 g baby spinach
  (optional)
200 g cheese, grated

METHOD

Pre-heat the oven to 180°C. In a large pot of salted boiling water, cook pasta until just al dente.

Meanwhile, in a smaller pot, melt butter, add flour and cook until you obtain a paste (roux). Add milk slowly, whisking to break up any lumps. Cook until you obtain a nice thick white sauce (béchamel). If too thick after you use all the milk, add a bit of the pasta cooking liquid. Season to taste.

Add Kikorangi, ham and spinach to the sauce. Drain the pasta, add it to the sauce and mix thoroughly. Pour into appropriate ovenproof dishes, either individual or family sized, and cover with grated cheese. Bake for about 25–30 minutes or until the grated cheese starts forming a nice golden crust. Serve straight away with a nice salad. Bon appétit!

TIPS

Replace the ham with bacon, or chorizo for extra spiciness – sauté bacon or chorizo in a pan first. The cheese can be cheddar or, a little more expensive, Gruyère. Remember, always blow on the hot macaroni cheese (just kidding)!

FRESH FRUIT & LEMON JELLY TRIFLE

Servings: 4 | Prep Time: 1 hour | Skill Level: 2 (Moderate)

INGREDIENTS

250 ml water
200 g sugar
juice and zest of
  2 lemons
3–4 gelatine leaves
¼ pineapple
4 tamarillos
4 passionfruit
8 small meringues
2 tbsp brown sugar
250 ml cream
1 tbsp coconut powder
4 sprigs fresh mint,
  to garnish
fresh berries, to garnish

METHOD

To make the jelly, place water and sugar in a pot, bring to the boil and stir until sugar dissolves. Add lemon juice and zest, measure the liquid, then take 1½ leaves of gelatine for each 100 ml of liquid and soak in cold water. When softened, squeeze excess water off and mix in with hot syrup until melted. Pour onto a deep tray and place in the fridge. Depending on the quantity, it will take up to an hour or so to set.

In the meantime, peel pineapple and cut into an 8 mm dice. Peel tamarillos and cut into a 4 mm slice. Cut passionfruit in half and remove pulp. Break up meringues.

Caramelise brown sugar in a pan on a low heat, add pineapple and sauté until slightly soft. Put on a tray and leave to cool. Whisk cream with coconut powder until soft peaks form, and keep refrigerated. Check the jelly. If set hard, cut into small cubes and keep refrigerated.

Take four tall glasses, milkshake-style, and start building the trifle in layers: cream, pineapple, tamarillo, jelly, meringue crumble, cream, passionfruit and repeat again to the top, finishing with cream then passionfruit. Garnish with mint and a fresh raspberry or strawberry, if in season.

Enjoy et bon appétit!

Kerikeri

COLIN ASHTON
FOOD AT WHAREPUKE

ORONGO BAY OYSTERS WITH THAI FLAVOURS
CHICKEN CHIANG MAI CURRY

Travelling through Thailand over the years made me fall in love with its healthy, fragrant and exotic cuisine.
The secret of cooking great Thai food is having the best ingredients, it's paramount to success.

Luckily these days most Kiwi's have access to fresh ginger, kaffir lime leaves, basil, coriander and chilli, the basics of Thai cooking. It's worth buying these ingredients and having a go at making your own pastes. Trust me, you can make a better Thai meal at home than you can buy as a take-away.

Colin

ORONGO BAY OYSTERS WITH THAI FLAVOURS

Servings: 4 | Prep Time: 15–20 mins | Skill Level: 1 (Easy)

INGREDIENTS

12 freshly picked large betel leaves
12 freshly shucked Orongo Bay oysters
1 lime

Dressing
½ medium-heat long red chilli
¼ teaspoon minced garlic
1 fresh lime leaf

1 stick of lemongrass
½ cup finely diced telegraph cucumber
¾ tsp very finely chopped fresh galangal
1 tsp chopped fresh coriander leaves
2 tbsp grated light palm sugar
2 tsp fresh lime juice
2 tbsp (or to taste) Megachef fish sauce

METHOD

Start by making the dressing. Finely dice chilli, mince garlic and finely chop lime leaf and lemongrass. Slice and dice the cucumber and use a micro-plane for the galangal. Chop coriander leaves.

In a mixing bowl, combine all chopped ingredients together. Add palm sugar and lime juice and stir in gently — try to fold the ingredients together with a spoon, to avoid bruising the cucumber too much.

Use fish sauce to season the dressing. Let it sit for 15–20 minutes before using, to allow time for the cucumber to be quickly pickled and the juices to come out.

Arrange the betel leaves on a plate and place an Orongo Bay oyster on each leaf. Spoon about ¾ teaspoon of the cucumber, palm sugar and lime dressing on top. Serve with fresh lime wedges.

TIPS

Use the freshest oysters possible; best to open and shuck them yourself.

Betel leaves are not easy to find, but you can substitute basil leaves (or no leaves if you like, as the dressing is great on its own). If you can't find galangal, use fresh ginger.

CHICKEN CHIANG MAI CURRY

Servings: 4 | Prep Time: 40 mins | Cook Time: 20 mins
Skill Level: 2—3 (Moderately challenging)

INGREDIENTS

Chiang paste (makes 500 ml)
10 large dried red chillis, medium heat
10 large shallots
1 tbsp grated galangal
5 tbsp finely diced fresh lemongrass
2 tbsp grated fresh ginger
5 tbsp chopped fresh garlic
1 tbsp salt
5 cloves
1 cinnamon quill
3 star anise
1 tsp coriander seeds
1 tsp cumin seeds
1 tsp ground cardamom
1 tsp ground turmeric

Curry
40 g piece of fresh ginger
20 shallots
1 kg free-range boneless, skinless chicken thighs
40 g dark palm sugar, grated
canola oil
500 ml chicken stock
10 lime leaves
½ a 300 ml jar pickled garlic, cloves only
2 tbsp salt
Megachef fish sauce, to taste
1 tbsp tamarind paste

To finish
½ cup blanched, roasted peanuts
1 cup fresh Thai basil leaves
crushed peanuts, to garnish
lime wedges, to garnish

METHOD

Soak chillis in boiling water for 10 minutes, drain and chop. Put chillis, shallots, galangal, lemongrass, ginger, garlic and salt into a mortar and pound with a pestle until smooth. If you don't have a mortar and pestle, put all the ingredients into a blender, add a couple of tablespoons of water and blend.

Toast cloves, cinnamon, star anise and coriander and cumin seeds in a pan until fragrant. Cool, then blend in a spice grinder until fine. Add cardamom and turmeric. Mix dry ingredients with the wet to form your paste.

Prepare the ingredients for the curry. Peel ginger and cut into fine julienne strips. Peel shallots and slice them fairly thickly. Dice chicken into 2½ cm cubes and grate palm sugar.

Sweat off the paste in some canola oil on a medium heat, for about 6 minutes, stirring constantly. Moisten with a little chicken stock, then add the rest of the ingredients except the palm sugar, remaining stock, fish sauce and tamarind. Stir well. Add half the remaining stock with half the palm sugar, and cook for about 20 minutes until the chicken is cooked through. Check flavour and season with fish sauce, tamarind, some stock if it needs it, and more palm sugar to taste. There should be a good balance of spiciness, sweet, sour and saltiness.

To finish, add blanched peanuts and Thai basil and garnish with crushed peanuts and a few lime wedges. Enjoy.

TIPS

Frozen lemongrass, frozen galangal and pickled galangal can be found in most Asian stores. If you can't find pickled garlic, you can just leave it out.

Megachef's fish sauce is my favourite brand, but any fish sauce will do.

NICK HONEYMAN
THE COMMONS

SHAVED VEGETABLES
BEETROOT & SNAPPER LASAGNE

Lasagne for me was my go-to dish as a child and my favourite time of the week was when my mother would crack one out. This recipe is my fun modern interpretation of a Kiwiana classic, using fresh beetroot as a replacement for pasta and snapper instead of meat sauce. These days, I prefer something a little bit lighter and fresher in an age where people are a little more conscious about what we are putting into our bodies each day. Having a good diet is pretty helpful to battle the stresses of the day so, if I can make food a bit healthier, I'm hopefully doing everyone a favour!

- Nick

Takapuna,
Auckland

SHAVED VEGETABLES

Servings: 4 | Prep Time: 15 mins plus chilling | Cook Time: 1 min | Skill Level: 1 (Easy)

INGREDIENTS

500 g any seasonal
  baby vegetables
  (e.g. radish, beetroot,
  carrot, turnip, fennel)
1 litre water
30 g salt
100 ml olive oil

METHOD

Cut each vegetable in half lengthways. Using a Japanese mandolin, slice each vegetable on its cut side to 2 mm thick. Place slices in a bowl of ice water for 1 hour.

Bring water, salt and olive oil to the boil. Strain the vegetables and blanch them in the olive oil water for 1 minute, until al dente. Strain, and serve immediately.

BEETROOT & SNAPPER LASAGNE

Servings: 4 | Prep Time: 45 mins | Cook Time: 4–6 mins | Skill Level: 2 (Moderate)

INGREDIENTS

2 large fresh beetroots
  (red or yellow)
4 pickling onions
1 clove garlic
1 snapper fillet, skinned
  (around 300 g)
30 g butter
2 tbsp olive oil
zest of 1 lemon
20 g chopped
  fresh parsley
200 g brie
50 g parmesan,
  finely grated

METHOD

Wash beetroot, place in a deep pot and cover with water. Add a tablespoon of sea salt and bring to the boil. Reduce the heat and simmer until cooked, around 35 minutes. Strain beetroot and peel the skin off straight away by rubbing them with a piece of paper towel. Using a mandolin or sharp knife, cut beetroot into thin ribbons around 2 mm thick. Irregular shapes are fine: it's the thickness that is important. Lay them on a tray and reserve until needed.

Peel onions and shave on a mandolin or finely with a knife, making sure to cut them across the grain to give perfect ringlets. Finely chop garlic and cut snapper into fine dice (3 mm). Pre-heat the oven to 180°C.

Place butter, oil and onions in a heavy-based saucepan. Gently heat the pan over a medium heat, seasoning the mixture with salt at the beginning to draw the moisture out of the onions. They will cook in 4–6 minutes over a medium heat; you do not want any colour but do want them to be translucent.

Strain onions out of the pot and reserve, returning the cooking liquid to the pot. Add garlic. Cook gently over a low heat until garlic takes on a light caramel colour, then add snapper and remove the pan from the heat. The snapper will cook in the residual heat of the pan – it will be ready as soon as it takes on a white colour. Season with lemon zest, chopped parsley and sea salt.

To plate, cut brie into four pieces, placing one in the centre of each plate and pushing it down with the back of a spoon until about 2 cm high. Place serving plates in the oven for 3 minutes, then remove and cover brie with beetroot slices, then a layer of onion and a layer of snapper. Repeat this one more time, then finish with beetroot slices on top. Season with olive oil and a little lemon zest, and finish the plate with a good amount of parmesan.

TIP

Take time in the cutting of all of the ingredients – this is a very important part of the cooking process and is often where people let themselves down.

SACHIE NOMURA
SACHIE'S KITCHEN

SALMON & AVOCADO SUSHI
TERIYAKI CHICKEN

I used to work for a large corporation until one day two colleagues' friends passed away from heart attacks - I knew then that I quickly needed to change jobs! I love people and have always been passionate about food so I decided to open a cooking school that would be like a bridge between the East and the West by teaching Kiwis how to cook Japanese and Asian food. I'm fortunate to have met a lot of different people from all walks of life here. The moment they walk out this door they have the smiley on their faces and full tummies that's what I love!!

— SACHIE

Parnell,
Auckland

サーモンとアボカドの巻き寿司
SALMON & AVOCADO SUSHI

Makes: 16 | Prep Time: 10 mins | Cook Time: 10 mins | Skill Level: 2 (Moderate)

INGREDIENTS

400–420 g cooked white rice (short/medium)

3 tbsp sushi vinegar

300 g salmon, raw sashimi-grade

½ avocado

2 sheets of nori

Garnish

sushi ginger

soy sauce

wasabi

METHOD

You will need a sushi rolling mat for this recipe.

Put warm or hot cooked rice in a large non-metal bowl. Pour sushi vinegar over and mix well. Use a cutting rather than a stirring motion, otherwise the rice becomes very mushy. Try to coat each rice grain with the sushi vinegar. Cover with a wet cloth and set aside.

Cut salmon into strips and slice avocado.

Place a nori sheet on top of your sushi rolling mat. Wet your hands (this is to avoid having rice stick to your fingers!) and put two handfuls (about 160 g) of sushi rice on the nori. Spread the rice evenly, leaving a 1 cm gap at the top of the nori sheet.

Place salmon and avocado on top of the rice, near the bottom end. Lift the bottom edge of the mat upwards and over the filling, using your fingers to keep the ingredients in the centre of the roll. As the rice meets the nori, squeeze the roll to make it firm and lift the top edge of the mat out to stop it getting caught in the roll. Continue until the roll is complete.

Wet a sharp knife with water and cut each roll into 8 pieces. Serve with sushi ginger, soy sauce and wasabi.

TIPS

Making a sushi roll is just like riding a bicycle. Once you know how to do it, then the skill is yours forever. If the first one doesn't come out right, don't worry! Try again; practice makes perfect.

Don't put too much rice on at the beginning – otherwise there won't be much space left for you to add your other ingredients.

照り焼きチキン
TERIYAKI CHICKEN

Servings: 4 | Prep Time: 5 mins | Cook Time: 20 mins | Skill Level: 1–2 (Easy–Moderate)

INGREDIENTS

Teriyaki sauce
35 g brown sugar
75 ml mirin
75 ml cooking sake
75 ml soy sauce

Chicken
4 large boneless
  chicken thighs
3 tbsp plain flour
oil for cooking

Garnish
shredded cabbage
sliced cucumber
toasted sesame seeds

METHOD

Start by making the teriyaki sauce. Mix all sauce ingredients in a small saucepan and bring to the boil. Reduce the heat to medium and simmer for 2 minutes. Remove from the heat and set aside.

Score the chicken to flatten it, and dust with flour. Put a pan on medium to high heat, add cooking oil and place the chicken in, skin-side first. Cook for 2–3 minutes, then flip to cook the other side for another 2–3 minutes or until it has cooked through.

Add the teriyaki sauce to the pan, and cook until the sauce becomes thicker and lightly caramelised.

Slice the chicken and serve with cooked rice. Garnish with cabbage, cucumber and toasted sesame seeds.

TIPS

I have found that teriyaki chicken is one of the most popular Japanese dishes and a favourite with everybody. But don't feel restricted to chicken – the sauce goes well with beef, pork, salmon or even just stir-fried vegetables and tofu.

I normally make a lot of teriyaki sauce and keep it in a bottle in the fridge! It will keep for three to four weeks.

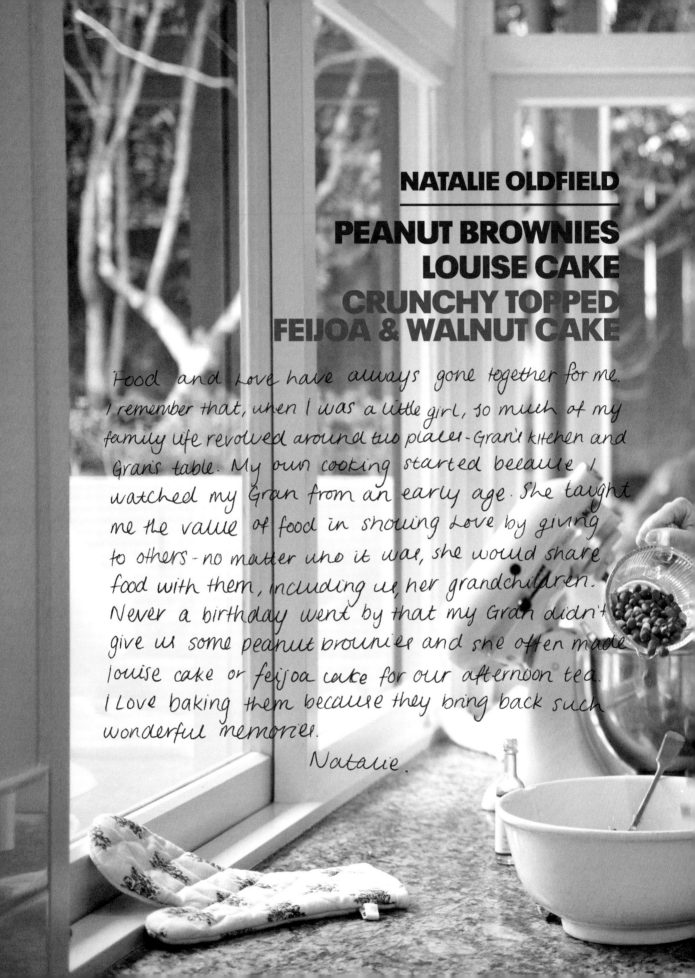

NATALIE OLDFIELD

PEANUT BROWNIES
LOUISE CAKE
CRUNCHY TOPPED
FEIJOA & WALNUT CAKE

Food and love have always gone together for me.
I remember that, when I was a little girl, so much of my
family life revolved around two places - Gran's kitchen and
Gran's table. My own cooking started because I
watched my Gran from an early age. She taught
me the value of food in showing love by giving
to others - no matter who it was, she would share
food with them, including us, her grandchildren.
Never a birthday went by that my Gran didn't
give us some peanut brownies and she often made
louise cake or feijoa cake for our afternoon tea.
I love baking them because they bring back such
wonderful memories.

Natalie.

Remuera,
Auckland

PEANUT BROWNIES

Makes: about 24 | Prep Time: 20–25 mins | Cook Time: 20–25 mins | Skill Level: 1 (Easy)

INGREDIENTS

250 g butter, softened
2 cups sugar
2 eggs
2 tsp vanilla essence
2 cups plain flour
2 tbsp cocoa
½ tsp salt
1 tsp baking powder
2½ cups roasted peanuts
1 cup coconut

METHOD

Pre-heat the oven to 170°C. Grease and line a baking tray.

Cream butter and sugar together until light and fluffy. Add eggs one at a time, beating well after each addition, then add vanilla and combine. Sift in flour, cocoa, salt and baking powder. Fold to combine. Lastly, add roasted peanuts and coconut. Mix together well.

Roll mixture into tablespoon-sized balls and press to flatten slightly when placing on baking tray. Bake for 20–25 minutes. Cool on a rack.

TIP

To roast your own peanuts, put them in a baking dish in an oven pre-heated to 120°C for 20 minutes, shaking them occasionally. You can keep their skins on – they're not too husky for this recipe.

LOUISE CAKE

Servings: 16 | Cook Time: 20–25 mins | Skill Level: 1 (Easy)

INGREDIENTS

Cake
150 g butter, softened
¼ cup white sugar
2 egg yolks
2 cups self-raising flour
¾ cup raspberry jam

Meringue
2 egg whites
½ cup sugar
1½ cups coconut

METHOD

Pre-heat the oven to 180°C. Grease and line a 30 cm x 20 cm slice tin.

Cream butter and sugar together until light and fluffy, then add egg yolks and beat well. Sift flour and stir in, then use your hands to achieve an even consistency.

Press mixture into slice tin, then spread jam over the top.

To make the meringue, beat egg whites and sugar until thick, then fold in coconut. Spread the meringue on top of the jam and cake.

Bake for 20–25 minutes. Cool in the tin before slicing.

TIPS

Don't be afraid to get your hands into this when preparing the base!

When spreading the meringue over the top, you can use a hot knife to help.

CRUNCHY TOPPED FEIJOA & WALNUT CAKE

Servings: 8 | Prep Time: 15 mins | Cook Time: 1¼ hours | Skill Level: 1 (Easy)

INGREDIENTS

2 cups self-raising flour
½ cup wholemeal flour
1 tsp ground cinnamon
½ tsp ground nutmeg
1 cup sugar
185 g butter, melted
½ cup water
3 eggs, lightly beaten
1½ cups chopped fresh feijoa flesh
½ cup chopped walnuts

Topping
60 g butter
½ cup brown sugar
¼ tsp ground cinnamon
¼ tsp ground nutmeg
½ cup chopped walnuts

METHOD

Pre-heat the oven to 180°C. Grease and line a 20 cm round or square cake tin.

Sift the flours and spices into a large bowl and stir in the sugar. In a separate bowl, mix together butter, water and eggs. Add wet ingredients to flour mix and fold together. Lastly, fold in feijoa and walnuts. Pour into tin.

For the topping, melt butter and mix in the other ingredients. Pour over cake mixture and cook for 1¼ hours. Cool in the tin.

Gisborne

THOMAS BOYCE
USSCO BAR & BISTRO

SESAME BEEF DUMPLINGS
STUFFED CHICKEN ROLL WITH ROASTED KŪMARA & PAN-FRIED HALOUMI

I was born and bred in Gisborne and I am proud to call it home. The dishes that I have chosen represent life growing up in a small town and also my love of travelling overseas.

This classic chicken wrapped in bacon dish with roasted kūmara goes down well with the locals, it's hearty, familiar and you get a decent portion.

The inspiration for the beef dumplings came after a trip to Japan with my wife Christine and daughter Lucia. The seaweed we use in this dish comes from our local beaches after it washes up after storms. It's processed into Kombu (ie made edible) and has the most beautiful and intense flavour.

We host quite a few Japanese businessmen here at Ussco so it's nice to be able to offer this dish.

Tom

SESAME BEEF DUMPLINGS

Servings: 4 | Prep Time: 30–40 mins plus cooling | Cook Time: 1 min | Skill Level: 2 (Moderate)

INGREDIENTS

2 cups plain flour
1¼ cups water
pinch of salt
250 g diced beef
a little cooking oil
1 tsp ground ginger
1 tbsp tahini
  (sesame paste)
1 tbsp sesame oil
1 tbsp hoisin sauce
1 tbsp shrimp paste
100 g chopped fresh
  coriander
4 leaves of kombu

METHOD

With the flour on a work surface, make a well in the middle and pour in the water and salt, then use your fingers to slowly bring it all together into a dough. Knead until the dough starts to strengthen (at least 5 minutes), then rest in the fridge.

In a hot pan, sear the beef in a dash of oil until brown and then add ginger, tahini, sesame oil, hoisin sauce and shrimp paste. Stir and cook, reducing it down until shiny. Season with salt and pepper and toss coriander through. Place in the fridge to cool.

Roll dough out thinly into 10 cm squares using a rolling pin or pasta roller. In the centre of the dough, place a tablespoonful of sesame beef. Use a pastry brush to brush the edges with water, then fold the dough over the filling and press down to seal. Brush the folded corners with water, bring them together and press firmly.

Poach dumplings for 1 minute in 2 litres of boiling water seasoned with kombu. Serve warm.

TIP

Kombu (dried brown seaweed) is available in Asian food stores.

STUFFED CHICKEN ROLL WITH
ROASTED KŪMARA & PAN-FRIED HALOUMI

Servings: 4 | Prep Time: 25 mins | Cook Time: 40–50 mins plus cooling | Skill Level: 2 (Moderate)

INGREDIENTS

1 whole chicken (1.5 kg)
200 g cream cheese
8 slices streaky bacon
a little cooking oil
500 ml beef jus
4 medium or
  8 small-sized kūmara
200 g haloumi
handful of young fresh
  celery leaves
1 tbsp olive oil
lemon juice, to taste
butter, for serving

METHOD

Bone chicken, keeping it all in one piece and the skin on, or ask your butcher to do this. Spread plastic wrap out on a work surface and place boned chicken on top, skin-side down. Spread another sheet of plastic wrap on top, and use a meat mallet to bang the chicken until it is evenly flattened to approx. 5 cm thick. Remove the top layer of plastic wrap and discard.

Spread cream cheese over chicken and fold chicken into a sausage shape with the cheese on the inside. Fold the plastic wrap over and twist the ends closed. Wrap in several more layers of plastic wrap so that the sausage is firm.

Place a roasting tray half full of water on the stovetop and bring it to a simmer. Place chicken roll in the water and cover tray with tinfoil. Simmer for 35–40 minutes, no longer. Remove from water and allow to cool.

While the chicken is simmering, bring beef jus to the boil and reduce just until it is glossy. Pre-heat the oven to 200°C. Boil kūmara, skin on, in salted water until you can pierce it with a knife, then remove from water and allow to dry. Season with salt and pepper, toss in some olive oil and roast in oven for about 20 minutes.

Once chicken roll is cool, it should be firm and easy to cut into four pieces. Wrap each portion in bacon and roast in a hot frying pan with a little oil, until heated through and golden. Cut haloumi into four slices and grill in a hot, non-stick frying pan (no oil). Brown both sides, and season with pepper. Toss celery leaves with olive oil and lemon juice and season to taste.

Serve chicken with a spoonful of beef jus, alongside haloumi on a bed of celery leaves and a curl of butter in the kūmara.

Growing up on a farm with food all around us, my parents didn't need to buy much because they could grow it. I love that mentality and that's what I hope to impart to my kids. I'm hoping this fast-food trend will pass and people will go back to cooking at home or having backyard BBQs. We've got to remember here in New Zealand, we've got the best produce in the world that doesn't take long to turn into dinner. I realise that it's harder to feed our kids good food than it is to feed them rubbish but, if we can get them eating well early in life, hopefully they will carry that on.

Mike

Mt Albert,
Auckland

MICHAEL VAN DE ELZEN

INDIAN-INSPIRED REVITALISING
SALAD WITH KASUNDI
BARBECUED BEER-CAN CHICKEN

INDIAN-INSPIRED REVITALISING SALAD WITH KASUNDI

Servings: 6 | Prep Time: 15–20 mins plus cooling | Cook Time: 1¾ hours | Skill Level: 1 (Easy)

INGREDIENTS

Kasundi
3 tbsp canola oil
2 tbsp sunflower seeds
2 tbsp pumpkin seeds
1 tbsp black mustard seeds
1 tbsp turmeric powder
2 tbsp cumin powder
2 tsp chilli powder
1 cup diced white onions
¼ cup grated fresh ginger
4 cloves garlic, crushed
1 small fresh red chilli,
  thinly sliced

30 ml water
400 g canned diced tomatoes
4 tbsp brown sugar
½ cup malt vinegar
1 tsp salt

Salad
2 red capsicum
2 tbsp olive oil
1 red onion, finely diced
1 large beetroot, grated
3 large kale leaves, sliced

100 g black rice
100 g quinoa
1 cup tamari almonds, toasted
2 cloves garlic, crushed
½ cup sultanas
200 g packet of sprouting peas
2 tbsp pumpkin seeds
1 cup puffed amaranth
100 g fresh mint leaves
3 tbsp plain dukkah

METHOD

For Kasundi, heat oil in a frying pan and fry off the seeds, turmeric, cumin and chilli powders for 5 minutes to release the flavours. Prepare onion, ginger, garlic and fresh chilli and add, with water, cooking for 5 minutes to soften. Add tomatoes, brown sugar, vinegar and salt. Simmer for 1½ hours. Allow to cool. If bottled while hot, it will keep (unopened) for three months.

Pre-heat the oven to 200°C. Brush capsicum with oil, season with salt and pepper and put in the hot oven for 10–12 minutes. Allow to cool slightly, remove the skins and slice. Finely dice red onion, grate beetroot and slice kale.

Cook rice and quinoa separately according to the packet instructions and place in a large bowl. Allow to cool. Add almonds, garlic, red onion, sultanas, sliced capsicum and beetroot, then mix in kale, sprouting peas, pumpkin seeds and puffed amaranth. Finally, chop mint leaves and add with dukkah. Transfer to a large serving bowl and serve with Kasundi.

BARBECUED BEER-CAN CHICKEN

Servings: 4–6 | Prep Time: 4 mins | Cook Time: 30–40 mins | Skill Level: 1 (Easy)

INGREDIENTS

1 size 16 free-range
  chicken
2 tbsp olive oil
sea salt and pepper
650 ml can of beer

METHOD

Pre-heat a Weber or charcoal barbecue and allow the flames to burn down. To prepare the bird, remove the winglets with a sharp knife, rub skin with oil and season inside and out.

Open the can of beer and place the bird over the top of the can, ensuring the chicken can stand up and hold its own weight. Slowly cook for the next 30–40 minutes with the barbecue's lid down. Test that the meat is cooked by inserting a small knife in the side of the leg – if the blood runs clear, it's ready to rumble!

RUTH PRETTY
RUTH PRETTY CATERING

BACON & EGG PIE
CARROT CAKE WITH CREAM CHEESE FROSTING

Te Horo

Bacon and Egg Pie is sort of the Kiwi psyche. My mother and all her sisters always made it. Maybe because we always had bacon, eggs and puff pastry and perhaps because it's something that can be made ahead and taken places as it is eaten cold. I hate it served hot. If you can, use streaky bacon as it has the best flavour and it is malleable. Aim to use free-range eggs as they taste better and have better colour. By the way, not all pastry, and especially puff pastry at the supermarket is created equal. You definitely need one made with butter. Pack up the picnic basket with your pie, an iceberg lettuce salad, a few cornichons and a generous carrot cake (my mother would have included a sultana cake). You have the makings of a classic Kiwi picnic.

Ruth

BACON & EGG PIE

Servings: 6–12 | Prep Time: 45 mins | Cook Time: 45 mins | Skill Level: 2 (Moderate)

INGREDIENTS

250–300 g puff pastry

200 g rindless middle bacon rashers

10 eggs plus 1 yolk

1 tbsp finely chopped onion

1 tbsp finely chopped fresh parsley

freshly ground black pepper

½ tsp flaky sea salt

METHOD

Take a deep-sided, round 17 cm cake tin. Our tin has a depth of 4½ cm. On a lightly floured surface, roll out about a third of the pastry and use the tin base as a guide to cut out the base of the pie. Place this into the tin.

Roll out another third and cut out a second round the same size to use as the top of the pie. Place on a lightly floured tray.

Roll out the remaining pastry to a strip which will form the sides of the pie. Make it the same height as your tin and long enough to go all the way around the inside. Join the pastry if you do not have the full length in one piece.

Place pastry strip inside the tin, around the sides. Using your fingertips, gently push the edge of the base onto the sides to adhere and form a seal. Place the tin and tray in the refrigerator to rest pastry for 20 minutes. Pre-heat the oven to 210°C.

Cut each bacon rasher into three. Line pastry base with half the bacon, allowing the bacon slices to sit side by side rather than overlapping. Break whole eggs into a cup, one by one, and gradually place each one onto bacon, taking care that the yolks remain whole. Sprinkle onion, parsley, pepper and salt onto eggs. Lay remainder of bacon over eggs.

Make a very small hole in the centre of the pastry lid. (A piping nozzle is ideal to do this.) Brush a very small border around the inside edge of the lid with cold water. Place lid on pie. Gently fork around lid edge to seal the pie and, if you wish, use any leftover pastry to make a decorative twist to go around the pie, and/or decorative leaves to sit on top.

Place egg yolk and 1 tablespoon of water in a bowl. Mix together and brush the glaze onto the lid. Place the pie into the oven. After 20 minutes, reduce the heat to 180°C. Cook for a further 25 minutes or until the pie is light golden brown and the base is cooked through.

Cool and serve, or place in refrigerator to serve within 2 days. When the pie is cold, tip out of the tin and invert onto a serving plate.

TIPS

Please note the change of oven temperature midway through cooking.

Preferably, use all-butter puff pastry.

CARROT CAKE WITH CREAM CHEESE FROSTING

Servings: 14–16 | Prep Time: 20 mins | Cook Time: 1½ hours | Skill Level: 1 (Easy)

INGREDIENTS

420 g caster sugar
315 ml flavourless oil (e.g. canola)
2 tsp pure vanilla essence
2 tsp finely grated lemon zest
3 eggs, lightly beaten
270 g grated carrot
195 g peeled and grated apple
250 g unsweetened crushed pineapple,
  juice reserved
65 ml pineapple juice
40 g desiccated coconut

420 g plain flour
1 tsp ground cinnamon
2 tsp baking soda
½ tsp salt

Cream cheese frosting
375 g full-fat cream cheese
10 g butter, softened
1 tbsp plus 1 tsp finely grated lemon zest
2 tbsp lemon juice
375 g icing sugar

METHOD

Pre-heat the oven to 170°C. Lightly grease a 23 cm round cake tin with baking spray or additional oil. Line base with baking paper cut to fit.

Place sugar, oil, vanilla and lemon zest in a large bowl and whisk with a hand whisk to mix. (Do not use an electric mixer because it will create too much air.) Add eggs and mix well. Add carrot, apple, pineapple, juice and coconut and stir together.

Sift dry ingredients together, add to bowl and gently fold in.

Pour batter into prepared tin and bake for approx. 1½ hours or until a cake skewer inserted comes out clean, and the cake bounces back when you prod it. Remove from the oven. Place the tin on a wire rack and allow to cool for 10 minutes, then remove cake from the tin and place on a rack to cool completely.

In a medium-sized bowl, beat cream cheese until smooth and creamy. Dice butter and add with lemon juice and zest, and combine well.

Sift icing sugar into the bowl and beat until combined and the frosting is smooth. Use to ice cooled cake immediately or cover and refrigerate for up to one day, before icing.

TIPS

A peaky cream cheese frosting is too sweet for me – I prefer a citrusy flavour and I don't mind that it sits smooth and flat like this icing.

If you wish, garnish with culinary flowers such as thyme flowers, calendula petals, violas or nasturtiums.

Northcote Point,
Auckland

CARL KOPPENHAGEN
THE ENGINE ROOM

VEAL SCHNITZEL WITH RÖSTI, SLAW & CAPER BUTTER

Schnitzel is one of my father's favourite meals
so we grew up eating it once a week.
It's kind of the signature meal in a lot of New Zealand
homes and let's be honest who doesn't like schnitzel!
The reason we have it on our menu is everyone
can relate to it and chefs come to eat it on
their days off. Plus it's bloody delicious!
Spend your money on some good quality meat,
we use veal but you can use pok, chicken or beef.
Bash it out, crumb it and fry it up.
A small amount goes a long way and potatoes and
cabbage are cheap.
I love cooking, I never get sick of it and I think
when you find something you love doing, it never
        feels like work. Enjoy!
            — CARL.

VEAL SCHNITZEL WITH RÖSTI, SLAW & CAPER BUTTER

Servings: 6 | Prep Time: 40 mins | Cook Time: 30 mins | Skill Level: 1 (Easy)

INGREDIENTS

Rösti
4 large Agria potatoes
freshly grated nutmeg
canola oil for frying
sea salt

Slaw
1 bulb fennel
2 radishes
1½ cups thinly shredded
  white cabbage
1½ cups thinly shredded
  red cabbage
1 cup chopped fresh
  flat-leaf parsley

Dijon vinaigrette
30 ml white wine vinegar
60 ml extra virgin olive oil
1 tsp Dijon mustard

Schnitzel
2 eggs
½ cup milk
1 cup flour
2 cups panko
  breadcrumbs
6 x 140 g veal scaloppini
8 tbsp clarified butter
6 tbsp baby capers
6 tbsp butter
6 tbsp sour cream
lemon wedges, to serve

METHOD

Peel and halve potatoes, then place in a medium-sized saucepan, cover with water to 5 cm above the potatoes and season well with salt. Bring to the boil and continue to boil for exactly 5 minutes, then immediately drain the potatoes and place on a tray to cool and dry.

To make the rösti, grate potatoes using a coarse grater and season with salt, pepper and freshly grated nutmeg. Shape into round cakes around 5 cm in diameter and 2 cm thick. Shallow-fry until golden brown on both sides. Season with sea salt.

To prepare the slaw, finely slice fennel and radish, shred cabbages and chop parsley. Make up vinaigrette by whisking all ingredients together with salt and pepper to taste. Set aside. At the very last minute, toss vegetables and parsley together, dress with vinaigrette and season with salt and pepper.

To prepare the veal, whisk eggs and milk together in a bowl to make an egg wash. Set up a crumbing station of three bowls or trays: the first with flour seasoned with salt and pepper, the second with egg wash and the third with breadcrumbs. Pat veal dry with paper towels, then place in flour and coat well. Shake off the excess, then dip into egg wash. Let the egg drain off, then place into breadcrumbs and coat well, pressing the crumbs onto the veal. Place veal on a plate or tray in a single layer, or separate using baking paper, so they stay dry.

Heat a heavy-based skillet or frying pan until hot, add clarified butter and fry veal on both sides until golden brown. Place on plates. Wipe out the pan with paper towels, return to a medium heat and add capers and butter. Swirl the pan around until the butter turns nut brown and the capers start to pop. Pour butter and capers over the scaloppini and serve straight away with rösti, slaw, a dollop of sour cream and lemon wedges to squeeze over.

TIPS

We serve this schnitzel with the dollop of sour cream alongside to smear over the rösti, and squeezing lemon over the tender, buttery schnitzel is absolutely essential.

And yes, the butter quantity in this recipe is correct – this is definitely not the Weight Watchers version! Don't feel guilty, though; enjoy it every so often, just not every night.

TOM HUTCHISON
WBC/CAPITOL

ZUCCHINI & BUFFALO MOZZARELLA SOUP
ROAST PUMPKIN & BASIL RISOTTO

I cooked my first soft-boiled egg on the family coal range when I was four and apparently it turned out perfectly so from a young age my family gave me positive encouragement to cook. Maybe I was destined to become a chef like my great-grandfather – he was a chef at Scotland Yard!

I love cooking. I love the industry, the food, the produce, the people and the environment. It's just part of my soul.

tom

Wellington
Central

ZUCCHINI & BUFFALO MOZZARELLA SOUP

Servings: 4 | Prep Time: 20–25 mins | Skill Level: 1 (Easy)

INGREDIENTS

1 large white onion
4 cloves garlic
½ fresh red chilli
800 g zucchini
4 sprigs of fresh thyme
5 cm parmesan cheese rind, washed
½ cup olive oil
1 litre chicken stock

zest of ½ lemon
¼ cup chopped fresh basil leaves
¼ cup chopped fresh Italian parsley
1 tbsp chopped fresh chives
1 tbsp chopped fresh marjoram
½ cup grated parmesan cheese
125 g buffalo mozzarella cheese

METHOD

Dice onion and garlic, finely slice chilli and roughly chop zucchinis. Put all these in a heavy-bottomed soup pot together with thyme sprigs, parmesan rind and olive oil, then gently sauté until zucchinis are tender. Do not allow the vegetables to colour. Add chicken stock and lemon zest. Simmer for 3 minutes.

Remove parmesan rind and pass soup through a coarse mouli, or pulse in a food processor. Return the soup to the pot and bring it to heated (not boiling). Add herbs and parmesan. Break mozzarella up into 1 cm chunks and stir gently into the soup. Season to taste with salt and freshly ground black pepper and serve immediately with crusty bread.

ROAST PUMPKIN & BASIL RISOTTO

Servings: 4 | Prep Time: 10 mins | Cook Time: 55 mins | Skill Level: 2 (Moderate)

INGREDIENTS

600 g crown pumpkin
extra virgin olive oil
100 g pine nuts
1.5 litres chicken stock
1 medium-sized brown onion
2 cloves garlic

150 g parmesan cheese
2 cups Carnaroli or Arborio rice
75 g butter
80 g fresh basil leaves, ripped
juice of ½ lemon

METHOD

Pre-heat the oven to 180°C. Remove the skin and seeds from pumpkin and chop into 2 cm cubes. Drizzle with olive oil, season generously and roast for about 20 minutes, until just soft and golden in colour. Keep warm.

In a dry frying pan, toast pine nuts over a low heat. Heat chicken stock and keep it ready on a low heat. Finely chop onion, crush garlic and grate most of the parmesan, reserving some to be shaved for garnish. Over a low heat, sauté onion and garlic with a lug of olive oil in a heavy-bottomed skillet for about 4 minutes, until soft. Increase the heat and add rice, stirring to coat each grain.

Reduce the heat to medium, then add chicken stock to rice ladle by ladle, adding more as stock is absorbed. Stir frequently, and continue adding stock until rice is cooked to al dente (about 20 minutes). Remove from the heat and add butter and grated parmesan, stirring vigorously to create a creamy risotto. Taste and season with salt and freshly ground black pepper. Gently stir basil leaves in with warm pumpkin and toasted pine nuts. Drizzle with lemon juice, and serve with black pepper and fresh parmesan shavings.

LAURAINE JACOBS

CHRISTMAS MINCE TARTS
RICH CHRISTMAS CAKE

This Christmas cake has been one of our family traditions for as long as I can remember. I don't know where Nana Laura got the recipe from, but it must be over one hundred years old as my ninety-year-old mother has been baking it all her life.

The secret to our family Christmas mince tarts is using Granny Smith apples, grated into the mixture, instead of suet, which makes for a lighter, delicious fruit mince. The pastry can be sweet or savoury and, in our family, we make a batch of each to keep everyone happy!

Lauraine

Remuera,
Auckland

CHRISTMAS MINCE TARTS

Makes: 36 | Prep Time: 1 hour | Cook Time: 30 mins | Skill Level: 2 (Moderate)

INGREDIENTS

250 g seeded raisins

250 g sultanas

60 g candied peel

400 g Granny Smith apples

500 g currants

250 g brown sugar

pinch of salt

¼ tsp freshly ground nutmeg

¼ tsp mixed spice

juice and zest of ½ lemon

juice and zest of ½ orange

3 tbsp brandy

250 g flaky puff or sweet shortcrust pastry

icing sugar, for dusting

METHOD

Put raisins, sultanas and peel into the food processor. Peel and core apples, then cut into chunks and add. Process together until finely chopped but not completely pulverised. Turn out into a large bowl and add currants, sugar, salt, spices and lemon and orange juice and zest. Mix well until all is combined. Add brandy and place in well-sterilised preserving jars until needed. Makes two 950 ml jars and will keep for several months if well sealed.

Pre-heat the oven to 200°C. To make the mince tarts, roll pastry out to ½ cm thick. Using a pastry cutter, cut circles to match the size of your tart tin and ease these into the tin. Take a generous teaspoonful of the Christmas mince, smooth it into each pastry case and then cut more circles, slightly smaller, to cover the tops of the tarts. Allow the tarts to rest at room temperature for at least half an hour before cooking, until the pastry is golden.

Serve warm, dusted with a little icing sugar.

TIP

Use flaky puff pastry for lighter and more savoury pies, or sweet shortcrust for more traditional pies.

RICH CHRISTMAS CAKE

Servings: 60 | Prep Time: 30 mins plus standing | Cook Time: 4 hours | Skill Level: 2 (Moderate)

INGREDIENTS

1½ kg mixed dried fruit, including sultanas, raisins and currants

500 g butter

385 g brown sugar

8 eggs

1 tbsp golden syrup

4 tbsp blackcurrant jam

500 g flour

1 tsp baking soda

1 tsp baking powder

½ tsp salt

1 tsp mixed spice

1 tsp ground cinnamon

150 g glacé cherries

100 g blanched almonds

¼ cup dark rum or brandy

apricot jam (optional)

METHOD

Place all the dried fruit in a large saucepan and cover with water. Bring to a boil and simmer for 5 minutes. Drain well, cool and let stand overnight.

Pre-heat the oven to 160°C.

Beat butter and sugar well until light and creamy, then add eggs one at a time, beating well between each addition so they are well incorporated. Add golden syrup and blackcurrant jam and beat that in well too.

Sift dry ingredients together four times. Add the dry ingredients and fruit in small alternate batches to the creamed butter, sugar and egg mixture, and finally fold in the cherries.

Line a 24 cm cake tin with several layers of greaseproof paper and tip in the mixture. Press almonds onto the surface.

Bake the cake for 4 hours. When cooked, pour dark rum or brandy over the surface while the cake is still warm. Cool, and place in an airtight container to mature for 2–4 weeks.

Immediately before cutting the cake, glaze the top with melted apricot jam for a professional-looking finish.

GEOFF SCOTT
VINNIES

———

**WILD VENISON LOIN
WITH MULLED WINE GLAZE
& CARROT PURÉE**
HOKEY POKEY ICE WHISKEYS
WITH SALTED CARAMEL SAUCE

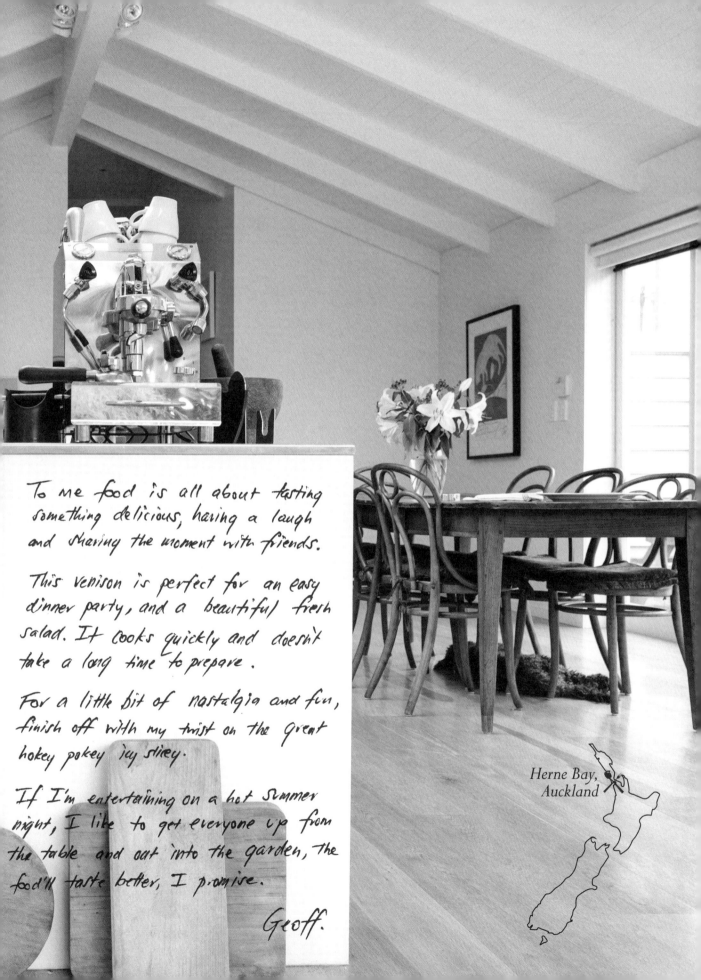

To me food is all about tasting something delicious, having a laugh and sharing the moment with friends.

This venison is perfect for an easy dinner party, and a beautiful fresh salad. It cooks quickly and doesn't take a long time to prepare.

For a little bit of nostalgia and fun, finish off with my twist on the great hokey pokey icy slicey.

If I'm entertaining on a hot summer night, I like to get everyone up from the table and out into the garden, the food'll taste better, I promise.

Geoff.

Herne Bay,
Auckland

WILD VENISON LOIN WITH MULLED WINE GLAZE & CARROT PURÉE

Servings: 4 | Prep Time: 1 hour | Cook Time: 30 mins | Skill Level: 3 (More challenging)

INGREDIENTS

Carrot purée
2 cups peeled and
   diced carrots
2 tbsp butter
½ tsp sea salt
1 cup milk

Mulled wine glaze
2 tsp mixed spice,
   plus a little extra
1 tbsp sugar
2 tbsp orange juice
2 tbsp lemon juice
1 cup red wine

600 g venison loin
1 tsp flaky sea salt
2 tbsp rice bran oil
½ cup baby peas
½ cup finely sliced raw fennel
2 baby carrots, finely sliced
8 sliced orange segments
½ cup fresh mesclun
   salad leaves
olive oil, for dressing
½ cup puffed black rice

(GF)

METHOD

Pre-heat the oven to 180°C.

Gently fry diced carrots in butter and salt for 10 minutes, then add milk, cover with a lid and simmer until cooked. Drain milk off and purée carrots in a blender. Strain through a fine sieve and keep warm.

Lightly toast mixed spice in a saucepan, then add sugar, juices and wine. Reduce down to a syrup.

Trim venison of any sinew or silver skin, and cut into four even portions. Season with sea salt. Heat an ovenproof frying pan to very hot, add oil and sear venison until caramelised all over (2 minutes). Place in the oven for a further 2 minutes. Remove from the pan and allow to rest before slicing.

Bring peas to the boil in salted water, drain and season with salt. Mix together fennel, sliced carrots, orange segments and salad leaves, and dress with salt and olive oil.

To serve, spoon carrot purée onto hot plates. Lightly dust venison with extra mixed spice and slice each portion into three. Arrange on top of purée, spoon peas and rice onto plates, place mini salad and finish with mulled wine glaze.

TIP

To make delicious puffed rice, boil 1 cup wild or black rice in 3 cups of water until fully cooked. Drain, then spread rice on a tray and leave in a cool oven (90°C) overnight to completely dry out. Use a metal sieve to deep-fry rice, for 1 minute, in very hot oil (200°C). Season with salt.

HOKEY POKEY ICY SLICEYS
WITH SALTED CARAMEL SAUCE

Servings: 10 | Prep Time: 30 mins plus freezing | Cook Time: 20 mins | Skill Level: 2 (Moderate)

INGREDIENTS

2 litres hokey pokey
   ice cream
180 g butter
180 g brown sugar
1 tsp vanilla extract
2 eggs
220 g plain flour
220 g wholemeal flour
1 tsp baking powder
½ tsp bicarbonate of soda
380 g tin caramel
   sweetened
   condensed milk

Salted caramel sauce
125 ml water
125 g sugar
125 ml cream
1 tsp salt

METHOD

Line a 20 cm x 30 cm slice tin with greaseproof paper. Tip ice cream into tin and press down flat, then freeze until hard. Use an 8 cm plain cookie cutter to cut 10 rounds and re-freeze.

Pre-heat the oven to 180°C. Cream butter, sugar and vanilla together in a food processor, then add eggs and mix. Add flours, baking powder and bicarbonate of soda, and mix to combine and form a dough.

Split dough in half, and roll each half out to 4 mm thick. Place on baking trays lined with baking paper and rest in the fridge for 30 minutes. Use a 9 cm crinkle cookie cutter to cut 20 rounds, placing on fresh baking paper back on the trays. Cook for 10 minutes until golden, then remove to a rack to cool.

For the salted caramel sauce, bring water and sugar to the boil and cook until the syrup begins to turn golden. In a separate saucepan, gently heat cream. Take caramel-coloured sugar off the heat and carefully whisk in the hot cream. Stir salt in.

To assemble, spread half the biscuits with caramelised condensed milk, place ice cream rounds on top and finish with a second biscuit lid. Dip into lightly warmed salted caramel sauce or drizzle it over.

TIPS

The ice cream is best left overnight to freeze solid.

Have pre-cut ice cream rounds laid out on plastic wrap in the freezer to make for quick assembly and easy serving.

MEGAN MAY
LITTLE BIRD UNBAKERY

TROPICAL PINEAPPLE & MINT MOJITO SMOOTHIE
RASPBERRY MILKSHAKE (HOLD THE MILK)
CASHEW & MACADAMIA MILK
RAW RASPBERRY BROWNIE

little bird came from me trying to feed and heal myself
as I've always had allergies and ended up seriously ill
and unable to work. My philosophy is that we should be
eating foods that make our bodies feel good, whatever
they might be. It's about health. Everybody should eat some
raw food every day and most people have a salad or a fresh
piece of fruit, which is great. Raw foods generally make
people feel a lot better and more energised, who doesn't want that?

Megan

*Kingsland,
Auckland*

TROPICAL PINEAPPLE & MINT MOJITO SMOOTHIE

Servings: 2 | Prep Time: 5 mins | Skill Level: 1 (Easy)

INGREDIENTS

handful of fresh
  mint leaves
½ handful of
  basil leaves
handful of chopped
  kale leaves
juice of 1 lime or
  ½ lemon
½ cup chopped
  pineapple or mango
  (fresh or frozen)
⅓ cup chopped
  cucumber
½ banana, frozen
½ cup coconut water
½ cup filtered water
½ cup ice cubes

METHOD

Blend all the ingredients in a high-speed blender until very smooth.

For garnish, add a slice of lime to the edge of the cup.

TIPS

Green smoothies are a great way of getting some unsuspecting greens into kids (big and small) – if they are anti-greens, make up some great names you think they will go for, like Monster Juice or (for older kids) a Tropical Mint Shake.

You can also use fresh banana; just add a little extra ice. If you don't have coconut water, just use extra filtered water.

RASPBERRY MILKSHAKE (HOLD THE MILK)

Servings: 2 | Prep Time: 5 mins | Skill Level: 1 (Easy)

INGREDIENTS

1 cup cashew and
  macadamia milk (see
  recipe over page)
1 cup ice cubes
1 banana, frozen
2 tbsp raw agave syrup,
  organic maple syrup or
  raw honey
½ tsp vanilla extract
¼ cup frozen
  raspberries, plus extra

METHOD

Blend all the ingredients except the raspberries in a high-speed blender until smooth. Pour half the smoothie mixture into two glasses (leaving half in the blender).

To the remaining mixture in the blender, add half the frozen raspberries and blend until the mixture is a lovely pink colour. Pour half of the contents into each glass to create berries and cream.

To finish, lightly crush a few extra raspberries and sprinkle on top.

TIP

While not your typical milkshake, this does taste like a familiar Kiwi favourite, reminiscent of a jelly-tip ice cream – but without any gluten, milk or sugary substances or those additives you can't recognise the names of which are present in most milkshakes or ice creams.

CASHEW & MACADAMIA MILK

Makes: 500 ml | Prep Time: 5 mins plus soaking | Skill Level: 1 (Easy)

INGREDIENTS

⅓ cup cashew nuts
¼ cup macadamia nuts
2 cups filtered water
pinch of salt
pinch of vanilla paste or
  1 tsp vanilla extract

METHOD

Soak cashew and macadamia nuts separately in cold water for 2–4 hours. Drain.

Next, blend all ingredients on high in a regular blender or a VitaMix for 1–2 minutes. Strain through a cheesecloth or a nut milk bag, and place in a sealed jar or bottle.

Keeps in the fridge for two days.

TIPS

When dairy is off the menu, nut milks make a wonderful substitute or addition to your repertoire. Cashews are one of the creamiest of nuts and, when mixed with macadamias, the taste of the nut milk is even closer to the dairy flavour people are familiar with. You can use it in almost any way you would regularly use dairy milk.

RAW RASPBERRY BROWNIE

Makes: 6–8 | Prep Time: 10–15 mins plus setting | Skill Level: 1 (Easy)

INGREDIENTS

2 cups Brazil nuts
2½ cups pitted dates
1 tsp sea salt
2 tsp vanilla extract
1½ avocados, pitted
  and peeled
¾ cup raw cacao
  powder or good-
  quality organic
  cocoa powder
3 tbsp melted coconut
  oil or cacao butter
¼ cup freeze-dried
  raspberries or ½
  cup fresh or frozen
  raspberries

METHOD

Pulse Brazil nuts in a food processor until slightly chunky, then add dates, salt, vanilla, avocado, cacao powder and coconut oil or cacao butter. Pulse for approx. 30 seconds until the mixture comes together well but there is still texture to it.

Add two-thirds of the raspberries and pulse them in.

Line a baking tray approx. 12 cm x 20 cm with plastic wrap or baking paper and press the mixture in. Top with the remaining raspberries, cover and leave to set in the fridge for 2 hours or the freezer for 1 hour.

Cut into 6–8 squares. Enjoy! It will keep in the fridge for one week or in the freezer for one month.

TIPS

When serving, be aware that it will soften at room temperature. If you're taking it to a friend's place, transport it in a cooler bag or put in the fridge when you get there.

If you can't get freeze-dried raspberries, use fresh or frozen raspberries instead; just increase the amount to half a cup (freeze-dried products always have a more concentrated flavour). You will need to store the brownie in the freezer if you are using fresh or frozen raspberries, as otherwise it will have a very short shelf-life – which is fine if you are going to eat it straight away.

MICHEL LOUWS
HUKA LODGE

COLD-SMOKED TAUPO TROUT

SLOW-COOKED LAMB SHOULDER

TOMATO & CHILLI SALSA

JAPANESE-STYLE RICE & VEGETABLE SALAD

Taupo

New Zealand is full of so many amazing farmers, suppliers, hunters, gatherers, fishers — people with respect for food, who know what they are doing — it's mind boggling! BBQ'd lamb shoulder is so Kiwi and I love to use a charcoal BBQ as the flavour is so superior. I have way more fun too — I can make more mess, chill out more and drink more beer!

Although this rice salad may look daunting from the picture, give yourself an hour, make it for a big group and honestly — you will steal the show!

Trout is unique in that you cannot go into a shop & buy it — you either have to catch it or have it given to you. I really recommend cold smoking — it is not so traditional and all you need is an old chilly bin or a box. The flavour is absolutely incredible, once you have tried it you won't want it any other way.

Michel

COLD-SMOKED TAUPO TROUT

Servings: 4–6 | Prep Time: 5 mins plus chilling | Cook Time: 1–4 hours minimum | Level: 1 (Easy)

INGREDIENTS

1 kg trout fillets

Cure mixture
200 g sea salt
100 g brown sugar
10 black peppercorns,
  crushed

METHOD

First get your trout, as they are not for sale – I guess you should go fishing (and don't forget a licence!). Fillet and pin-bone it or, better still, look helpless and ask a seasoned angler to assist with both. If all else fails, you could also substitute with any oily fish, like salmon or kahawai for example.

There are lots of different techniques and so many recipes, but I will share with you a basic one that most people love.

Mix together cure ingredients and place some in the bottom of a deep ceramic, plastic or glass dish. Place fish on top and cover with remaining cure mixture. Refrigerate, uncovered, for 8–12 hours.

Remove from fridge and quickly rinse under cold water to remove cure mixture. Be careful not to over-handle the fish or waterlog it. Pat fish dry with paper towels, place uncovered in fridge for another night; then it will be ready to smoke.

I recommend using a cold-smoke – the same principle as hot smoking, just without the ongoing heat. You will end up with a firm product that will hold its shape when sliced and is absolutely delicious.

Find a container big enough to hold the fish and yet also deep enough to add a pan with the smoke dust underneath. A large old chilly bin can be perfect (depending on the size of your fish fillets) or, if you decide to do this frequently, investing in an old bar fridge is a good idea.

Take an old metal oven dish and put wood dust or fine smoking chips (mānuka, oak, alderwood – your choice) in the bottom. Place a footed wire rack on top of the wood dust/smoking chips mixture and rest the fish fillets on top of this, in a single layer.

Wrap the top of the dish tightly with tinfoil and place over a gas hob or a campfire for about 3–4 minutes, until you see smoke coming out from under the sides of the foil.

Remove from the heat and place pan and contents into your chilly bin or bar fridge. Make sure the hot pan does not touch any surfaces where it could melt the plastic; if necessary, create a heat barrier with bricks or stones. The fish should ideally stay below 30°C. Put the lid on the chilly bin or close the door of the fridge and leave for a few hours until the smoke has disappeared.

Repeat the whole process (replacing the wood dust/smoking chips each time) until you achieve the degree of smokiness you like. It can take up to three smokings for this to be the case.

TIP

Multiply the cure mixture for larger quantities of fish.

Please don't try this on a hot summer's day, because the outside temperature will be too high.

SLOW-COOKED LAMB SHOULDER

Servings: 4 | Prep Time: 3 mins | Cook Time: 12 hours or overnight
Skill Level: 1 (Easy)

INGREDIENTS

1 'oyster cut' lamb
  shoulder (1.2 kg)
salt and white pepper
olive oil

METHOD

Rub lamb with salt and freshly ground white pepper and drizzle with olive oil.

Now you have two options: ask your friendly butcher to vacuum-pack this for you and cook it overnight at around 70°C (in a ham kettle), or wrap the lamb shoulder in an excess of heat-safe plastic wrap (don't hold back, use heaps) and place it in a deep-sided tray in your own oven, for about 12 hours at 70°C. Remove from the oven and allow to cool as quickly as possible, keeping it within the layers of plastic.

Half an hour before you want to serve it, remove lamb from the refrigerator, light your charcoal barbecue, unwrap or unpack the shoulder, sprinkle generously with salt and 'colour' over hot coals to obtain a great smoky flavour and a roasted-brown colour.

Now carve, or remove the bone first to make carving easier. You will find that because the meat is so tender, the bone will come away clean! Serve with tomato and chilli salsa (see below).

TIPS

This lamb will keep for up to a week if treated carefully and refrigerated. This process cooks the lamb very slowly to make it tender, without the flesh falling off the bone.

TOMATO & CHILLI SALSA

Servings: 4 | Prep Time: 10 mins | Skill Level: 1 (Easy)

INGREDIENTS

2 medium-sized
  tomatoes, skin on
1 medium-sized onion
1 clove garlic
5–10 sprigs fresh
  coriander, chopped
chilli, to taste (go nuts!)
juice and zest of 1 lime

METHOD

Chop tomato and onion finely, and garlic very finely. Combine in a bowl and season with salt.

Add coriander and chilli, tasting all the time, but be aware that the flavours will develop, so season to an 80 per cent level at this stage and wait to see if you need more. Add the lime juice and zest to taste.

Leave covered for a while, complete seasoning if required and serve alongside the lamb (see above).

TIP

The ingredients are a guide only; they can vary considerably according to your own personal taste. I personally always aim for a zingy, tangy, spicy salsa with loads of coriander. Feel free to experiment (add cucumber or avocado, and how about replacing the lime juice with some red wine vinegar and chopped oregano?). Ground cumin is a favourite, too!

JAPANESE-STYLE RICE & VEGETABLE SALAD

Servings: 4 | Prep Time: 1 hour | Skill Level: 2 (Moderate)

INGREDIENTS

Rice
1 cup sushi rice
2 cups water
sushi vinegar, to taste

Wasabi mayonnaise
75 g good-quality mayonnaise
15 g wasabi paste

Marinated vegetables
50 g caster sugar
170 ml white wine vinegar
pinch of ground white pepper
200 ml water
10 kaffir lime leaves
¼ raw parsnip
¼ raw carrot

Salad
¼ telegraph cucumber,
  peeled and sliced thinly
small piece of raw pumpkin,
  peeled and sliced very thinly
1 medium radish, (washed and) sliced thinly
3 raw green beans, cut into small pieces
4 cherry tomatoes, peeled and cut in half

To finish
2 tsp mixed black and white sesame seeds
sushi seasoning
Colonna mandarin-infused extra virgin olive oil
¼ sheet toasted nori (dried Japanese seaweed)
6 slices pickled ginger
fresh coriander leaves

METHOD

Wash rice and soak in cold water for 15 minutes, then drain through a sieve. Add rice and water to a saucepan and bring to the boil, then turn the heat down, cover and simmer for 5 minutes. Remove from the heat, keeping the lid in place, and allow to stand undisturbed for 5–10 minutes. Uncover and allow to cool a little.

Tip rice mixture into the bottom of a large bowl and score the mixture with a spatula. Sprinkle sushi vinegar over, tasting as you go. Allow mixture to cool – at room temperature is best, covered with a clean tea towel. (If you refrigerate this mixture it will go hard and the texture becomes unpleasant.)

Combine mayonnaise with wasabi and mix well. Set aside, at room temperature.

Place marinating ingredients (except parsnip and carrot) in a saucepan and bring to a simmer, stirring until sugar is dissolved. Remove from the heat. Peel and thinly slice parsnip and carrot and marinate separately. (Personally, I add some crushed juniper berries to the parsnip and the peel of half an orange to the carrot.)

Prepare salad vegetables.

Toast sesame seeds in a dry, clean frying pan until they start to smell good, then transfer to a cold plate.

To serve, place rice on the base of a large serving platter. Dress vegetables with the sushi seasoning and infused oil, season with salt and place on top. Add dollops of wasabi mayonnaise. Add all the remaining ingredients, placed evenly on top and arranged attractively around the platter.

TIPS

The marinated vegetables can be made in advance, as they keep well in the refrigerator for a few weeks. Sushi seasoning and nori are available at Asian food stores, and Colonna infused oils at specialist food stores.

NICI WICKES

FRAGRANT GINGER & CHICKEN BALINESE CURRY
SAGO GULA MELAKA

Port Waikato

New Zealanders are famous for their O.E: packing up their backpacks and heading off around the world for adventure. Food is such a fabulous gateway to learning about the culture of a place. When I come back to NZ, rather than bore people with endless photos from my travels (no one's actually interested, let's be honest!), I'll cook a meal from where I've been recently — to me that's a much more generous and fun way to share the experiences. It's a terrible cliché but you really can travel with your taste buds.

Nici

FRAGRANT GINGER & CHICKEN BALINESE CURRY

Servings: 4 | Prep Time: 10 mins | Cook Time: 40–45 mins | Skill Level: 1 (Easy)

INGREDIENTS

4 chicken breasts, skinless

1 medium-sized onion

3 cloves garlic

2 mild red chillies

½ cup cashew nuts

1 heaped tsp ground turmeric

5 tbsp lemon juice

2 tbsp dark soy sauce

3 tbsp grated palm sugar

2 tbsp grated fresh ginger

2 tbsp rice bran oil

¾ cup coconut milk

½ cup water

METHOD

Cube chicken and roughly chop onion. Combine onion, garlic, chillies, cashew nuts, turmeric, lemon juice, soy sauce, sugar and ginger in a blender or food processor, or a mortar and pestle, until the mixture forms a smooth paste.

Heat oil in a heavy-based pan and add the blended spice and nut mixture. Fry this, stirring to prevent sticking, for 4–5 minutes to let the flavours develop and the sugar to caramelise. Add chicken and cook for a further 15 minutes.

Add coconut milk and water, reduce the heat to low and simmer uncovered, stirring occasionally, until chicken is tender and sauce has thickened (about 15–20 minutes).

Serve with rice or salad.

TIP

You can use brown sugar in place of the palm sugar.

Serve with thinely sliced fresh pineapple, mango or cucumber flecked with finely chopped fresh red chillies.

SAGO GULA MELAKA

Servings: 4 | Prep Time: 20 mins | Cook Time: 20 mins plus chilling | Skill Level: 1 (Easy)

INGREDIENTS

10 cups water

2 cups sago

1 cup coconut milk

pinch of salt

Palm sugar syrup

250 g palm sugar

½ cup water

METHOD

In a large saucepan, bring water to a rolling boil. Gradually add sago, stirring as you add it so it doesn't clump. Cook for 5–7 minutes, then turn the heat off, cover and let it sit for 10 minutes until sago is translucent.

Drain in a sieve and rinse starch out with cold water. It will seem very 'gluey' at the start but, as you begin to wash the starch away, the little sago pearls will appear.

Pour sago into a bowl, add ¼ cup coconut milk and a pinch of salt and mix through. Pour into small individual tumblers and chill.

Make the syrup. Put palm sugar and water in a small saucepan and bring to the boil, breaking up the sugar as it begins to soften. Swirl and keep an eye on it until it begins to bubble and thickens slightly to form a syrup. (If it gets too toffee-like or thickens too much, add a small amount of extra water to loosen it.)

To serve, pour remaining coconut milk over each chilled tumbler of sago, then pour syrup into the middle of the sago — this will form a layer on top and eventually settle at the bottom. Serve chilled.

JONNY SCHWASS
HARLEQUIN PUBLIC HOUSE

FRIED CHICKEN
BBQ PULLED PORK
FENNEL, GRAPEFRUIT
& RADISH SALAD

There are four things I need every day
a good sandwich, a kiss from my wife, a
smile from my baby girl and a nice glass
of wine. Other things come and go but
the simplest things make me the happiest.

Kiwis love the idea of a BBQ, but we're
stuck in this antiquated way of throwing
everything onto a hot plate and letting it
stew. These recipes need to be cooked
slowly so take your time, kick back, relax
and enjoy the process.

For me, food is as much about the
journey and who I share it with as it is
about the final enjoyment.

I'm a bit old-school in that ultimately,
all I want to do is sit around a table,
share a plate of food, listen to great music
and reconnect on a human level. —Jonny

Christchurch
Central

FRIED CHICKEN

Servings: 6–8 | Prep Time: 15 mins plus marinating | Cook Time: 20–30 mins
Skill Level: 1 (Easy)

INGREDIENTS

Marinade
4 cups buttermilk
¼ tsp cayenne pepper
2 tsp Old Bay seasoning
2 tsp salt
1 tsp freshly ground
   black pepper
2 tsp Tabasco sauce
2 tsp honey

Chicken
2 small chickens,
   cut into pieces
1200 ml cooking oil
4 tsp paprika
2 tsp chilli powder
2 tsp garlic powder
2 tsp onion powder
2 tsp Old Bay seasoning
2 tsp cayenne pepper
2 tsp ground celery seed
4 tsp salt
1 tsp freshly ground
   black pepper
4 cups plain flour

METHOD

In a large mixing bowl, whisk the buttermilk together with the rest of the marinade ingredients. Add the chicken pieces and submerge them in the buttermilk marinade. Cover the bowl with plastic wrap, put it in the fridge, and let the chicken marinate for at least 12 hours.

Take the chicken out of the fridge and let it come up to room temperature, still in the marinade (this will take about 45 minutes).

Pre-heat the oven to 90°C. Heat cooking oil in a deep pot or a deep-fryer over a high heat. The oil should be 15 cm deep, and it should be so hot that it starts popping (about 175°C). A good rule of thumb: if you drop a pinch of flour into the oil and it fries up immediately, you're good to go.

While the oil is heating, combine all the remaining ingredients except the flour in a large mixing bowl. Mix things around with your hands so everything is distributed evenly. Pour half the mixture into a small bowl and set aside. Add flour to the large bowl and mix well.

When the oil is hot, pull a piece of chicken out of the marinade. Put it right into the dredging flour bowl and heap flour on top of it; flip it around until the chicken is completely coated. Do the same with each piece until there's no more space in the bowl.

Pick up a piece of chicken, give it a light shake (just enough to get rid of the really loose bits of flour), and use your hands or a pair of tongs to drop it into the frying pot. Do the same with the rest of the chicken pieces. (You will definitely need to fry your chicken in batches, unless you've got some really big bowls and pots.)

Let the chicken fry for about 8 minutes, until golden brown. Pull the chicken out of the fryer with tongs and place on a rack set over a baking sheet. Sprinkle each piece of chicken with the seasoning mixture, using the tongs to turn the chicken so it's coated on all sides.

Place the baking sheet and chicken pieces in the oven. The chicken pieces should rest in the oven for at least 10 minutes, so that the cooking process finishes. Meanwhile, fry up the next batch of chicken.

Keep the fried chicken in the oven until all the pieces are fried and rested and you're ready to serve it up. Then pile the chicken on a big plate, put it in the centre of the table together with biscuits, collards and coleslaw – for a Kiwi spin on this, bread rolls and a crisp green salad would work – and let everybody start grabbing pieces. I guarantee it will disappear fast.

TIP

Old Bay is an American blend of herbs and spices, first sold in 1939 in Baltimore, Maryland. You can get it from www.unclesams.co.nz or there are many recipes online. Otherwise, give me a call at the restaurant and I will share my recipe with you.

BBQ PULLED PORK

Servings: a table of hungry pork fans | Prep Time: 5 mins | Cook Time: 12 hours (mostly unattended)
Skill Level: 1 (Easy)

INGREDIENTS

1 pork shoulder (larger than your head but smaller than your oven)

dry spice rub (optional)

about ¼ cup BBQ sauce per person

METHOD

Barbecue means different things to different people all over the world. Unfortunately, in New Zealand a barbecue often means simply warming food up outside. When I think of barbecue, I think of pork — or, more precisely, smoked pork shoulder grilled over charcoal then pulled into meaty shreds with fingers or a fork. Doused with sauce and eaten with a tart and tangy grapefruit salad, it is one of the most delicious things on the planet and requires only one special ingredient: patience.

First, rub pork generously with sea salt and freshly cracked black pepper. If you want, you can use a dry spice rub instead of the salt and pepper; as it's important to allow the shoulder to absorb the rub, this takes a minimum of 3 hours. I prefer to taste the flavour of the pork, the smoke and the joy of something cooked slowly.

A true pit master will light a fire, burn his coals down until the temperature reaches 145°C, then cook the shoulder slow and low for 6–10 hours while he tends the coals, balancing the smoke with the addition of different woods and sitting with the shoulder as it moves through various stages to barbecue nirvana. The best method I have found, however, is to cook the shoulder overnight in your kitchen oven at 85°C for at least 10 hours. This allows the meat to be safely cooked all the way through and allows you to spend time on other pressing issues like sleeping.

The following day, fire up your wood grill, charcoal pit, brick oven, or whatever — as long as it smokes and creates heat, you can finish your shoulder on anything.

Take your shoulder to your prepared fire and give it a good lick of flame, smoke and flavour; allow the skin to crackle, blister and char and the flavour to develop. This process will take as long as you care to spend until the desired colour and flavour are reached or until your dining table is full of guests — but allow a minimum of 1 hour to build the flavour.

Once cooked to your liking, shred the pork with a fork and add your favourite barbecue sauce. Put everything in the tray the pork was cooked in so that pork, sauce, pork fat and crackling combine for porky goodness.

FENNEL, GRAPEFRUIT & RADISH SALAD

Servings: 8 | Prep Time: 15 mins plus steeping | Skill Level: 1 (Easy)

INGREDIENTS

⅓ cup olive oil

2 tsp fennel seeds, lightly crushed

4 medium-sized fennel bulbs

20 radishes with greens, trimmed

4 pink or red grapefruits

1 medium-sized clove garlic

½ tsp salt

¼ tsp black pepper

METHOD

For this recipe you will need a Japanese Benriner or other adjustable-blade slicer.

Heat oil with fennel seeds in a small heavy saucepan over a moderate heat until seeds are fragrant and pale golden, 1–2 minutes. Remove from heat and let them steep for 2 hours.

Meanwhile, cut stalks off fennel and quarter the bulbs lengthwise, cutting out and discarding most of the core – leave just enough core to keep the fennel quarters intact. Cut fennel lengthwise into paper-thin slices with the slicer. Transfer to a large bowl.

Cut radishes crosswise into very thin slices (slightly thicker than the fennel) and add to the fennel.

Cut peel, including all white pith, from grapefruits using a small sharp knife. Working over a bowl, cut segments free from the membranes and squeeze the juice from the membranes into a bowl. Transfer segments to a cutting board, reserving the juice, and coarsely chop, then add to fennel and radishes.

Pour fennel oil through a fine-meshed sieve into a small bowl. Discard seeds.

Mince garlic, and mash to a paste with a pinch of salt using a large heavy knife, then transfer to another small bowl. Whisk in salt, pepper, fennel oil and 5 tablespoons grapefruit juice. Pour this over the salad, tossing gently to coat.

TIPS

Fennel oil can be made a day ahead and chilled in an airtight container. Bring to room temperature before using. The dressing can be made 2 hours ahead and kept (covered) at room temperature or chilled.

Fennel and radishes can be sliced up to 6 hours ahead; cover with dampened paper towels and chill. Grapefruit can also be chopped up to 6 hours ahead, covered and chilled. Chill the juice separately.

PETA MATHIAS

PRESERVED DUCK LEGS
POTATOES IN DUCK FAT
ROLY POLY PUDDING

I discovered when I was young that, if you can cook, people will like you. Being able to cook means you can have something of yourself which doesn't cost anything. The magic of recipes is that they connect you to the past.

Roly poly pudding is an old-fashioned dish that my father used to make us kids. My mother was a plain cook and Dad had a sweet tooth so we had dessert every night.

Duck confit is a great recipe from my French life. It's a good recipe for a dinner party because you can do the cooking the day before then sauté just before serving. Duck fat is not like any other fat; it gives food an unctuousness, a mouthfeel that is like nothing else. Putting duck fat and potatoes together is like dying and going to heaven.

Peta

Westmere,
Auckland

CONFIT DE CANARD
PRESERVED DUCK LEGS

Servings: 6 | Prep Time: 5 mins plus marinating | Cook Time: 2 hours plus maturing
Skill Level: 1 (Easy)

INGREDIENTS

6 duck legs
2 tbsp rock salt
1 tbsp crushed black
  peppercorns
2 cloves garlic, sliced
4 sprigs fresh thyme
2 bay leaves, crushed
2 litres melted duck fat
½ tsp ground white
  pepper

METHOD

Cover duck legs with all the ingredients except the fat and white pepper and marinate for 24 hours. Rinse the legs with cold water to remove the marinade.

Lie duck legs, skin-side down, in a large pot, add melted duck fat and white pepper and simmer very gently for 2 hours.

Allow to cool, then transfer legs and fat to an earthenware dish. Leave for at least a week in a cool place to mature before eating. The confit will keep in the fridge like that for up to two weeks. If you seal the pot with a salt-sprinkled cloth and then cover it with thick brown paper tied with string, the confit will keep for several months, either in a cool place or in the fridge.

To serve, allow the confit to sit in a warm place until the fat runs (this can be done in a gentle bain-marie). Drain the legs, then heat up a little of the duck fat in a frying pan and sauté the legs, skin-side down, until golden and crispy. Alternatively, grill them.

TIPS

In France, confit is usually served with sliced potatoes fried in duck fat (see below) and a salad. I suggest a chicory and dandelion salad splashed with walnut oil and tarragon vinegar.

Duck fat gives a creaminess and depth to dishes that is incomparable. It is all melted off during reheating, so try not to think of the fat transferring to your own legs! The fat can be strained and reused.

POMMES SARLADAISES
POTATOES IN DUCK FAT

Servings: 6 | Prep Time: 10 mins | Cook Time: 20–30 mins | Skill Level: 1 (Easy)

INGREDIENTS

1 kg waxy potatoes
  (Desirée, Draga or
  Jersey Benne)
8 tbsp duck fat
2 cloves garlic, finely
  chopped
3 tbsp chopped fresh
  flat-leaf parsley

METHOD

Peel potatoes and slice very thinly. Dry with a tea towel. Melt half the duck fat, pour it into a bowl, add salt and pepper and toss the potato slices in it.

Heat the rest of the duck fat in a large, heavy-based frying pan. Tip the potatoes in and cook on medium heat for about 10 minutes to get a golden base. Now start moving the slices around so that other layers can take on some colour. When they are all golden and cooked through, you can either stir in the garlic and parsley and serve, or serve and scatter the garlic and parsley over the top.

ROLY POLY PUDDING

Servings: 6 | Prep Time: 15 mins | Cook Time: 30 mins | Skill Level: 1 (Easy)

INGREDIENTS

225 g self-raising flour
1 tsp baking powder
½ tsp salt
110 g suet
150 ml water
300 g strawberry,
  raspberry, blackcurrant
  or plum jam
milk, for glazing
whipped cream,
  to serve

METHOD

Pre-heat the oven to 180°C.

Sift flour, baking powder and salt together, then mix suet in. Add water and quickly mix to a soft, wet dough.

Roll dough out roughly on a floured surface until it measures about 30 cm x 15 cm. Spread jam all over, but not quite to the edges. Dip a pastry brush in milk and brush the edges, then roll up loosely, starting at a short end.

Place on a greased baking sheet, brush with milk and bake for at least 30 minutes or until golden on top. Serve hot, sliced thickly, with whipped cream.

PETER PEETI
KAI TIME ON THE ROAD

MĀNUKA-SMOKED VENISON
WITH PIKOPIKO & WATERCRESS
WILD FOOD SALAD

For as long as I can remember, I've always
wanted to be a chef.
When I started hunting, the first thing
I said to myself was I will never
shoot and kill anything unless I
plan to eat it.
My whole life has been dedicated to
gathering food for whānau & friends.
I love chasing wild pigs and deer
with Chum, my favourite dog, he's
sharp as, very clever.
Every day I spend out in the hills,
roaming the bush is magic.
As I always say to people...
Every day is a beautiful day,
          Sweet As — Ka Rawe!

Mourea

MĀNUKA-SMOKED VENISON WITH PIKOPIKO & WATERCRESS

Servings: 4 | Prep Time: 45 mins | Skill Level: 1 (Easy)

INGREDIENTS

200 g fresh pikopiko

1 cup fresh watercress

4 x 250 g venison striploin (also known as backstrap)

4 tbsp olive oil

3 large kūmara (1 red, 1 orange, 1 gold)

For smoking meat

200 g mānuka sawdust

Sauce

port or red wine (optional)

200 ml venison jus

100 g fresh or frozen blackberries

METHOD

Blanch pikopiko in hot, salted water until soft, about 7 minutes. Bring water back to boil and blanch watercress until just wilted, up to 1 minute. Drain. Season venison with salt and freshly cracked pepper. With a sharp knife, cut a hole through the centre of the meat and stuff each piece of venison with both pikopiko and watercress. Place venison on a wire rack.

Place mānuka sawdust in a pan and heat on a direct flame until mānuka starts to smoke. Place rack of venison on top and cover with a larger pan or tinfoil to trap the smoke. Smoke venison for about 10 minutes.

Heat olive oil in another frying pan and sear venison on all sides, then continue to cook gently until rare to medium-rare, about 8 minutes all up. Don't overcook, as it can easily become dry. Remove from the pan and rest for 10 minutes before serving.

In the same pan used for frying, deglaze the meat flavours with port or red wine (or a little jus if not using these). Add jus, simmer gently, then fold blackberries in. In the meantime, peel kūmara, cut into 2 cm cubes and cook in boiling salted water until just soft. Strain cooking liquid off, adjust seasoning, and mix gently together with a large spoon.

To serve, place a large spoonful of kūmara onto the plate, slice the venison striploin in half to reveal the stuffing, and gently pour a little blackberry venison jus over. Serve hot!

TIPS

Pikopiko is best picked with someone who knows which type is used for cooking – only a few of the many varieties are edible. My good friend Charles Royal at www.maorifoods.com can supply fresh pikopiko to order. Blanching the pikopiko helps to break down the grainy fibres which can otherwise be quite chewy.

WILD FOOD SALAD

Servings: 4 | Prep Time: 15 mins | Skill Level: 1 (Easy)

INGREDIENTS

200 g pikopiko

200 g wild pork bacon

4 field mushrooms

1 medium-sized onion

small bunch of fresh watercress

oil, for cooking

Dressing

100 ml extra virgin olive oil

50 ml white wine vinegar

1 tbsp whole-grain mustard

1 tsp sugar

METHOD

Blanch pikopiko in hot salted water until soft, about 7 minutes. Chop pikopiko and bacon, slice mushrooms and finely dice onion. Wash watercress.

Gently fry bacon, onion and mushrooms in a little oil. Toss into a bowl with the watercress and pikopiko and season to taste with salt and freshly ground black pepper.

Mix dressing ingredients together and drizzle over salad. Serve warm or cold.

Oxford

JO SEAGAR

CHOCOLATE CHUNK OAT COOKIES
BANANA CAKE
CARAMEL OAT SLICE

Food is my passion and I love teaching and sharing my knowledge for easy straightforward cooking — I guess its that "New Zealand Mother Thing". I always dreamed I'd have a little country cooking school and now I'm living my dream in Oxford, North Canterbury, in the foothills of the Southern Alps. These classic kiwiana recipes will always be well received at morning or afternoon tea — great for "filling the tins" and loved by all, not just sheep shearers!

Jo x

CHOCOLATE CHUNK OAT COOKIES

Makes: 24 | Prep Time: 10 mins | Cook Time: 15–20 mins | Skill Level: 1 (Easy)

INGREDIENTS

250 g butter, softened
3 tbsp sweetened
  condensed milk
¾ cup sugar
1½ cups plain flour
1½ cups rolled oats
1 tsp baking powder
200 g dark chocolate,
  roughly chopped

METHOD

Pre-heat the oven to 180°C. Line two baking trays with baking paper.

Beat butter, condensed milk and sugar together until light and creamy. Add flour, rolled oats, baking powder and chocolate chunks.

Flatten spoonfuls on the prepared trays and cook for 15–20 minutes until golden brown. Cool on a wire rack and store in an airtight container.

TIP

To save having to chop the chocolate, use large chocolate buttons.

BANANA CAKE

Servings: 10 | Prep Time: 15 mins | Cook Time: 50–60 mins | Skill Level: 1 (Easy)

INGREDIENTS

1½ cups sugar
150 g butter, softened
4 eggs
3 bananas, mashed
¾ cup milk
1 tsp baking soda
200 ml plain natural
  yoghurt
2½ cups plain flour
3 tsp baking powder

Lemon icing
25 g butter
juice and grated zest
  of 1 lemon
2–2½ cups icing sugar

METHOD

Pre-heat the oven to 160°C. Spray a 23 cm round springform tin with baking spray. Line the base with baking paper.

Beat sugar and butter together until creamy and pale. Add eggs and beat until thick and creamy and well incorporated. Add bananas and mix in well.

Heat milk in a small saucepan or microwave-proof bowl until nearly boiling. Stir baking soda into milk and then stir this into the banana mixture. Add yoghurt, flour and baking powder. Mix well and pour into the prepared cake tin.

Bake for 50–60 minutes until the cake is cooked in the middle and just pulling away from the sides of the tin. Cool in the tin for 5 minutes, then release the spring sides and cool completely on a wire rack. When fully cold, ice with lemon icing.

For the icing, place butter, lemon juice and zest in a small microwave-proof jug or bowl. Microwave on high for 30–40 seconds until the butter is melted. Beat in enough icing sugar to make a smooth icing. Spread over the cooled cake and allow to drip down the sides.

CARAMEL OAT SLICE

Makes: 16–20 | Prep Time: 12 mins | Cook Time: 30 mins | Skill Level: 1 (Easy)

INGREDIENTS

Base
2 cups plain flour
1 cup self-raising flour
1 cup coconut
2 cups brown sugar
3 cups rolled oats
2 eggs
300 g butter, melted

Filling
200 g butter
400 g sweetened condensed milk
4 tbsp golden syrup
1 tsp vanilla essence
dark and white chocolate melts (optional)

METHOD

Pre-heat the oven to 180°C. Grease a large 25 cm x 35 cm slice or sponge roll tin and line with baking paper. Make sure the paper has a good over-hang.

For the base, combine dry ingredients in a bowl. Add eggs and butter. Mix well, then press two-thirds of the mixture into the prepared tin.

For the filling, slowly melt butter, condensed milk and golden syrup together. Mix well, then add vanilla essence. Pour onto the base. Sprinkle the remaining crumbly mixture on top of the filling and bake for 30 minutes. Cool and refrigerate.

TIPS

Best to cut the next day, to get beautiful slices. Can be drizzled with melted dark and white chocolate to decorate.

Kumeu,
Auckland

HIPGROUP
SCOTT BROWN & JACKIE GRANT

WOOD-FIRED BREAD
ASHED CHILLI &
TOMATILLO SAUCE VIERGE

HAND-CUT PASTA WITH ZUCCHINI, MINT, ALMONDS & PARMESAN

LATE SUMMER FRUIT, FRESH CHEESE & BUCKWHEAT

RASPBERRY SORBET

Sourcing the finest ingredients on a consistent basis for our cafés + restaurants has always been a challenge. So we thought let's try and grow all our produce as the first step towards our goal of being fully self-sufficient; not only with fruit and vegetables but with everything we source.

It's been a wonderful journey of discovery for us, our chefs and team members to really appreciate the magic that goes into growing and producing the ingredients we use.

New Zealand can produce the finest of everything we need and there is something enormously satisfying about serving produce through the seasons to our customers, knowing every step that the food has taken from our farms to their plates.

Scott and Jackie

WOOD-FIRED BREAD

Makes: 6 small loaves | Prep Time: 35–40 mins | Cook Time: 7 mins | Skill Level: 2 (Moderate)

INGREDIENTS

700 ml water at
  approx. 20°C
10 g dry yeast granules
1 kg high-grade flour
flaky sea salt
30 ml olive oil, plus
  extra for drizzling
4 tbsp chopped fresh
  oregano leaves

METHOD

Get your wood-fired oven going to a nice high heat. If using a conventional oven, pre-heat it to 300°C (or as high as it will go), and put a pizza stone in to heat up.

Pour water into an electric mixer with a dough hook, add dry yeast and mix to dissolve, then add flour, salt and olive oil. Mix for 2 minutes on slow speed, then approx. 6 minutes on medium speed or until dough reaches a temperature between 27 and 28°C.

Cover dough and rest for at least 20 minutes before dividing into 200 g pieces and shaping. To shape, flatten the dough with your fingertips, then roll out to a thickness of 1 cm using a rolling pin. Drizzle olive oil over, sprinkle with sea salt and oregano. Bake for approx. 7 minutes in a wood-fired oven or 10–12 minutes on the pizza stone in a conventional oven. The bread will be golden with a hard crust when done.

ASHED CHILLI & TOMATILLO SAUCE VIERGE

Servings: 6 | Prep Time: 25 mins | Skill Level: 1 (Easy)

INGREDIENTS

1 red onion
4 red cayenne chillies
5 medium-sized
  tomatillos
4 oxheart tomatoes
10 pitted Kalamata
  olives
8 capers
zest and juice of
  2 lemons
50 g chopped fresh
  coriander
2 cloves crushed garlic
50 ml olive oil
sea salt

DF GF V

METHOD

Prepare coals and a grill for direct-heat cooking. Peel onion, leaving root end on so it doesn't fall apart, then nestle onion and chillies directly into the hot coals. Leave for 3–5 minutes, until blistered and blackened, then turn and continue to cook until the other sides are black. The chillies will blister and turn black before the onions, so turn and remove those first.

Place 2 tomatillos and 2 tomatoes on the grill over a blazing fire and cook for 3–5 minutes until the skins are partially charred, turning when needed. Transfer all blackened vegetables into a bowl and cover with plastic wrap. When cool enough to handle, remove the stems from the chillies and cut the root end off the onion, and discard. Place charred vegetables into a food processor and blend on a high speed until smooth.

Finely dice remaining tomatillos and tomatoes, olives and capers and place in a mixing bowl with lemon zest and juice, coriander, garlic and olive oil. Transfer the blended charred vegetables into the mixing bowl, mix and season with sea salt.

TIPS

Fresh tomatillos and oxheart tomatoes can be found in summer at fine food stores or farmers' markets. Oxhearts can be substituted with any similar variety, like Roma or San Marzano. Tomatillos can also be bought canned and could be used if fresh ones are hard to get.

HAND-CUT PASTA WITH ZUCCHINI, MINT, ALMONDS & PARMESAN

Servings: 6 | Prep Time: 45 mins plus resting | Cook Time: 10 mins | Skill Level: 2 (Moderate)

INGREDIENTS

80 g raisins
white wine vinegar
water
4 zucchinis, yellow
  and green
4 zucchini flowers
100 g toasted natural
  almonds
30 ml olive oil
80 g butter
20 g fresh mint leaves
10 g chopped
  fresh parsley
juice of 1 lemon
grated parmesan,
  to serve

Pasta dough
300 g high-grade flour
200 g fine semolina
25 ml olive oil
1½ tsp salt
4 eggs
4 egg yolks

METHOD

Cover raisins with equal parts of vinegar and water, soak for 30 minutes and drain. Cut zucchinis into strips about 2 cm wide, tear flowers into strips and cut almonds in half.

Combine all pasta dough ingredients in an electric mixer with a dough hook, mixing for 10 minutes or until the dough is smooth and elastic. Wrap in plastic wrap and rest in the refrigerator for 1 hour. Roll rested dough through a pasta machine, fold it onto itself and roll again, then repeat twice more. Fold again and roll the dough to a thickness of 2 mm. Dust with flour and cut into strips.

Blanch the pasta in boiling salted water for 2 minutes. Meanwhile, to a hot pan add olive oil and cook zucchinis until tender, then add cooked pasta and ½ cup of pasta cooking water. Remove from the stove and add butter, raisins, almonds, mint, parsley, zucchini flowers and lemon juice. Taste and season with salt, sprinkle with parmesan, and serve immediately.

LATE SUMMER FRUIT, FRESH CHEESE & BUCKWHEAT

Servings: 4 | Prep Time: 30–40 mins plus cheese (1½ days) | Cook Time: 45 mins plus cooling
Skill Level: 2 (moderate)

INGREDIENTS

Fresh cheese
4 litres unhomogenised
  whole milk (silver top)
1/16 tsp mesophilic
  starter culture

Baked pears
2 large pears
4 large fig leaves
50 ml olive oil

Buckwheat crumble
100 g butter
100 g sugar
100 g ground almonds
1 tsp salt
100 g buckwheat flour
100 g buckwheat groats
60 g honey

To plate and garnish
50 g buckwheat groats
2 ripe Black Doris plums
4 ripe figs
20 g puffed buckwheat
edible viola flowers
baby sorrel leaves

METHOD

Start the cheese the day before. Ensure all equipment is sterilised before use. Warm milk to 30°C and stir in mesophilic culture. Keep at warm room temperature for 24 hours (a hot-water cupboard is fine). Transfer curds to a cheesecloth and hang for 6 hours to allow the whey to drip off. Whip cheese with a whisk until smooth and place in a piping bag. Refrigerate until needed.

Pre-heat the oven to 180°C. Peel pears and slice in half. Brush fig leaves generously with olive oil. Wrap fig leaves around pear, place on a baking sheet and bake for approximately 25 minutes until just cooked – test for doneness with a knife or skewer.

Turn the oven down to 170°C. Rub butter, sugar, ground almonds, salt and buckwheat flour together with your fingertips until fine crumbs form. Mix buckwheat groats through and spread in a thin layer on a baking sheet. Bake for approx. 20 minutes, stirring every 5 minutes until an even golden colour. While still warm, mix honey through. Cool down and store in an airtight container until needed.

Warm pears back through in the oven, remove from fig leaves and slice into eighths. Toast buckwheat groats in a dry frying pan for a few minutes. Slice plums and figs into quarters. Pipe small drops of cheese onto each plate. Arrange alternating slices of fruit in a straight line, sprinkle with buckwheat crumble and puffed and toasted buckwheat, and garnish with flowers and sorrel. Serve with raspberry sorbet (see below).

TIPS

If you don't have time to make the cheese, try lactic curd, hung yoghurt or quark instead. Puffed buckwheat can be bought in wholefood stores, and fig leaves (in season) can be sourced through a friendly greengrocer or grower.

RASPBERRY SORBET

Servings: 8 | Prep Time: 15 mins plus cooling and freezing | Skill Level: 1 (Easy)

INGREDIENTS

1 kg fresh or frozen
  raspberries
75 g sugar
75 g water
20 g lemon juice

METHOD

Blitz raspberries in a food processor, then press through a fine sieve to remove seeds. Bring sugar and water to the boil. Cool, then add lemon juice and raspberry purée. Mix well and freeze in an ice cream machine according to the manufacturer's instructions. Freeze until shortly before required.

INDEX

CONTRIBUTORS

AL BROWN (20)
www.albrown.co.nz

(148) **DES HARRIS**
www.clooney.co.nz

DAME ALISON HOLST (258)
www.holst.co.nz

(278) **DIMITRIS & NIKOS MERENTITIS**
Facebook: Dimitris Greek Food

ALLYSON GOFTON (286)
www.allysongofton.co.nz

(116) **EMMA METTRICK & PAUL HOWELLS**
www.thelittlebistro.co.nz

ANDREW & JULIA CLARKE (224)
www.victoriastreetbistro.co.nz

(98) **FLEUR SULLIVAN**
www.fleursplace.com

ANNABELLE WHITE (300)
www.annabellewhite.com

(364) **GEOFF SCOTT**
www.vinnies.co.nz

ANNE THORP (62)
www.annethorp.co.nz

(144) **HESTER GUY**
www.hgcatering.co.nz

ANTHONY HOY FONG (46)
Twitter: @AnthonyHoyFong

(126) **JACOB BROWN**
www.thelarder.co.nz

ANTONIO CRISCI (30)
www.podericrisci.co.nz

(72) **JAY SHERWOOD**
www.amisfield.co.nz

BEN BAYLY (56)
www.thegroverestaurant.co.nz

(52) **JEREMY RAMEKA**
www.pacificarestaurant.co.nz

BEVAN SMITH (192)
www.riverstonekitchen.co.nz

(88) **JIM BYARS**
The Friday Shop ph: 03 4777 605

BRENTON LOW (176)
Facebook: A Deco Whangarei

(404) **JO SEAGAR**
www.joseagar.com

BRONWYN KELLY, KATIE RICHARDSON & MATT WILSON (282)
www.maranuicafe.co.nz

(388) **JONNY SCHWASS**
www.jonnyschwass.com

BRUCE MAUNSELL & TEAM (84)
www.boscocafe.me

(262) **JOSE CARLOS DE LA MACORRA**
www.mexicanspecialities.co.nz

CARL KOPPENHAGEN (352)
www.engineroom.net.nz

(104) **JOSH EMETT**
www.ratadining.co.nz

CAZNA & PAT GILDER (254)
Facebook: Mrs Clark's Cafe, Riverton

(206) **JUDITH TABRON**
www.soulbar.co.nz

COLIN ASHTON (314)
www.foodatwharepuke.co.nz

(186) **JULIE BIUSO**
www.juliebiuso.com

DAVID GRIFFITHS (152)
www.misterd.co.nz

(120) **JULIE LE CLERC**
www.julieleclerc.blogspot.co.nz

DEAN BRETTSCHNEIDER (230)
www.globalbaker.com

(160) **KATE FAY**
www.cibo.co.nz

SIR DES BRITTEN (220)
Former restaurateur,
Wellington City Missioner,
author and presenter

(216) **THE KERR FAMILY**
www.curlytreewhitebait.com

ACKNOWLEDGEMENTS

We would really like to thank all those who have contributed to *The Great New Zealand Cookbook* and would especially like to thank the following people: Catherine Abbott; Alvin the Irishman; Trey Anderson; the crew of oyster boat *Argosy*; Beth Astle; Tyson Barnard; Debbie Barry; Prue Barton; Maria Batiz; Steve Bayliss; Cara Bayly; Jeremy Bennett; Remo Biuso; James Blackie; Kim Boshier; Matthew Bowcock; Christine Boyce; Mike Bradshaw; Simone Brandon; Lorraine Britten; Sarah Bullock; Rachel Byars; Troy Caltaux; Brian Campbell; Rae Candy; Kylie Cederman; Johnny Clark; Rebecca Clouston; Chrissy Conyngham; Rachel Cooper; Rosie Cox; Ben Crawshaw; Dylan Crummer; Louis de Bievre; Michael de Vries; Deepika; Helene Dehmer; Rachel Dewhurst; Gavin Doyle; Jared Durham; Helen Emett; Hugh Enbersey; Craig Erasmus; Vivienne Farnell; Christine Fernyhough; Rob Finn; Madeleine Furley; Nick Gemmel; Rachel Goldfinch; Rodney Greaves; Eugene Hamilton; Athalia Harper; Pearl Harper; Nicky Harrop; John Hedges; the Hedley family; Rose Hibbard; Thomas Holroyd; Simon Holst; Michael Hood; Tierney Hos-Cuthers; the Hoy Fong family; Kate Hutchison; Jesse Jensen; Mary Johnson; John Kerr; Moana Kerr; Joan Mackenzie; Robyn Martin; Shaun Martin; Paul (Dougall) McDougall; Christos Merentitis; Despina Merentitis; Kirsten Merentitis; Toni Mitchell; Creghan Molloy-Wright; Nadia Monaghan; Debbie Mortensen; Scott Muir; the O'Sullivan family; Darryl Parker; Michelle Pattison; Jo Pearson; Andy Pettitt; Martin Phillips; Garry Phipps; Dave Poole; Liam Poole; Ming Poon; Rebecca Rameka; Chand Sahrawat; Natalia Schamroth; Alexandra Schwass; Hayden Scott; Jane Scott; Lou Sellars; Monique Smith; Steve Smith; Louise Smythe; Dirk Stark; Gareth Stewart; Chris Tapp; Rachel Taulelei; Miriama Te Huia; Anne Thom; Sam Thom; Sarah Thom; Mike Tod; Dan Tosswill; Jeremy Turner; Belinda Van de Elzen; Karl van Wynbergen; the Vette family; Gary Ward; Mary Wells; Jim Wheeler; Paul & Lisa Wigglesworth; Luke Wigley; Jodi Williams; George Willis; Debbie Zampieri.

We would also like to extend special thanks to the following organisations for their invaluable assistance in making *The Great New Zealand Cookbook*:

Air New Zealand Limited

Canon New Zealand

Foodstuffs (N.Z.) Limited

CREATED & DIRECTED BY:
Murray Thom & Tim Harper

PRODUCER: Murray Thom
ART DIRECTION: Tim Harper
COVER ART: Dick Frizzell
DESIGN: Tim Harper, Bridget White
PHOTOGRAPHY: Lottie Hedley
VIDEOGRAPHY: Hayley Thom
PRODUCTION COORDINATOR: Wendy Nixon

PUBLISHER: Geoff Blackwell
EDITOR IN CHIEF: Ruth Hobday
FOOD EDITOR: Teresa McIntyre
ADDITIONAL EDITORIAL: Abby Aitcheson, Mary Dobbyn

www.thegreatnewzealandcookbook.co.nz
Copyright © Thom Music Ltd www.thommusic.com

All images copyright © Lottie Hedley www.lottiehedleyphotography.com other than images on pages 286–287, 289 copyright © Rachael Hale McKenna www.rachaelmckenna.com

This edition produced by PQ Blackwell Limited www.pqblackwell.com

Find and follow us on:

ISBN: 978-0-473-27740-6
Printed in China by 1010 Printing International Limited